W9-APJ-403

Writing Poetry

Writing Poetry

By JOHN HOLMES

Boston

THE WRITER, INC.

Publishers

Reprinted 1966

Part Three was originally published in book form under the title, *The Poet's Work.*

Library of Congress Catalog Card Number 60-8935

Printed in the United States of America

To All My Students

Foreword

The small book called *The Poet's Work* had its lifetime, gratifyingly long, if quiet. Now it has been enlarged, to continue even more in the image of the sort of book I wanted it to become, above all for "the young poet who is smart enough to wish to live to be a great poet."

The four hundred, more or less, brief quotations from prose and poetry, in five sections, each with an introductory essay, stand as they were in the original book, with a few corrections. This is Part III of *Writing Poetry*. I believe in its power to exhilarate the creative mind. I had the excitement and pleasure and weariness of copying it from the first page to the last, essays and quotations, five times over, revising with each new manuscript. But each time I was carried away by the sheer accumulating power of the words I copied. I believe they will do the same thing for new readers. These quotations are rich reading and should not be taken in quantity, but eaten of many times, a little at a time. Some of the passages concentrate whole essays, and the poems say more than books.

The new parts of the present edition are two. One is "Knowing That You Know," and is Part I, consisting of five essays of my own. Four of them first appeared in *The Writer*. For this book I have combined some of them and re-written all of them, some extensively. The fifth essay,

"My Style, My Face," was written especially for this book. These five chapters do not proceed from one to the next or pretend to be all that might be necessary. But one intention runs through them, as it did in choosing the nine essays in Part II. That intention is to be suggestive, to set forth a great number of ideas, analyses, opinions, and reports, each one of which leads out and forward to a great many more.

The other new part is the addition of essays by contemporary poets and critics. The intent in adding these longer prose pieces by writers on poetry is to provide a larger, a richer, and a more specifically useful section, to which the writer may go for particular help. This group of nine essays (Part II) is entitled "A Great Quickness," from the piece by Richard Eberhart. Some of these are in their effect much like the briefer passages in Part III, "The Poet's Work." The selection of aphorisms by Wallace Stevens might have been used in the appropriate places in the original book, except that Samuel French Morse, his literary executor, had not then made them available, nor had Stevens ever published them. The excellent and deeply searching examination of a poem of R. P. Blackmur's by Donald Stauffer gets down to the fiery moment of the actual bursting forth of the poem in the heat of the poet's work, writing. This is the more specific example. Marianne Moore is specific, too, as she shows how the expression of feeling may be made precise, and gives examples of precision and the lack of it. Auden talks of his earliest thinking about poetry and of the example of Thomas Hardy, a great lesson we may well re-learn. Although Auden calls Hardy his master, we may be sure that Hardy did not know it. Nor could we know it until Auden told us. A poet's master must be the poet's secret. Richard Wilbur answers to the best of his scrupulous and penetrating ability a series of questions about his way of writing. These, too, may be compared with answers the reader could or would give.

My gratitude for assistance in preparing this book is owing more than I can indicate here: to my wife; to Richard S. Beal, Harrison M. Hayford, Myron J. Files, Harold H. Blanchard, Charles Gott, and the staff of Eaton Memorial Library, at Tufts College; to Louella D. Everett, Edgar Lee Masters, Theodore Roethke, Ruth Blodgett, Malcolm Cowley, Jessica Nelson North, Ford Madox Ford, John Cournos, E. M. Forster, Robert Frost, Christopher Morley, O. Kenneth Wrigley, Lucien Price, R. P. Blackmur, Max J. Herzberg, Helen Davies McGlade, John Ciardi, Charles Manning, and Welborn Hope for permission to quote their work, or for the generous loan of valuable books, or for patient answers to my questions; and to the *Atlantic Monthly* for permission to use in a revised form an essay which appeared with the title "Great Rich Vine."

Acknowledgment is hereby made to other magazines for permission to reprint verse or prose which first appeared in their pages: to *The Commonweal* for part of a poem by Eileen Duggan; to *Poetry: A Magazine of Verse* for a passage from an editorial by Jessica Nelson North; to the *New York Herald-Tribune Books* for some prose by Malcolm Cowley and part of a verse by John Jay Chapman; to *The Nation* for a sentence from an article by Conrad Aiken; and to the *Saturday Review of Literature* for extracts from the writings of Christopher Morley, Archibald MacLeish, William Rose Benét, Arthur Davison Ficke, Henry S. Canby, Frank Jewett Mather, Stella Benson, and Welborn Hope.

Acknowledgment of permission to quote from books is hereby made to Charles Scribner's Sons for extracts taken from *The Middle Years,* by Henry James; *Soliloquies in England,* by George Santayana; *The Enjoyment of Poetry,* by Max Eastman; *Axel's Castle,* by Edmund Wilson; *Tatterdemalion,* by John Galsworthy; *Adventures in Criticism,* by Sir Arthur Quiller-Couch; *Preludes for Memnon* and *Selected Poems,* by Conrad Aiken; *The Wind in the Willows,* by Kenneth Grahame; and *Across the Plains,* by Robert Louis Stevenson.

To the J. B. Lippincott Co., for permission to quote from *Romany Stain, Inward Ho!, John Mistletoe,* and *Human Being,* by Christopher Morley; and from *The Art Spirit,* by Robert Henri.

To Doubleday, Doran & Co., Inc., to Mrs. Rudyard Kipling, and to Messrs. A. P. Watt & Son for permission to quote from *A Book of Words,* by Rudyard Kipling.

To Doubleday, Doran & Co., Inc., for permission to quote from *The Right Place,* by C. E. Montague; *Harriet Hume: a London Fantasy,* by Rebecca West, copyright, 1929; *Notes on My Books,* by Joseph Conrad, copyright, 1920, 1921; *The Nigger of the Narcissus,* by Joseph Conrad, copyright, 1897; *Intellectual Things,* by Stanley Kunitz, copyright, 1929; and *A Writer's Notes on His Trade,* by C. E. Montague.

To Alfred A. Knopf, Inc., for permission to quote from *The Journal of Katherine Mansfield* and *The Letters of Katherine Mansfield; The Hill of Dreams,* by Arthur Machen; *Peter Whiffle,* by Carl Van Vechten; *Prejudices, Third Series,* by H. L. Mencken; and *Two Gentlemen in Bonds,* by John Crowe Ransom.

To the Viking Press, Inc., for permission to quote from *Studies in Classic American Literature,* by D. H. Lawrence, copyright, 1925; *The Letters of D. H. Lawrence,* copyright, 1932; *The Flowering Stone,* by George Dillon, copyright, 1931; *A Portrait of the Artist as a Young Man,* by James Joyce, copyright, 1916; *A Story-Teller's Story,* by Sherwood Anderson, copyright, 1924; and *Blossoming Antlers,* by Winifred Welles, copyright, 1933.

To Random House, Inc., for permission to quote from *Poems* by Stephen Spender; and *Poems* by W. H. Auden.

To Modern Library for permission to quote from William Butler Yeats's introduction to their edition of the poems of William Blake.

To Houghton Mifflin Co., for permission to quote from the essays and journals of Ralph Waldo Emerson; the journals of Henry David Thoreau; *Poems*: 1924-1933, by Archibald MacLeish; *Writing Poetry,* by Marie Gilchrist; *The Trusty Knave,* by Eugene Manlove Rhodes; *The Dance of Life,* by Havelock Ellis; *John Keats,* by Amy Lowell; *The Architecture of Humanism,* by Geoffrey Scott, and the journals of John Burroughs.

To G. P. Putnam's Sons, for permission to quote from *The Art of Writing,* by Sir Arthur Quiller-Couch.

To the Condé Nast Publications, Inc., for permission to quote from "Work and Echo," by Arthur Schnitzler.

To Sheed & Ward, for permission to quote from *Form in Modern Poetry,* by Herbert Read.

To the Caxton Printers, for permission to quote from *Streams from the Source,* by Helene Mullins.

To the G. & C. Merriam Co., for permission to quote from *Word Study* part of an article entitled "Marlowe's Mighty Line," by Max J. Herzberg.

To W. W. Norton Co., for permission to quote from *Exile's Return,* by Malcolm Cowley; *The Meaning of Culture,* by John Cowper Powys; *The Notebook of Malte Laurids Brigge,* by Rainer Maria Rilke; and *Discovering Poetry,* by Elizabeth Drew.

To the Bobbs-Merrill Co., for permission to quote from *Everyman's Genius,* by Mary Austin.

To Henry Holt & Co., for permission to quote from *Language,* by Otto Jespersen; *Motley and Other Poems,* by Walter de la Mare; *Address to the Living,* by John Holmes; *A Boy's Will, West-Running Brook, New Hampshire,* and *A Further Range,* by Robert Frost.

To Farrar & Rinehart, Inc., for permission to quote from *A Draft of XXX Cantos,* by Ezra Pound.

To Harcourt, Brace & Co., for permission to quote from *On Reading Shakespeare, Afterthoughts,* and *The Prospects of Literature,* by Logan Pearsall Smith; *The Imagination,* by I. A. Richards; *Play in Poetry,* by Louis Untermeyer; *Collected Essays,* by T. S. Eliot; *Abinger Harvest,* by E. M. Forster; *Orlando, To the Lighthouse,* and the *Common Reader, First and Second Series,* by Virginia Woolf.

To the Oxford University Press, for permission to quote from *The Letters of Gerard Manley Hopkins to Robert Bridges,* and the *Correspondence of Gerard Manley Hopkins and Richard Watson Dixon,* edited by C. C. Abbott; *The Notebooks and Papers of Gerard Manley Hopkins,* edited by C. C. Abbott; and *Poems,* by Gerard Manley Hopkins.

To the Macmillan Co., for permission to quote from *Strict Joy,* by James Stephens; *Collected Poems,* by William Butler Yeats; *Essays,* by William Butler Yeats; *Autobiographies,* by William Butler Yeats; *Selected Poems,* by Æ (George Russell); *Collected Poems,* by John Masefield; *A Shakesperian Grammar,* by E. A. Abbott; *Designed for Reading,* edited by H. S. Canby, Christopher Morley, William Rose Benét and Amy Loveman; *Poems,* by Eileen Duggan; and *Letters,* by R. L. Nettleship.

To Alfred A. Knopf, Inc., for permission to reprint a selection from "Adagia" from *Opus Posthumous,* by Wallace Stevens, Copyright 1957 by Elsie Stevens and Hollie Stevens.

To The Clarendon Press (England), for permission to reprint "Making, Knowing, and Judging," by W. H. Auden.

To McDowell, Oblensky, Inc., for permission to quote from *The Selected Letters of William Carlos Williams,* Copyright 1957 by William Carlos Williams.

To the Viking Press, Inc., for permission to quote from *Predilections,* by Marianne Moore, Copyright 1944 by Marianne Moore.

To Harcourt, Brace and Company, Inc., for permission to reprint "Genesis, or The Poet as Maker," by Donald Stauffer, from *Poets At Work,* edited by Charles D. Abbott, Copyright 1948, by Harcourt, Brace, and Company, Inc.

To Meridian Books, Inc., for permission to reprint Robert Frost's "Maturity No Object," the preface to *New Poets of England and America.*

To Stephen Spender, for permission to reprint his essay, "Can't We Do Without Poets?"

To R. P. Blackmur, for permission to reprint his poem, "Missa Vocis."

To Richard Wilbur, for permission to reprint his essay, "The Genie in the Bottle."

To Richard Eberhart, for permission to reprint his essay, "What I Say in Verse."

Such laborious acknowledgments clear one's debt to the holders of copyright, which is fair and right; there are other obligations to be discharged, though they are not easy to define. In the first place, I am painfully aware that, though I have been at some pains to thank both persons incorporated and persons as yet private and alive, I have by no means recalled and thanked the friends, students, writers, enemies, rivals, relations, critics, publishers, and people at large who are always helping to make a book whether they know it or not. My thanks are hereby extended to them.

But all this is not enough. In the prefatory mood (which is of course not at all prefatory but backward-gazing) I should like to summon from their exaltation the spirits of Ralph Waldo Emerson, and Henry David Thoreau, and Gerard Manley Hopkins, and Thomas Carlyle, and John Donne to thank them for having written what they wrote. They had more books in them than they published, and mine is least among them. I am glad for the industry and curiosity of Samuel Taylor Coleridge; the heartiness of William Hazlitt; the visions of William Blake, and Walt Whitman, and Thomas Traherne, who said, "You never enjoy the world aright, till the Sea itself floweth in your veins, till you are clothed with the heavens, and crowned with the stars." What would these be without the warmth and light of John Keats, without the shrewdness of Montaigne, Jonson, Schopenhauer, and Shakespeare? Much more than to publishers and interested friends I owe, and they owe, gratitude to these men who made their own names live, and made life better for their special energy spent among us. Looking back from this foreword (which ought to be at the end of the book) I think these poets have merely found, in these pages, another way to speak. My part is now obvious: I say, listen!

—John Holmes

Contents

Foreword vii

PART ONE ◆ KNOWING THAT YOU KNOW

CHAPTER

I Definition of a Poet 3
II Parable of Poetry: Devotion 11
III Born or Made 23
IV Biographies of Five Poems 36
V My Style, My Face 51

PART TWO ◆ A GREAT QUICKNESS

VI Making, Knowing, and Judging *W. H. Auden* 79
VII Maturity No Object *Robert Frost* 84
VIII Why I Say It in Verse *Richard Eberhart* 87
IX Adagia *Wallace Stevens* 91
X A New Measure *William Carlos Williams* 99
XI Can't We Do Without the Poets? *Stephen Spender* 104
XII Feeling and Precision *Marianne Moore* 111
XIII The Genie in the Bottle *Richard Wilbur* 120
XIV Genesis, Or the Poet as Maker *Donald A. Stauffer* 131

PART THREE ◆ THE POET'S WORK

CHAPTER

XV	The Poet's Words	143
XVI	The Poet's Knowledge	169
XVII	The Poet's Difficulties	211
XVIII	The Poet's World	242
XIX	The Poet's Nature	263

Writing Poetry

PART ONE

Knowing That You Know

I

Definition of a Poet

If you see three men walking down the street together, and one of them happens to be a poet, although at the moment you do not know it, nothing the poet does will reveal which one he is, and nothing about his looks will set him apart. Someone said the other day that businessmen and poets can't be told apart, unless the tweedier, pipe-smoking, rather literary-looking fellows seem to be off by themselves, and they're the businessmen. But in these days, poets live, act, and appear like any other normal human beings, which is as it should be. They must be close to life, and share it equally with men and women of their times. It is a cruel and stupid legend in comic strips, farce movies, and the minds of the thoughtless that poets wear long, ragged hair, live in attics, and are happier to be poor, and happiest in an unreal world of rhymed imagination. The fact is that poverty withers any human growth, and the lack of books, of the company of other writers, of travel, of good food and clothes, would kill a poet, or anyone else. And since above all, poets wish to live, it is a fact that they go about it like anyone else.

One prejudice against the poet, and literally a pre-judgment, is that he is highbrow. This leads to the assumption that what he writes is too obscure for easy understanding, that his occupation is somehow unmanly, and certainly unprofitable. The common prejudices are ignoble remnants of our pioneering age, when a right man had no time for idling with words, and the weak or lazy man who could, could find only women or children to listen to him. Naturally, the vigorous, fortune-founding, active men were suspicious of poetry. It seemed to exclude them—though they considered it beneath them—and they resented such inequality, especially when the cause of it could not be bought, sold, or seen. Everyone resents rejection, but rejection by a fool is outrageous. At present, and always, teachers, lecturers, and the poets themselves must acknowledge that these prejudices exist, that the charges of superiority, unmanliness, and obscurity are made, and that they must be met.

A lesser handicap to poetry is the conception of the poet as a bearded man of great age, a Santa Claus named Longfellow. He lived a hundred years ago, but the pictures hung in schoolrooms ever since have established in the minds of generations of students astonishing ideas of a poet. The hanging of pictures of poets as young, living poets, would be a movement worth starting—young Keats, young Rupert Brooke, or Archibald MacLeish, Richard Wilbur, Mark Van Doren, Dylan Thomas.

To the eye of the physician, psychologist or literary critic, there would be a difference between the strolling poet and his friends. Though all would appear active and alert, the poet would be even more eager and vigorous, awake and sensitive, observant and wondering. In a literal sense, the poet is more alive than other people, and it shows most when he writes. Ordinarily we know the world through our five senses. We see red and green lights, smell smoke, touch cloth or warm rough stone, taste seasoned meat, hear voices. Now the poet has all these senses, much heightened, and is equipped with twice as many more, perhaps three times as many. This is where he differs.

Hearers and lovers of poetry are endlessly curious about this difference. How does a poet know the things he knows? Where does he get the things he puts into a poem? How, they ask, is poetry written? Sometimes they say, I don't see how you do it; I couldn't. They should be answered, You don't have to; that's *my* business, or, that's my *business.* And it is. Good poetry is what is written by good poets. When a good poet looks at an object with the eyes in his head, he sees more than merely accurately. Most people see inaccurately or not at all, like the third monkey in the little group. Sight is the sense that most enriches poetry. Everywhere we read it, we come with amazement upon examples of this fact. Winifred Welles, writing about pale-colored caterpillars, says that they are "pleating and unpleating," and that "some wear dark spots, some have small dreary faces." The sense of sight (like all the others) relates closely to the sense for words, which is one of the great extra senses given a poet, along with the sense of analogy, and the sense of curiosity. When she had first seen pleating, she felt it was formation true not only of cloth.

Gerard Manley Hopkins speaks of the hawk's "wimpling wing," which happens also to be a word for the draping of cloth, here used of a bent wing; and he also knew that ancient word. The poet's knowledge is a sense, too, reaching into the past, and searching the present. When the caterpillar moved, Miss Welles had the right word for it, and again when it looked her in the face. "The difference," Mark Twain said once, "between the right word and the almost-right word is the difference between lightning and a lightning-bug." The curiosity, which is simply the urge to take a close look, is a most useful sense, and the poet begins to die, Conrad Aiken says, when he begins to be incurious.

Curiosity, the sense, is a kind of love, and so is wording. Eyesight is illuminated by a second seeing we call analogy. Winifred Welles wrote:

THE BODY OF THE ROOTS

The hand that up the dark and twisted stair,
  Carries the tulip's candle in its case,
The shoulder and the thigh, that, straining, bear
  Up to their shelf each gossamer urn and vase,
Are tense and knotted, lean and veined and spare.
  Not with deft swiftness nor with delicate grace,
But in slow agonies of strength and care,
  The burden of a flower's ephemeral face
Is lifted and unhooded in the air.

Seeing a person (or herself) stretch up to put something on a shelf, or urge the leaning body upstairs, she felt the quality of growth, what all growth is, slow and careful and upward. Probably the poem was made then in her mind, saying that a tulip growing is a flower being carried up as if a candle by an unseen hand. As if, as if—in these two small words lies the seed of poetry. And a poet is one who sees "as if."

Poets are extremely sensitive to life manifested as sound. Volume and pitch in their million gradations are separated in the poet's ear, and named. In usual people sound is noise. But the poet listens as eagerly as he looks. Sometimes it is as if he can hear grass grow or time pass. Sound becomes almost visible to him, especially the arranged and developing sounds we call music. Music makes images all its own, and these are as much design as sound, to the poet.

Poets, especially the more greatly imaginative poets, have a strong sense of space. It can be Archibald MacLeish in his "You, Andrew Marvell," with the cosmic sense of the dark coming round the earth, pouring like a tall wave toward him where it is noon. This sense makes a man feel his riding of the earth as it lunges over and over slowly on its axis in the middle of the sea of air. He has a compass swinging in his breast. Or he feels the strange float of being in a block of space, a room, between other blocks, and huge night outside the thin walls. Design is an arrangement of space, so that all slightest combinations of parallels, curves, and angles are recognized, and the balanced spaces between—by a poet. A poet feels the off-design, the imbalance. He might be a good deal of a nuisance around the house, forever straightening up the magazines on the table, moving chairs back, or picking up perfectly good litter. But he's more likely to do it imaginatively, or later on fix things up by creating the order of a poem.

Poets bother some people because they appear to live disorderly lives. In fact, many of them do, but it seems an ominous clue to something probably mixed up in the poets' art. Indifference to outward disorder is really certainty that in a poem all may be ordered, and the world's imperfections revenged. But never trust a poet. He is silent like a bomb. He is motionless like a gyroscope. When nothing much seems to be going on, a tremendous great deal is going to happen. Of course, he may merely be thinking about his clothes, or his car. He does have his human moments. In spite of much claim here for the poet's high-strung awareness, he may be as blank as blankness while some metaphor of extraordinary potentiality is before him, and be as blank inside as out. But his habit saves him, his involuntary reaction; like the barest blob of an amoeba, he opens himself, closes on the metaphor, and years later he writes it. This rescue takes place because the poet comes equipped with a highly associative mind, a metaphor-making mind. He is forever likening, even if he has to reach back through years of muscular memory to make the connection.

The poet's sense of time is powerful in him. It tells him that at every latest breath he draws, time is at the same point for everyone all over the world. Everyone is as far from his day of birth as the poet is; time is running through millions of people. In a poem of high vision, of strange exultation, called "Hot Afternoons Have Been in Montana," a prize poem of three decades ago, by Eli Siegel, we feel this sense reaching backward and forward. When he says that in the field where he sits there were once Indians fighting on a hot afternoon, and that "we live now and it is hundreds of years after," we are in both places in time. When the Indians fought and yelled, monks in cool black monasteries thought of God and studied Vergil. That was at that same time. With a more obvious magnitude than some of the other senses, the senses of time and space make the poet feel alive and complete in the life of man. There is such vibration of life in poetry that to read it is like taking hold of a naked wire—it stings and flashes and it quickens all the perceptions.

All these senses can be related and cross-related, and all have in common the quality of intense life—sight, words, movement, space, time, design, likeness—but words always and most of all. The poet is taut with life, shivering with the stroke of life upon him. If shivering seems a poor word here, it might be a good test, even so. Anyone still curious about those three men in the first paragraph can step up and twang them. The poet is the one that gives off a high humming sound; the others plonk. But the researcher is warned that the poetic twang is often inaudible; the poet doesn't rattle all over, he twangs, with that high humming sound. He receives the world through his own heightened senses, and because one of them is a sense for words and their most exciting and most beautiful order, he transmits the world to all who will read poetry. He transmits the world alive, even more alive than in reality. Poetry is a great reserve of life on which we may draw when our own supply is low. It comes to us beating with the intensity of the man who felt it and wrote it down. That very beating is still another of his special senses, the sense of rhythm.

But rhythm is the space between things, or the time between. Movement has rhythm when it repeats, divides, doubles and repeats. Rhythm is likeness with variations. It occurs in sound, and also in sizes, and at different levels. The one meaning of design is rhythm, and words spread out in patterns. Praise of poets comes in many forms, but none is more valued by the poet than to be told that he has a good ear. This ear is like no actual aural equipment seen on a human being, because it signifies the skilled-working-together of all the special senses—of the sense for his native language, for its literature, for the voice, for tones under and over that tell of experience.

The ultimate, and of course absolutely indispensable, special sense in the poet is the sense of truth, or it may be called the sense of salvation. At some time every poet writes the one poem that sums up everything on which he would be willing to stake his chances of salvation. At what time? Every time he writes. Every new poem is another bid for being snatched up by angels into life everlasting. But this is usual enough. Everyone tries it, and some, the artists, are trying it every day they live, for fear they will die. Beyond this sense of salvation, no other special senses are necessary to the poet—except, of course, a sense of humor. The perception of incongruity is the basis of a sense of humor, and having such a keen sense of congruity, the poet will surely have a lively sense of humor. And the sense of wonder should be added. The poet should also be able to detect subtle odors, exercise a well-instructed historical sense, and have the moralist's sense of significance and of discrimination. All these are of course absolutely indispensable. This completes the list of the special senses the possession of which, and the use of which, defines the poet. He has, of course, the sense of excellence, that which is good of its kind however unfamiliar the kind. He is helpless, or he must completely understand how to become completely helpless, that is, to surrender to event, to impression, to anything at all and drown in it, be lost. And find himself again. It is absolutely indispensable as a special sense that the poet know how to find himself. And how, although this subject is endless, to stop.

II

Parable of Poetry: Devotion

Becoming a poet may be likened to running in a race. There are strange things about this race, not the least of them being that there are tens of thousands of starters at the beginning of the long course, and more tens of thousands coming up behind them to the starting line. The race never begins; it has always been going on. Most of the runners are not very sure what the goal looks like, but some more than others sense the glory that attends the winning. This, too, is strange, because the real winners hardly ever know they have won; years pass, after their deaths, before they are declared to have won, are crowned with the wreath, and have the glory. Those few who approach the goal and find themselves running almost alone discover that the goal recedes as they come nearer. They can know, however, the great satisfaction of never falling back, of being always about to cross the line, and of running well.

The competition dwindles fast in this race. Hundreds upon hundreds drop out after the first spurt, and feel no disappointment, and never again move faster than a walk. Thousands more are content to endure a mile, four miles, seven miles, and to run standing still at that point for the rest of their lives. It is also true that these and some others admit to themselves their limitations and are bitter, cursing fate and such skill as has been allowed them. The most unhappy ones curse the runners disappearing in the distance ahead, and the runners coming up from behind and passing them, and those who are all around them running standing still.

Sometimes an incredibly fleet runner passes the beginning mob, the steady-moving hundreds up ahead, and seems to match stride for stride the little group running first. Those who watch the race pay more attention to him than to anyone else—his remarkable speed, his brilliant performance, his power! The watchers look away for a moment, and when they look back he is not there at all, and he is never seen again, and after a while the watchers forget that they have forgotten his name.

One of the strangest of all the strange things about this race is that many of those who attain real distance, respectable and even admirable distance, and go no further, are happy in their continuing effort. They do not expect to win any more, but they greatly enjoy having run, and keeping on running—standing still. It is good exercise, and they are good at it. Actually the watchers come back again and again to the place in the race-course where these runners are, to watch and admire them. In the watchers' hearts is no jealousy of the leading runners and no contempt for the early quitters, but a great deal of satisfaction in doing what they are doing, and affection and respect for those about them, still running in the one place. They are doing their best, and their best is good.

Far out in front, a long way ahead, about a dozen runners are strung out along the road. They often shift position. One who has been back in ninth place will draw ahead slowly and reach second or first place. Another will come up from fourth place and run ahead for a little while, or maybe for a long time. They run smoothly and steadily; they have no thought now of giving up; but they race mostly against themselves, and all of them will be remembered by those who remember good running.

However, out of sight in the distance are two, perhaps three, runners who see the goal very clearly and very near. Theirs is a joy unknown to any of the thousands and thousands behind. They know they will cross the line. They know they are better runners, faster, stronger, more enduring than all the rest in their generation. There is no doubt that each one has a secret belief that he is to be, and ought to be, the first to reach the goal. But these great runners can do no more than they are doing. They are doing their best, and if their best is so nearly equal that differences are imperceptible, they know, and all the watchers know, and all the runners know that their best is infinitely better than any other in the race.

It is the sense of that power, the perspective of that understanding, that is the glory the tens of thousands hoped to know, and one by one, and score after score discovered they could never know. There is a serenity in that self-knowledge, and a richness of the memory of reward, for the rewards have been many. It may be—in fact, it is probably only too true—that what the starters hoped for was the world's reward, the cheers, the medals, the worship, and that they mistook it for the true glory. The starters were too likely to wish *to have run* the race, not to run it. The immortal two or three are glad to be running, to be nearing the goal, to know the goal is surely theirs.

Now that the parable has been told—and drawing out the metaphor to the limit, maybe beyond the limit, has been real pleasure, like writing a poem—suppose we translate some of it.

Everyone has written a poem sometime in his life. One may have been enough to drain off all the poetry in his being. Still, a great many people have written a great many more than one, even if these poems were never shown to anyone. The reason for this is that poetry begins with emotion, and that poetry is a release for emotions otherwise unbearable in the intensity of their pain or pleasure. Over a period of years, it has been my experience that young people most frequently are stirred to write (what they think is) a poem when girl has met boy, and boy has left girl. There is some curious compulsion to probe the hurt again and again, as we tongue a sore tooth. Then girl (sometimes boy) wants professor or someone to look at his poem. But it isn't a poem at all; it is an entry in a diary, containing just enough stimuli to reawaken the pleasure-pain of the great experience, and not anywhere near enough to move or interest anyone else. Brutal remark, but true. And there we lose the first few thousand starters in the long race. This is good for everyone. Maybe some of the happiest people there are living are those who don't want to write poetry, and are not writing poetry, and don't even know that they don't want to. Next are probably those who quit early. They will never know how gentle that early criticism was, compared to the bruising, withering brutality later to be risked, or felt. The pains of love become new pleasures (girl meets new boy), but the wounds of severe, true, and deserved criticism bite deep, and the good writer does not live who does not flinch with pain on wet dark days, years after.

There is a better chance of making some distance if the young sufferer in love cares more about how she says it, and not what she says. The *how* will not only carry her past the break-up of the love-affair, but will carry her on toward satisfactions of growth in technical skill and clear thought. The Irish poet, James Stephens, knew it:

> And cared it into song—strict care, strict joy!
> Caring for grief he cared his grief away:
> And those sad songs, tho' woe be all the theme,
> Do not make us grieve who read them now
> Because the poet makes grief beautiful.

A sure sign of intention to try for the distance is a real concern with form and technique, and a discipline of the subjective, the I, my, me. Later on it can come back, and as Christopher Morley said:

> Cries the poet every day,
> Ego, mei, mihi, me.

But there must be discipline of technical skill, and that takes time to learn. *Ego* and *mei* are interesting only when the pronouns have verbs, nouns, not too many adjectives, and some real word-music to go with them.

The young poet begins to get interested in an audience, usually long before any audience of more than three or four could possibly be assembled, but it is nevertheless a good sign. It is the death-wish, pure and simple, to write poems and hide them away, never to want them to be seen and heard. What kind of person does this is beyond human understanding, because he is inhuman by self-definition. Poetry is the life-wish, life put to words. A poet, someone (probably Auden) said, is one who when he has nothing to do, does something. He writes, therefore he wants to be read. Good. The normal behavior at this stage is one of vast day-dreams, born of night-long sessions of writing, tremendous-excitement, tremendous-words, I-am-a-poet, my-poems, Shelley, Shakespeare, etc. So he writes to Louis Untermeyer (I did) and sends him poems (too many) and asks, "Will you give me a criticism of all these poems, and tell me whether or not I should continue with my writing?" And Louis Untermeyer writes back (he did) with more patience than is deserved, and a rebuke well-deserved, and some never-to-be-forgotten advice: "I can't possibly write about your poems, I'm a busy man. If you're any good, *you're* the one who really knows it. And as for continuing with your writing, if you *can* stop, for God's sake do, and there'll be that much more room for the rest of us." All I wanted was an audience, praise, cheers for my genius. Not forthcoming from Louis, bless him for this and many good deeds for poetry's sake.

If you were really running in a long race—to return to the parable—would you stop off at the side of the road, and ask, "Do you think I should keep on running, in order to win this race?" What would the watcher say?

Oddly enough, many good runners, meaning good young poets, do foolish things like this, because they want recognition, any recognition, from anyone at all. If the urge to write poetry has really come from a need for ego-satisfaction, a build-up, it had better stop right here. And a great many people drop out of the race here and spend the rest of their lives running standing still, asking for criticism—by which they mean praise—seeking a soothing of some hurt in the psyche. But if it is good listeners these people want, they will work to learn how to reach an audience. "To have great poets there must be great audiences too," said Walt Whitman. To have average poets or good poets, there must be audiences. All poets have audiences; every audience has its poet. There is no such thing as a large audience with no poet, and no such thing as a Milton unwept, unhonored, and unsung. Without doubt Whitman meant that greatness of the audience will bring forth poets with like greatness in them, nobility summoning up nobility, and wisdom begetting wisdom. However we try to change this shape, it still has two parts, poet and audience. The poet, the real poet, will not seek merely praise.

The wiser young poets, who submit their poems to magazines and abide by the decisions of the editors, will last longer in the race. It is simple sense not to send poems to the two or three best-known magazines in the country—their names come first to mind with every college undergraduate, every hopeful everywhere. Arithmetic will tell you that twelve numbers in each year can carry an average of about three poems per issue, no more. Try smaller magazines first, the little magazines that don't pay, but show by their content a respect for poetry. Study lists of all the magazines, or study the magazines themselves. But when two or three of the smaller magazines have accepted and printed your work, *move up*. The parable again—thousands drop out at this point. Once having been accepted by one or two little magazines, they go on sending their work, knowing everything will be taken. Dare the next step. Try better magazines. Prove you can do it until you have proved you can go no higher.

Of course, higher is not necessarily bigger, and eminently respectable is not necessarily good, in the magazines. Range is what the poet is testing, the limits and areas of the kind of audience he can get to listen to him. Nothing puts an exact rating on a poet, in the eyes of other poets, quicker than his list of magazine publications. In the front pages of first books it happens, that list of acknowledgments, that fine little bundle of scalps hung from the belt of, "Some of these poems first appeared in . . . and grateful acknowledgment for permission to reprint is made herewith." Grateful be damned. It's his ticket to the assembly. Will it get him in? Into what company? It's a badge, and he wears it in very plain sight. For this reason, the somewhat more than beginning poet will choose his magazine appearances with care. There are several kinds of prestige in this matter. But let it be said that the real best, early and late, is publication in the strong little magazines, those literary quarterlies of small circulation, highest critical standard, and intellectual energy. Whichever eight or ten flourish at any one time, the quality is about the same, and the distinction of publication in them about equal. This is where the really good things happen, and happen first; in this company one is rightly proud to be welcome.

During this time of range-finding—and time ought to pass rapidly, with good clear-cut results coming fast—the poet will still want recognition, but will have learned how to get it with modesty and confidence. He may seek membership in the best local organization there is, where he can get criticism, maybe win a few prizes, and share and compare himself with others at somewhere near the same stage of development. Fear of adverse criticism, fear of comparison, result in inverted pride, a vast suppressed conceit, and a deep unhappiness. Certainly now try for an audience, through companionship and publication (itself good company), and as it is deserved it will be found.

It might be said here that many a backward look at the annual collections of magazine verse made by William Stanley Braithwaite from 1915 to 1929 will teach sound lessons in what to do and what not to do. Revisions of standard anthologies; the periodic evaluations of a decade or a half decade, in the United States and in England; the annual book-publication awards in poetry—these tell the story. From ten or twenty years away one is sometimes astounded by bad poems in poor magazines signed by good names. Simultaneously one is depressed by the endless alphabetized no-names, the adequate and briefly persevering and long-since-forgotten names, which far outnumber the good names under the bad little poems. The good runners started where all the rest of them started, but they kept on coming.

How did they keep on coming? How did they outlast the tens of thousands, then the thousands, the hundreds, and get up forward? How did they last? There's the real secret, the unvoiced problem, the thing we all want to know. Who didn't win the Yale Series of Younger Poets publication award last year, and why? If one publishes long enough and well enough in magazines (though God and the goalkeeper certainly know that the magazine is not the golden gate), there will be a book at last. What sort of book? Who is the publisher? His name is another part of the badge. *Who'll buy it?* It had better be the best book you can put together of all you have written—ruthlessly, savagely, grimly the best choices. By and large, publishers like about seventy-five pages, but sixty will be a better book. Even that is a lot of good poetry, a very great deal of good poetry. Have you that much? Wait, if you haven't, and don't take any short cuts. There are publishers who will show you short cuts, the obvious one being payment from your own pocket. But right there you, too, drop out of the race, and begin to run standing still. You can run and run, just as long as your bank account lasts, and no one much cares. The only right publication of a book is that done by an established publishing house, one so sure of your poetry's worth that it will risk the large sum of money necessary to manufacture a book. My publisher. Ah! Wonderful, wonderful words, even if you say them quietly and not very often.

The competition is getting really tough now. Here many

hundreds of runners drop out. They know no one will invest in them, and wisely they withdraw. Here more scores (I think not hundreds—there aren't that many left) tighten their manuscripts, gird their loins, screw up their courage a bit higher, and keep trying. Some of them achieve a book. I think there are a few unhonored junior Miltons here, but not unwept, because I'll drop a tear now for them, the very good and somehow overlooked few poets in each generation, stones of the house, maybe ornaments. And after the book come the reviewers, who say what they think in print, and the unknown readers who think to themselves.

But this is really only the beginning, and nowhere near the sight of even the dwindling middle group of runners. A book is—a book. There are many books. There are too many books, in fact, and, in poetry, too many for the number of willing or possible buyers. So the next hurdle is the second book. The second, and the third, and the fourth books of poems—a progression lifting at a dizzy geometrical speed—begin to tell what the poet's place in the race may be. It is assumed that each line of each poem of each of these new books is good, better than the last, better than anything anyone else is doing, but best of all the best you can do, in a way that no one else but you could do. Take about ten years for that. Ten years.

How have you been earning a living all this time? Not from writing poetry. Not even if you teach it somewhere, and lecture about it in many other places? No, not even that way. How have you managed to marry, and have a family, and live in a house that has heat and hardware, books and boys and love and electric light, and all the human warmth a poet needs to help make? The stupid, persistent picture of the poet in an attic is a cruel and terrible lie; more life cannot come out of no life. You want a house and a home, of course. And here several more hundred runners drop out, as they should.

Those who are still in the race have somehow (how?) been skillful, energetic, ruthless, and gifted enough to have this and poetry too. Now we are still further up, and now the competition is worse than tough. It is a fight with or against one's own bone, muscle, and mind; with or against time, and age, and the ultimates. Because the ultimates, by which we mean the goal, are forever there. How much you care about reaching the far-off sight of the ultimates, the greatness and its fame—that is what brings you forward out of the mob, through the middle crowd, into the smaller persistent group, and within sight of the leaders. Someone asked Dylan Thomas if he thought himself a great poet, or perhaps pronounced him to be, and he said, "I am first among the second." That seems to me one of the humblest, wisest, and proudest things I know of a poet saying. It doesn't matter at all if I disagree, or you disagree with me. That he said it is memorable. He understood the meaning of the race.

But it isn't really the fame, it isn't being one of the leaders, that you want. *It's knowing that you know how to write*. It all comes back again to being very much alone, and being wholly yourself. The aloneness is not loneliness, and the being wholly yourself is not peculiarity. Devotion to the craft of writing may do as much as anything else to bring you up toward the front—devotion—a most difficult state of mind to maintain and enlarge through forty years. But it is clearly to be seen, on the shelves, that devotion to poetry is what has put the big volumes of collected works into the libraries, and consequently into hearts and memories.

Poetry is not a part-time thing. Poetry is not a hobby, a

little talent with beadwork or whittling, or a happy skill with sketching in one's off hours. Poetry is not something you do after you've finished something else; it's what won't let you finish anything else. Poetry is not ease, or easy. Poetry is one of the major arts, and demands of its practitioners a major effort, and a major ability, sustained, perfecting, and triumphant. The greatest artists of all time are the happiest human beings of all time. They know a joy beyond anything anyone else can know: they have used their gift.

And in the light of this parable we must question ourselves. Should I go on with my writing, against such very long and very severe odds? Why, of course, of course you should. Should I quit right now? No. No, of course not. Unless you have it in you to be discouraged by the few minutes you have spent reading these few hundred words. If you are as near as that to giving up, it can't make much difference. But what if I think I know exactly my place in the race, and know I'll never get ahead? What about running standing still?

How do you know you're standing still? The condition of life is change, and it is more than likely that, whether you think so or not, you're changing. Take the long view. Admit to yourself the conditions of the race you've committed yourself to. It has only just begun. And with all the grace of spirit, and all the craftsmanship and art you have in you, keep on writing. *The word is, devotion.*

III

Born or Made

The old question of whether the poet is born or made is very simply answered: He must be born partly a poet, and his urgent, peculiar, uncultivated talents will find the way to completion. I propose here to examine the qualities with which the poet may be born, and what he is likely to do with them; and also the latent possibilities that can be developed, what they are, how they can be recognized, possessed, and used. There is one condition. We are going to discuss real poetic ability, the real gift for creating poetry. We are going to reject the feeble stirrings, the fake gestures, and the facile but immature persistence that make rhymes and print them, getting nowhere with great energy. The proof of the born poet is that he makes this rejection in himself, and for himself, and goes on from there. He has an impatience that grows to harshness at the less than best, and in others as well as himself. It is a gnawing and dreadful hunger, and it grows more fierce after a few tastes of the true sustenance. Nothing less will satisfy, and there is not enough to go around; it's eat or die, and die they do, though thousands of them still walk around. But not the longest shelf of published volumes, not daily verse in all the newspapers, nothing, can make a poet where no poet is.

It is said that everyone has a novel in him. This probably means that every life has the making of a novel in it, not that each living person could, if he would, write it. It is far truer that everyone has at least one poem in him, and almost a certainty that he has written it, too. Scratch the most unlikely person you can think of, and there'll be a poem or many poems. It is necessary to realize that it is as natural as physical growth to exude at some time or other a few poems. Somewhere in emotional and bodily enlargement a written statement that looks and sounds like a poem will appear, as surely as the bones and voice and glands change. It is usually as personal a matter, too. But it should not be mistaken for the emergence of a literary gift. Too often it is, and years are wasted in tending it. The same overflow of emotion, or pricking of perception, or articulation of an ideal, will soon and naturally modify, and the doctor, or teacher, or manager will go on to be what he was always meant to be, which is not a poet. This time of pre-definition is a natural phase, and poetry is a natural part of it. But as soon as a stronger inclination shows, and the poetry takes second place, that phase is over. Poetry never takes second place.

Not to write poetry is a decision that will take care of itself for most people. They simply stop. But for some it is years before they know for sure whether it is worth going on with. This can be a really agonizing period, and can go on for summers of writers' conferences, winters of extension courses, season after season of lonely pounding and scribbling. Whether in late adolescence, or more or less middle age, the troubled ones should face the question and answer it. The question has two ways of showing itself:

Should I go on with my work? and, How can I go on with my work?

There are two ways of looking at it. One is the rather curious notion of refraining from writing poetry in the hope that this abstention will be curative or restorative. The other is the more active view, that of doing something immediate and practical about those dismal times when one can't write, hasn't been writing, and is scared (not really frightened, just scared) that maybe nothing more will get written. At least, not by this particular poet. There is a third way of looking at it, which we can save for a while; the first two are the important ones.

In order to accept at all the thought of ceasing to write poetry, voluntarily and of necessity, of course you have to know what it feels like to want to write. This goading need never really lets up. The man or woman who is apparently an official or a designer or a wife or a musician, but is really a poet, has always at the back of his mind a memory of the time a poem got written, and written right. This poem seems to have been fated to come out in exactly the right words and the pattern it happily achieved, with this poet's hand holding the pencil. No matter how the poet earns a living, no matter what name other people know him by, for this once he was a poet, and wrote the poem. This experience is important. It is secret, unforgettable, and one of the few greatly satisfying experiences in all life. The words rush, the picture grows and lifts, the lines come strengthening and lengthening into stanzas and forms, and suddenly there it is—the poem that meant itself to be written. You softly and silently pound the tabletop with clenched fist. This is it. And you taste for a little while alone the real, the only satisfaction, after which you rush out to read the poem to someone, and thereafter to mail it to an editor. And as a matter of fact, an editor is likely to print a poem written under such warm compulsion, with such inevitability.

So far, so good. You have had this high creative experience, which nothing can take away from you, even if an editor obtusely rejects the poem. What matters is the great feeling of having done it. Then, of course, what comes next is the desire to have that feeling again, to find yourself again at the desk late at night, the pattern fulfilling itself, the next poem coming to life, and your hand doing it.

And it doesn't come to life. It falls cold and clumsy. You tear it up. Next night you try again, and it's still all wrong. And this goes on. You have to have known the ultimate achievement coming now and then through a long period of time, and to have known times of failure to recapture it, before you will even understand the meaning of the simple words, "Stop writing poetry for a while, say for a month, maybe six months."

It's a nice theory. I never tried it. But I still believe that if I forbade myself, or if some circumstance I can't quite imagine prevented my writing poetry, that enforced silence would be a very good thing for me. There is nothing so agonizing as the long periods of harried anxiety, fallow and futile and miserable, during which one daily and hourly wishes to be writing and is not writing. Why not take the hard advice of the critic I do not name, and stop trying; but stop for only a stated period? Stop wishing to write. Stop looking for poems. Stop torturing yourself because you aren't writing. At the end of a month or six months, you will do one of two things: You will have discovered you honestly don't care about starting again, or you will begin writing so fast and so happily that the abstinence will have been more than worth it. I would, of course, hope the latter would be the result. The poet needs periods of restoration and should write when he must, not merely when he wishes he were writing.

But suppose, to pass on to the second consideration, that you don't need this drastic cure and don't want to try it, but simply want to stir into action and haven't been writing very much. The poet, since he knows nothing is foreign to him, and since he is curious about all things, is always open, always receptive. If, however, there comes a brief interval in which he ceases to shape and state all that he has been taking in, he becomes most unhappy. A sort of crust forms as the days lengthen between today and the last day he actually wrote a poem. The longer this goes on the worse it is. It becomes necessary to use some arbitrary method, self-imposed, of breaking the crust. One method, suggested by Stephen Vincent Benét (all poets have this trouble sometime), is to vow to write a fixed number of poems in a stated number of days, say, ten sonnets in a week. The sonnet, because it is a set form, and short, and the poet is freed of the problem of a choice; the week, because it is rather a short time, and one must grasp at and use anything and everything, and hammer it into a poem.

The amazing thing is that this cure works. Rhythms and phrases come out of the air, from overheard conversation, from the pages of books and papers, maybe from your own mouth. At such a time, more or less idly discussing the New England character (that twisty subject), I heard myself saying, "To be New England is to get up early and make the most of the day." That did for one poem; all I had to do was finish it—which was not hard, because I had reminded myself of something I knew all about. At first a sonnet, it became longer because there was more to say. Ideas are everywhere, in daily contacts, and in daily reading. Music does it. Faces, and familiar furniture, and ordinary routine, and the morning mail—all these bring something. That is, they bring something at which the poet, in his self-imposed new desperate need, will grasp. T. S. Eliot says somewhere that the poet in this hungry state is like the amoeba: he eats everything within reach. But what is happening is that he skims the forming crust off, and knows again what he always knew, that the material of poetry is all about him, but that he was out of the habit of seeing and using it. This discipline is a sort of sand-papering of the nerve-ends—one is thin-skinned again, which is only a way of describing what we wish were the normal emotional and working condition.

As for varying the assignment, demanding of one's self a certain number of poems in another form, or no form, I don't know what the answer is. But there are a few other cures.

There are always one's notebooks, or old work-sheets. Search slowly through them and glean—literally—the best and most suggestive phrases, lines, ideas, and give them another try. It is also often a stimulation and release to hear or to read poetry. Go to a club meeting, turn on a radio program, or best of all, break up household and professional routine by having a few hours of reading aloud. The poet, at this time, should not read his own work—should emphatically arrange things so he won't be asked to, and, if asked, still won't. His own poetry is old to him. He needs a new sound and pattern, if for no other reason than to feel jealous about it, competitive, assertive. He should listen, though, long and quietly; he can even make notes, off-shootings and extensions. When it is impossible to get people together, it is still always possible to read alone. Get out the books; take a trip through old scrapbooks; sit down with a new number of *Poetry*, or hunt out the verse in the month's periodicals. If the people who signed those poems did it (you will soon and irritably feel) then you can.

These are the direct ways. Personally, the big *U. S. Camera Annuals,* or, in fact, any of the several handsome books of reproductions of new and older art do things for me. The imaginative photographer composes his emotion in a design, and the poet feels the balance and opposition, the thrust of meaningful forces, the underlevels of symbolic suggestion. All this may be very much on the surface, and may not work when one's obstacles are deep, complex, economic, or spiritual, and very slowly curable, if at all. Yet even then these simple and workable ways of beginning to write again can be the first step.

A third way of looking at the idea of not writing is merely this: For every poet of any merit whatever, there are tens of thousands of human beings who never wrote a line, and never will, and never should. The poets are in a fortunate minority. The competition is not keen, except inside the group. Poets should be thankful for the great numbers of people who do not try to write poetry, who needn't even read it. They don't care. They get along perfectly well without it, they needn't be converted, they make good lives in their own ways, and that's that. Poetry is not for everyone.

But for those to whom poetry means a great deal, reading it or writing it, it is demanded that they look sanely and practically at the problems of keeping at it, or stopping. Nothing can be worse for poetry than fakery and pose and snobbishness of a highbrow sort. Let those who can, write poetry, and those who like to read, read it; and let both respect and live with those who don't do either. The ability to write poetry is only one skill among many that make life beautiful and endurable, but it should be honored according to its high place, and, if you have been given it, it should be cared for and made to grow.

If you are partly born a poet, it will be because your mother and father, and their mothers and fathers, were in some way poets. They may never have written one word. But some creative gift, some intensity of character, passed from one generation to another, and so to you, and made you partly a poet. You need not search in family history for orators, for highly educated ancestors, or necessarily for preachers. And it is a rule almost without exception that the children of poets are not poets. Look rather for carpenters. Ask your father what his mother collected or explored. Look for musicians, masons, or some aunt or uncle who liked amateur dramatics. Preachers are very useful ancestors for poets, if it can be so arranged, and so are teachers. But we know something about Shakespeare's parents, and grandparents, and the only trait we are sure of is ambition. That's good; that explains a lot. We are what we have inherited, but we should know what it is, to know ourselves.

The best way to find out about those men and women who gave you your own jaw, nose, forehead, bones, and inner drive, is by word of mouth. It is truer that way, and richer; but what you can read in family letters and diaries is also good, if you can illuminate it with your own understanding. Robert Louis Stevenson's father and several uncles built lighthouses, and there is a poem by R. L. S. that pays tribute to that more tangible creative genius. He apologizes in doing so, which is unnecessary and mistaken; they were all makers. The father of William Butler Yeats was a great conversationalist, painter, letter-writer, and observer of human affairs, as well as his son's best counsellor in the literary life. Emerson was strongly influenced by his aunt. Robert Frost's father was a newspaperman, his mother a schoolteacher. But these proofs are too obvious. What, in the blood and minds of the predecessors of these poets' parents, made them what they were? Browning's father was a banker, and Archibald MacLeish's father a well-to-do mid-western businessman. Charles Connick got as far as the eighth grade in the Pittsburgh schools and became one of the greatest designers of stained glass windows of our time. It was his mother who held their house together, she who gave him his stout courage and the drive of genius. No poet begins in and of himself.

As a usual thing, the poet's inborn gift tells him what he is, without recourse to genealogical libraries or family lore. It is part of his nature that he discovers himself. It is from his natural self that he will write. But there is a balance, always nicely kept, between conscious and unselfconscious awareness, and this special awareness is the first of the poet's inborn traits. The second is energy; not might, but a ruthless, persisting strength of purpose, single-minded and unkillable. The poet is largely ego, and this ego has a tremendous will to survive. To survive means to be heard, to be known by name. If a mute, inglorious Milton were to speak up, the sound would still be inglorious; there is no such thing as a Milton unheard.

The poet fears more than anything in life the diminishing and stilling of his given energy or its re-charging powers. He teaches himself every known trick and invents a few new ones for using the best energy he has while he has it. The third motivation in a poet is the wish for immortality. By this I do not mean a page in Palgrave, and he does not mean fame as such. He means an extension of his being beyond the usual span of life, because time presses in on him and seems too little and too swift. A man probably would not say, as Edna St. Vincent Millay did, "Read me! Do not let me die!" but that is exactly what he is working at: not to die. To project himself, to assert himself, to be read and talked about by people a hundred and more years after he is gone—a man wants that, and through his poetry he can have it. After the tributes paid to Robert Frost at his eightieth birthday dinner, he stood up, holding the book of his poems that had been printed in celebration of the day, and said, "All I have tried to do—what this tonight is all about—is to put a few poems in this book that will be hard to get rid of."

In a world where much is disorderly, much imperfect, the poet is impelled to clear at least one small space, and make at least one thing harmonious, orderly, perfect. This effort is his means of assertion and projection, his claim on a longer life than most men may have. As a designer, he knows that his hope of any future is in the best design he can make. His art will save. This powerful urgency is what makes him labor and experiment, shape and reshape, add and again add to his craftsmanship. He will seek his style and listen for his own voice. He will aim at bringing deepest awareness of himself, at a time when his energy is at its fullest, and all the lessons of tradition, all that he can add to what he has learned, and all that he most surely knows from thinking his own thoughts, to his poem. This concert of all his powers in an attempt to write a poem hard to get rid of may achieve just that. A man is easily lost, a voice forgotten. But to write an indispensable poem is to live, in the poem, in men's lives needed and remembered.

What are your gifts, if you still think you are a poet? You should have, and you probably do have, a good ear, a great heart, untiring curiosity, a definable moral sense, a retentive memory, a wide and unconventional reading experience, extra physical or nervous energy, some ego, human relations the richer the better, a sense of place, a sense of time passing—and maybe a hundred other things equally important. It is a good beginning, having been born thus, to make something with, possibly a poet. But these are samples at random. The five senses are only five of a possible twenty or thirty the poet should have and cultivate. Some others are communication, the present, the past, design, words—and perhaps a sense for words is one of the first a poet must have. The poet relishes words, knows a great many, makes new ones, is passionately exact about meaning, gives them extra levels of suggestion, delights and swaggers and swims in words.

Some of these given senses are intellectual or emotional, some sheerly physical. Anyone can name great poets who lack three or four, but the very best of all have the few necessities, and the necessities are those qualities that signify breadth and depth of sympathy, curiosity, and energy.

There is a real and nameless fraternity, in the best meaning of the word, always existent, made up of the best painters, actors, poets, the finest comedians, designers, and photographers, the leading builders, teachers, and creators. Where they come together they speak a common language. They are poets of our time. Given a real start, anyone may wish sometime to join this happiest of all company. Be sure, as sure as if this were a threat against your life, that you will never attain it unless you follow the greatest examples to the limit of your realized ability. First of all, you must want to be in the company that has one ruthless purpose, and that purpose, poetry. Next, you must be eager and open to learn from others and from yourself. No skill in another should find you indifferent: Why should you not be interested in wiring a house, or teaching Latin, or mixing ink? There is a right way to do it, and you are concerned in right ways to do. Next, you must never forget anything you have seen, heard, touched, smelt, tasted, or guessed. It cannot all be at once at finger tip and tongue's end, but you must know how to bring it there quickly, with delighted surprise that it comes. Memory is the great storage of your power, to be drawn upon and to be renewed every hour. And, if you are to be a poet, you must give yourself away to all things, even to the dirty and the evil. You must know they are that, before you deny and fight them. But from that extreme all the way up, you may keep nothing to yourself. You must see into, feel into, share, care, exult, and sicken. All life is your body, and you cannot push away the miserable or the difficult any more than you welcome the gay or golden. You must take them both.

What is there left to say? Something about training? Someone to tell you if you are really in love? If you know what you want, if you know who you are, then any specialized courses are just that: courses. The time to take courses and read rule-books in poetry is when they can no longer be anything but a review. You may very well need some work in the speaking of poetry, and you can always gain something—composition or interpretation—from the study of contemporaneous poetry. There are always books, but the books nearest at hand are not all there are; you have a lifetime of reading to do that no one can prescribe as you can for yourself. A wealth of special information is available on techniques, markets, critics, and how to wrap a manuscript. There are a surprising number of experienced poets with whom it is possible to make acquaintance, and so learn something the right way, which is first-hand. But however you do it, by courses, instructors, books, or hanging around with poets, it doesn't really count. These possibilities in you would push themselves out if there were no one to help. You don't need anyone to help, and if you do, then you are no poet, because the first, last, and best creation the poet puts his name to is himself.

Suddenly it seems necessary to say here that not all poets write words into patterns and print them for others to read. The creative gift may be handed down through the generations, changed and enriched, and produce you as a superior printer, librarian, mother, or grocer. Be a good one! God knows it is more pleasing in His eyes to be a really good grocer, a really good city councillor, than a third-rate poet. Be a good poet, or no poet at all.

IV

Biographies of Five Poems

It seems to me that very often the poet himself is not the one who knows most about the genesis of his poem; but for what it is worth, here it is:

THE NEW VIEW

There was an old stump of an old tree standing
All naked of bark, and brown, and ten feet tall
In the wrong place for our summer pleasure.
I pushed it over. I was glad to see it fall.

Let it lie there in the high grass till it rotted.
The roots broke when I rocked it where it stood,
The trunk split, and the shell in half-round pieces
Opened, and let fall something that had been wood.

But there were bees in it. Bees have a business
Not safely suddenly outraged by anything.
Nothing is left to an old man but his anger,
And I had hurried death that needs no hurrying.

The stump gone, we could look further and greener.
It was two June days before my wound was well.
That was all we got, and we had the spoiled honey
For sorrow, and a new view past where the tree fell.

We had been given for the summer a house in the green hills near Brattleboro, Vermont. It wasn't my house, so it wasn't my tree, either. But after a while I began actively to resent the tall old stump, sticking up between me and the other side of the valley like a pillar in a theater that cuts you off from the stage. It looked thoroughly dead to me, and I rationalized that my friends, who owned the house, would be glad of the obvious improvement I made to their estate by pushing the thing over one early evening.

What bit me was a wasp, not a bee. Bees, I think, don't store honey in such trees, but I looked at Article Four, Section G, of my poetic license, and decided I could and would mention bees and honey. Truth is truer than fact. I simply felt the red-hot sudden end of a wire in the back of my neck, and a somewhat similar prick of guilt, at the same time. When we set forth breakfast on the porch of that very pleasant house, next morning, I thought the view vastly bettered. But it was months later that I wrote the poem, and the poem is not about tree-stumps and bees (wasps) at all. It was sometime in the following winter that I had a brief, angry argument with my father, during which I showed the ignorant arrogance of a young man. He came back at me with considerable fire, truth, and authority, and it stung. The sting was that I had secretly harbored the thought that he was getting old; but he wasn't. The outburst, whatever it was about, was probably deeper down a fear and protest at the slow failure that had almost imperceptibly then begun. But there was plenty of temper and seniority left in him still, and I was ashamed and deeply stirred.

The emotional stir was what made me want to say something in a poem, something as retribution, I suppose, but anyway the stir. I think it is necessary to go further back for a cause. I notice that I have often written about, or used as an image, an old man, the tough old warm-spirited exasperating and terribly durable man. I don't know why this is. Maybe from reading much Yeats, and echoing to his bitter hatred of old age. Maybe, therefore, from a fear of my own old age, but maybe also because I hoped and hope to be one of the terribly durable old men. It could be carried deeper.

Suddenly I remembered the tree stump; it was my father, and I had tried to push him down. The actual tree, I now remembered, didn't push as easily as I had expected. It took a lot of rocking, and I did get stung for doing it. It was swift writing to set down the first eight lines. The decision was quite unconscious as to rhyme-scheme, alternate masculine and feminine (or was it?); the line-length, iambic pentameter, was merely habitual, I am afraid—though I still doubt that a shorter line or a fancier rhyme would have been appropriate. The tone was one of regret, even sorrow. I liked getting the effect of effort and heavy breathing in the divided fourth line, "I pushed it over. I was glad to see it fall," and the sound of satisfying vengefulness in the fifth, "Let it lie there—". There was also something that pleased me, and still does, like a lucky and graceful and successful stroke in a game, in the effect of running the seventh line over, from "the shell in half-round pieces" to "Opened, and let fall—" in the eighth. Nothing very wonderful, but a good rhythm, and the original emotion and action kept honest.

Then the real problem. How much was I to say about my father, or, if not of him, about old age? That's where I made it bees instead of wasps, because I needed, for myself at any rate, an image of something good damaged. Again, I did a little flourish of technique in bee-sound, "bees have a business—," but the key lines of the poem are the next two, "Nothing is left to an old man but his anger, And I had hurried death that needs no hurrying." I am dissatisfied now because I did not say more right there. The old man is not incidental, but central, and I suppressed, without wishing to, what was really the motive for the poem. From that point to the end, the double meaning is clear. It was years, not days, before my wound was well, if it is. The "further and greener" look was the new understanding I am still trying for. And the "spoiled honey" is that grief I felt and feel for what I so hastily said, for the tree stump I too impulsively pushed over to rot in the grass.

One summer we stayed in another house in a different part of Vermont. One August noon our ten-year-old son urged us to have the necessary mid-day meal out in the tree-ringed field in front of the old house. We did, and all three stayed there for a nap afterward. It was getting dark that night, and I was rounding up child, tools, car, toys, clothes, and all the things one learns to take care of in the country, when I saw from the front porch one of the blue chairs from the dining-room still out there in the field, incongruous, annoying, and somehow touching. But I felt again the urgency of my son's happy plan for that field picnic, a plan unexpectedly come from him when unknown to him it was desperately needed. I walked out through the grass, fetched the chair in, and still felt I wanted to save the particularity of the incident, his small stay made against the passing of life.

Here is an approximate reproduction of the seven worksheets I needed to write that poem. Here again, as I think back, was the same pull: anger and affection, and a need to clear my own feelings. The image seen was the one that meant most, and what I called the poem:

Chair in the Field

At half past six in August, two trees had begun to yellow
To bronze, two bordering our mowed field.
It was toward evening and September, growing cold.
A blue chair stood in the grass.

Crossings-out and fussings-about, and second, fifth, and seventh tries to get away to a clean fast start eventually changed these opening four lines to this final version:

At half past six in August, two trees,
Yellowing to bronze, bordered our mowed field.
It was toward evening and September, growing cold.
A blue chair stood in the grass.

The change here, which no one should be as slow as I am to make, is simply in the condensation of verb forms. "Had begun to yellow to bronze" is notebook stuff, first jottings. "Two" is unnecessarily repeated. "Bordering" is a weaker form than "bordered." And I was in a hurry to get on, to say:

This is what it was.
Wishing I do not know what rush of joy among us,
The boy child in the old summer farm house
At noon had us to the meadow with steak and corn,
Cloud mapping the blue as after
We three sprawled on blankets of sun
And almost slept.

I was in a hurry, and that was what I wanted to say, but there was fumbling, and wordiness, and clumsiness in line-division. At first I didn't get "at noon" in at all, for its sound and rhythm, and for the very necessary time-plot of the poem. The whole point had to be that I looked out the door at dusk, and then went back in my mind and emotions to explain and, as it happened, to rejoice in the chair out there. But one of the last touches was "blankets of sun" instead of the dull, literal first version, "blankets." I'd known enough to say "and almost slept," because that is what it was—we drowsed, murmured now and then, and the sun was hot, and the countryside quiet and vastly empty. But the heat, the pouring light, the sense of a skyful of it, and all for us!

But I still had to bring the time-scheme up to the point of the first "inspiration," that badly worn word. I had wanted to say, simply, "Johnny, darn you, I thought I told you to bring everything in, and you've gone and left one of the dining-room chairs out. How many times have I told you that the dew spoils our tools and baseball gloves and everything, if we don't bring them in?" But I was grinning to myself, out there on the porch. The lunch in the meadow had been his idea, wholly, for some deep need of family togetherness, and he had tirelessly carried the food and dishes to make it be. How could I be angry, or even mildly exasperated? No. It was an image, that blue chair in the field, that meant a great deal.

He later and we brought back to the house
The table, the milk, the spoons, the lucky idea.
Looking out after sunset I saw it,
The one chair blue there in green grass,
Human and his.

Time was ours and time goes
In shine and hurry as a boy grows.

I was for leaving it there to remember the day by.

That's the way the poem ends, in the version which was published in the *Atlantic* for August, 1947. By the time I put it into a book, *The Double Root,* 1950, I was dubious about the easy, redundant last lines. The whole feeling I had in that moment on the cool, darkening farmhouse porch, of a minor annoyance quickly turning into love, is in "Human and his," and "I was for leaving it there—." And I would have. I thought, I'll leave it out there, and not scold him. I'll tell him it reminds me of the good time we had yesterday. And he would look at me, a little puzzled, and maybe think I was trying to "teach him a lesson" in the often laborious and mysterious way grown-up people do. So I brought it in. And wrote the poem. But in the book the last lines are:

This is the way the world runs down.
But I was for leaving it out
To remember the day by.

Once I brought a poem that I had dreamed, and offered it, unrehearsed, as they say, to the unseen audience and my television colleagues on a program we called "Poets At Work." Donald Hall, Philip Booth, May Sarton, Edwin Honig, David Ferry, Adrienne Rich and I, in various combinations through six weeks of the hour-long program, read poems of our own that we felt were problem-poems. I said that my problem was whether or not a vivid dream has a right to be made into a poem, and if so, whether or not this particular poem stood up by itself. Would they know it had been a dream, I asked, but knowing, did that matter? Actually I had still another problem in mind, too long for television, which I will present here. But first, this is the poem:

ALL'S WELL THAT ENDS

Leaning ahead high at the knife-long bow of the motor-cruiser,
North air on his face, he felt it all slow down, the prow lower
Into the narrower, the civilized channel. He came down

To the talk on the so very varnished wideness of the after-deck;

To his hostesses; to three-foot trays of one-inch hors d'oeuvres,
Spread under the expensive sun. The boat steered itself.

Everyone took two, seven, the men more. From her white leather pillow-
Piled corner, a woman not the boat's owner laughed and said,
He gives the cucumber the chive the olive the anchovy

To everyone, so generous, and laughed and said again, So generous.
She had been blonde. Laughing, she said, It is incredible,
Is it not? The sort of thing one can no longer avoid,

She said, as the cruiser slowed into shallow water. He jumped overboard,
He waded ashore in not very deep water, mud, mud, some gravel,
Then white sand and coarse grass, and got away with it.

No one really noticed. Dodging left-handled doors, reaching right,
Somehow they all opened, he went through, mayonnaise and mud,
He was running in an oldtime movie, but he was ashore.

The sidewalks lined up for him, he slowed down at street-corners.
He knew what he was heading for, people who looked like him.
No one can hurt you if you look like people, he said.

First of all, I had tried hard, and I said so, to be complete, to be honest, to omit nothing, distort nothing, but simply to report, and be concise about it. I dream a good deal, and my wife says that unlike most people, I do not lose ego in a dream and let the id take over (I don't know what she's talking about) but retain my identity and my literary style. I dream in scenes, with plot-development, full dialogue, and significant overtones. Even so, I must have chosen this as one of my better dreams, one for writing down.

Booth and Hall, I noticed, laughed at the food in its quantity. That was not an important aspect, though true. The woman was important, a false, vicious, aimlessly dangerous person, and the involuntary mouthpiece for all the others. No one said that I did or didn't make her seem so; maybe I failed to. They accepted the mildly nightmarish flight. The great relief, the wonderful warm comfort and safety of being again among ordinary people in crowds that had made the dream happy for me, seemed not to be impressive one way or the other to the panel. Usually we were polite to one another. It was Hall who objected, I think rightly, that my word "civilized" was unfair. He said I couldn't have known that in the dream and that I rationalized afterward. Well, the whole thing was civilized, overcivilized, and I meant exactly that whereas the cruiser had been out in the bay, now it was moving in edged and engineered channels, artificial waterways. He also said I couldn't know the bow was like a knife; literary again.

The risk in reporting a dream as a poem is great, and the problem is in being objective, and utterly honest. I believe that if one is to use such material, a dubious source at best, one must risk confusing his own exciting mystification for the excitement of poetry. Who cares about another's dream life? No one. We wait out the telling impatiently so we can top it with a more unusual dream, and the whole performance becomes painfully selfish. I felt that I would be imposing on my listeners by reading this poem.

But the problem is this: Isn't the completely honest reporting of a dream, in the best and most economical style possible to the writer, a valid source of poetry? May not the poet extend and illuminate his always valuable self-discovery by using poetry this way? Having dreamed something that seems to him a valuable if involuntary exploration into the far places of his own country, may he not draw a map of what he has seen? Reading the map, will he not be wiser? What I'm sure of is that I have not forgotten it. I do not dislike rich people who have parties on yachts, with lots to eat. Nor do I ardently love crowds on the sidewalk. I deeply wish to be welcomed among my kind, which is probably neither of these. But I had returned with a good will to a group where I knew I did not belong, only to expose myself to a shrewd meanness. I escaped that particular willful ugliness.

There is also in *The Double Root* a poem called "Maybe for Love," which constructed itself in a curious rhyme-scheme, with the first three lines matching the second three, the third three matching the fourth three, and the fifth the sixth. The seventh is also matched by the eighth group of three lines, but this pair of triplets is the summing-up, a sort of coda, and is like the three pairs preceding it. The explanation of the triple framing is the fact that I once bought, at a summer sale of handicraft, three carved wooden animals, a duck, a mule, and a hound.

I let these determine the rhymes, and let the rhymes determine the three-line grouping, but had to stop somewhere, somehow. It was like writing a sort of super-terza-rima, which as everyone knows, especially Dante and John Ciardi, can go on forever. Perhaps I make the writing of the poem sound difficult. It was not at all difficult, but the pattern that immediately took shape was very rigid. It then became a wonderfully exciting contest, my wits against the inexorable Thing I had conjured up by idly buying some carved applewood objects at a garden sale in Nantucket. I had watched with amused superiority the women choosing cute little chickies, darling little bunny-rabbits, and had thought with what guilelessness people reveal themselves for what they are. Bunny-rabbits, indeed. So up I stepped and bought a wild duck, a mule, and a hound-dog. Nothing very revealing about that. My innermost soul, that's all. But the workmanship was excellent, the wood had come alive, and I had the subject of the poem the minute I paid my money, what I bought giving me the form. It was the carver I was slow to acknowledge, but now I praise him:

Maybe for Love

Set out in an old island garden behind boxwood hedges
Were all the small carved applewood animals to buy,
And I bought three, a hound, a mule, and a wild duck.

Boys and men last winter under the Carolina ledges
Knifed them out of the hard wood, and I wondered why.
Not for money—they cost so little. Maybe for luck.

The grain of the wood slides all round the small duck,
From the bent snaky neck to the fat feathered tail,
But applewood shines the same in hound or mule.

Maybe for love. I thought, yes, maybe the carver, struck
By his own thought of the dog, climbed a fence rail,
Sat, and cut to what wood meant to be, in the cool

Of the mountain evening, looking over the valley, alone.
Hundreds of miles from there, and a long year later,
I stare at and rub fondly the mule, the duck, the hound.

Drawn grain of applewood follows the mule's bone,
Hauled back, stubborn. Wood makes the hound a waiter,
A hunter for faint clues but true on the world's ground.

Something wild in an old man's heart I think cut wings
For the wild bird, and for me, for the flying in my mind.
Being stubborn, I bought the mule. I know how I will not.

The hound in my hand searches for me for the next things
I almost have, must have, will send him out to find.
Buying the three, I was the three meanings I bought.

The eye, if not the ear, will now perceive the rhyme-scheme: hedges, buy, duck, ledges, why, luck, and the rest in the same sequence. Copying it here, I feel again the surge of each even-numbered triplet, the second, fourth, sixth, and eighth, each line of which would come up against an unshakable wall, the rhyme I had set myself. I feel, too, the swiftness with which I used those lines to thrust in the necessary exposition. I knew the carving had been done at a mountain school in the Carolinas, and someone had hung a picture of an old man sitting on a fence-rail with a jack-knife and a hunk of wood. *Hedges* they had in Nantucket, and *ledges* they had in Carolina, just when I needed them. The *duck's tail* got me the *fence rail,* and so on. *Duck* made me speculate as to *luck,* and that led me to *love,* and the true title. I note now a sort of stranding within the tripled triple strands, of "a hound, a mule, and a wild duck" in the third line, and "the mule, the duck, the hound," in the fifteenth. I know that for some time before I set it down, I could see the last line coming, and it fell into place more with a final hammer-blow than a mere click. They talk about the inevitability of lines and whole poems: the thing that had to be, becoming. All I know for sure is that we have almost everything nowadays, but we don't have self-writing pencils.

Finally, here is a shortened version from my notebook of the making of a poem. In a friend's house I was shown a collection of hundreds of varieties of one kind of sea-shell; and an album of all the varieties of sea-weed from one (Irish) coastline; and briefly some enlarged photographs of a sea-shell cut across to show the spiralling outward growth. I carried the sound of the first line and a half in my head till I got home. The drafts, or gropings, are printed first; the completed or acceptable stanzas follow:

I. DRAFT

The infinite orderliness of the natural world
Is past all wonder. Only the ignorant wonder
And marvel, seeing the never-repeated curled
And colored and faithful patterns out of the

Seeing the never-repeated colored and curled

Seeing the colored and never-repeated curled
Slow growth of sea-shells. But find the founder

Only I ignorant wonder

COMPLETED STANZA

The infinite orderliness of the natural world
Is past all wonder. Only I ignorant wonder
At the common and colored and never-repeated curled
Slow growth of shells above the sea and under.

II. DRAFT

Seaweed is a green jungle of scum an inch wide

A scum of seaweed is a jungle a green inch wide,
A lifetime long, an age, if naming, caring
Maps it upon one page where spread and dried

A man's lifetime long for seeing, naming, caring
To map it on one page where spread and dried

To map it on one page. Spread there and dried
It is one pattern for the mind's comparing

With mind
With Mind

COMPLETED STANZA

A scum of seaweed is a jungle a green inch wide,
A man's lifetime long for seeing, naming, caring
To map it on one page. Spread there and dried,
It is one pattern for the mind's comparing

III. DRAFT

With Mind that remembers everything It made.
The government of water, like the art of teaching

humility
no pronoun *microscope*
birds
reaching searching arching marching

the government of water
greater

great calm of knowing law obeyed

Caverns of almost nothing, and heavens, discover
Alike a little of the great calm of law obeyed
As sun casts the year's same shadow over and over.

mover over
sever forever
cover

COMPLETED STANZA

With Mind that remembers everything It made.
Caverns of almost nothing, and heavens, discover
Alike a little of the great calm of law obeyed.
Sun casts the year's same shadow over and over.

IV. DRAFT

Out of shadow I, but no longer saying I,
Move myself from my self in an opening spiral
Toward what I speak of without knowing why

Toward what this poem speaks of, not

Toward what these words hope

Out slowly, outward, and must but may never die

To complete one cell of

The Spiral
title it

COMPLETED STANZA

Out of shadow I, but no longer saying I,
Move myself from my self in an opening spiral,
Drawn toward the light in understanding why
One cell may be one cell yet see the spiral

V. DRAFT

Whole, after slow accretion shaped the whole.

Whole, and what accretion shaped the whole.

But there is more, a world in a tall fountain's
One waterdrop, and more, the fire in coal

more, fire in a crumb of coal,

COMPLETED STANZA

Whole, and what slow accretion shaped the whole.
But there is more, a world in a tall fountain's
One waterdrop, more, fire in a crumb of coal,
And more worlds in the grains that make mountains.

V

My Style, My Face

The rules for writing poetry were made after the poems had been written. First, a man had an excitement, said a few words about it and repeated some of them, liked the way the beating of it went, and talked on to hear himself varying his own imitations of himself. This was a long time ago. After a while, a methodical kind of person, a man both careful and curious, gave names to the poet's play. The maker and player was a poet. The other man was an onlooker, a reporter. This second man noted that the poet's instinct seemed to be to use the same patterns of rhythm again and again, in variations, and re-combinations of the same sounds. Recurrent phenomena rouse expectation. Expectation always answered becomes a rule. Rules enough to fill a book always turn into a book of rules, and the methodical man wrote a book. Later on, some who wished to be poets read all the rules and found that something had been left out of the rule book. It was something about being a poet unlike any other poet, about writing so that a poem would be unmistakably one's own and no other's; something about how to achieve style. It has never been put into any one book from that day to this. No one can teach a writer how to write his poem, though some can teach the writing of poetry. The writer can observe how some poems have been written, but what he learns must forever be his secret; everything helps him, and nothing helps him. "The golden rule," said Bernard Shaw of this matter, "is that there is no golden rule."

But one rule of the highest value is, Do not sit down and read a handbook or dictionary of poetry from beginning to end and expect to rise a true poet—licensed, blest, and armed. It is tedious and confusing reading, and when taken as a whole, useless either as nourishment or information. Total reading of such books brings on, not humility for all one does not know, but humiliation. A handbook of poetics should be used only as a reference book in which to look up one thing at a time. It should be used for confirmation of something independently discovered. It is an excellent source of correct examples, but it is a backward-looking book, as indeed the one who compiled it looked back over all poetry ever written. The only reader who really understands it is the working poet who already knows almost everything in it, and he doesn't need to read it. He does read it, though, for professional polish.

But the beginning writer can find out how some poems have been written, guessing and feeling, disliking and liking, as he reads them. Reading poems is the best way to learn how to write them. It is the slowest way, but best. He can also learn that names have been given to some of the arrangements and devices in poetry he has noticed and chosen for his use. The time to learn these names is when they are needed, and one can live for a long time without needing them. What he teaches himself will be his golden rule. When he has mastered it, he will have mastered himself, and it will be said of him that he has achieved a style, or style. He will know only that he has to the utmost pleased himself. He has unknowingly followed rule book rules, because they are descriptions of the maker's instinct at work.

"Style is, like most other things that are worthwhile," said Irving Babbitt once, "the result of a difficult mediation. It goes without saying that a man's style should have about it something highly individual; but it is at least equally important that it should have about it something structural, and this structural quality can arise only from the subordination of the uniqueness that each one of us receives as a free gift of nature to some larger whole. Carl Sandburg is plainly using the word style in a very one-sided way when he writes:

> Go on talking
> Only don't take my style away.
> It's my face.
> Maybe no good
> but anyway, my face."

If that is one-sidedness, it has more natural life in it than Irving Babbitt's prose, and anyone wishes his own style were as unmistakable a face as Sandburg's. Babbitt says that style is uniqueness, and that uniqueness must be controlled by structure, and that such control is difficult, "a difficult mediation." The fact is that Sandburg has done it, and made it look easy. All the chapters in all the books on style have been brought into five short lines, which happen to have style as their subject, but are at the same time an example of it. Carl Sandburg has heard speech-rhythm, and knows the repetitiveness and balance of it. He knows exactly how the second statement has added some qualification, some humorous defiance in this case, before returning to the main statement. This is instinctive structure. Subordination to the larger whole? the poet would ask. I did what seemed natural, he would say. The natural *is* the larger whole, to Sandburg. There is a rule for this, never before stated: To subordinate uniqueness to structure as Sandburg does, one must be Sandburg. This rule applies to no one else, obviously. And it applies to every poet, by the substitution of his own name. But for how to do it there is no rule.

Yes, there is, too. Surely we can be contradictory in the smaller things. The rule in this matter of being yourself is that you must like yourself. You must believe that your feelings, and your words for your feelings, are important, more important than any others in the world in your time. That they are unique is a fact; that you believe they are unique is necessary. It is amazing that there are so few bold believers among beginning poets. The poet must be very bold indeed to like his own voice so well that he shuts out other voices and perfects his own, or perfects the transmission of it to the page. When a reader says, "I saw a poem of yours in a magazine the other day. It didn't have a name signed, but I'd know the sound of your voice anywhere," then the poet knows he has attained his style, which is the unaffected sound of his own voice. Untinkered with, not falsified, puts it better. The youngest poets too often begin to write by writing what they think is poetical, and it turns out to be a watery, a rather pinkish-watery, mixture of words, rhythms, and thoughts from the poets read in school. This young poet will read some of his poems aloud to a friend and between the poems will make some remark by way of describing or paraphrasing the next poem. These remarks are usually better than the poems. If he can begin his life's work by writing in the tone of voice of those remarks, he'll be off to a better start: He'll be starting with his own voice. The task is to keep on talking with it until you need not say, like Sandburg,

"Maybe no good but anyway, my face." No apologies are allowable except for failing to sound like yourself.

After a while one learns that the self is changing, and must change its voice; the change is for greater strength, variety, awareness, and reality, as one makes more and more connections with more kinds of life. New experiences add new groups of words to the vocabulary, both factual and emotional. Years of reading bring hundreds of examples of writers to be violently ignored or noted in passing or marked for full respect or a little learned from.

Almost every poet, while he is working toward his own style, discovers a poet he envies. It is improbable that the two poets are unlike. How dismaying it is, at first, to find a poet much further on his way and so much like you. But there are points of difference, and the discoverer uses not the manner but the reassurance the manner gives him; if one writer, working with a voice and feelings so similar, could make himself heard, then all the more hope. The still growing poet feels the force behind the manner, the urgency he recognizes, the temperamental likeness. This probably older poet becomes the master he more or less secretly acknowledges as the one he owes most to. A young poet needs a master in his trade. He will have teachers, actual teachers, and he will have friendly critics, and he will have great examples. But he will find his own master, who will never know he has an apprentice.

There is less possibility of making a rule about this than about anything else in the whole business. The obvious masters are obvious. There is only one master for each poet, and each must find his. Looking back from this time, he will see that an important step was taken when the master was found. But if he imitates his master, it will show like a rusty purple stain, and all the reviewers will note it, with contemptuous satisfaction. It might be said here that Gerard Manley Hopkins, Emily Dickinson, Edwin Arlington Robinson, and T. S. Eliot—not to mention W. H. Auden and Robert Frost—will color a younger poet's style beyond cleansing. These, of course, are poets who have so absolutely unmistakable a voice, so widely known, that the influence is deadly. The ideal is to acquire such an unmistakable voice, and let it be said of some other beginner that he has been reading you. But your own real master must be your secret, as he will be if you breathe his air, but are not blown off your own path by it. In the end he becomes part of your health and growth, and the body and the Voice are your own, and the face.

Now I am about to enunciate a profound concept. It is barely possible that it is not new, but I feel sure no one has ever set it forth as I will, or based so much wisdom on such a silly text. There is a great deal to it, I know, because I find proof of it everywhere. It delights me immoderately that I hold the comet by the tail, instead of having received the ball of fire in my middle, but the light is very bright. I call it the Lesson of the Unrhymed Limerick. The lesson was composed by W. S. Gilbert:

> There was an old man of St. Bees,
> Who was stung in the arm by a wasp;
> When they asked, "Does it hurt?"
> He replied, "No, it doesn't,
> But I thought all the while 'twas a hornet."

Coming on an unrhymed limerick among pages of rhymed ones, the reader feels acutely the bump of the unexpected at the end of each line, and the effect is hilarious. Or even if we come on this masterpiece by itself, as here, we have a heritage of the literature of the limerick, and relish the deviation from the well-known norm. But it is funny only because we know the norm, or rhymed, limerick. It is the simplest example of expectation denied or delayed or suggested, yet unfulfilled.

Of all the other arts, the poet can learn most from the graphic arts, and in the composition of pictures the principle of expectation with a surprise fulfillment is used all the time and in every possible way. Gradations of color, mass, and shape; changes of object having the same color; sequences of light-intensity; ratios of space; and opposition of line-direction are some of the devices of escape in composition. The escape sought is from the obvious, the promised. Something of the same is true in music. There the composer can divide notes by halves and halves again, or repeat but not quite repeat a melody in a related part of the key, or change keys, or give melody to another instrument. It is a greatly extended variation on a theme. In architecture and decoration the same principle holds. The long sweeping line is promised and given, or given and interrupted, and then resumed. To the eye, area has weight and so the architect, decorator, and painter balance and oppose areas and mass. All these artists count on our memory of the obvious, the norm. Our pleasure is in the degree and manner of the reminder of the norm, without having it thrust at us in equal dozens, or cubes, or identical sequences.

The eye of the poet is looking at any random spread of objects or events or emotions, hoping to find a hint of a norm; that is, a theme and a subject for a poem. The poet has also the power of inventing the random spread so that it does allow for a designed connection, the design being his poem.

Insofar as we live by ritual, which we call manners, or the customary behavior in a given place and time, we notice the deviation from the norm, and judge the difference.

Clumsiness is conspicuous. Grace, the light touch of certainty, is a mark of style. It acknowledges the convention but does not make a drill of it. There are surly poets and clumsy poets, but time, which has its own inexorable conventions and manners, finally excludes them. There are poets whose style is all mannerliness, all skill, and these are pleasant company, but we forget their names. Style makes reality acceptable. Style makes possible full communication, which, it must be remembered, is two-way. Style is the behavior of an appreciated person worth knowing. Each wishes to be individual and cannot help being, but as a stylist each one conforms at enough points so that the common likeness is observable.

There is no awkwardness in nature. There may be unfamiliar and unpleasing designs, but the law governing every growth is perfect and absolute. The infinite adaptations of form in seaweed, ditch-flower, fresh-water fish, carnivorous mammal, or cloud-mass are for one purpose—existence. The function is to live. This ultimate motive expands the families in kind, but the members are related. The poet lives only as he is related.

Sculpture is going through a runaway phase at present and seems not even a most distant cousin to any family or species. It asks a long memory indeed to get back to the norm or convention from which mid-twentieth-century sculpture is an escape. Observers are mightily confused, but so are the sculptors. Their suffering is of two kinds: They are very clearly making an enormous effort to cut themselves off from the familiar norm, and at the same time they are using new materials (metals, plastics) and new structural skills (welding, bending, riveting), and they are bewildered, though wonderfully eager, as they should be. The poets can learn from this phase in the history of sculpture, and it is only a phase. The long view is the secret of survival for all artists. Nature never forgets its past, but some artists, even if only with a wrenching effort of will, can go forward as if from this morning, with no yesterdays. I do not believe that the poet can move forward with such lunge as these sculptors, but he can profit greatly from them, if he translates their urges, rebellions, new materials, and failures into the analogous terms in words and metrics.

Our unrhymed limerick—we really ought to be taking all this more seriously—stands as a warning against runaway experimentalism. As long as we remember the rhymed limerick, the unrhymed one is very funny. But suppose everyone writes limericks unrhymed, and we forget what unrhymed limericks are a deviation from. There is nothing amusing, nothing satirical, nothing meaningful, about them. What a ridiculous world it is where molded plastic imitations of log-cabin walls, or even of bricks, are used by people who never came near a log cabin! What do children understand who watch on television a rapid-fire, half-parodied, and much-distorted version of an old story or an old song of which they never knew the original? It has gone beyond the humor of the unrhymed limerick into a region of dangerous meaninglessness and is heading toward some new system of values of communication in which the assumed foundation has disintegrated.

The poet cannot build on nothing or begin a style new to literature from himself as the only source. The poet's style comes from as much of the past as he can know, plus himself. The unrhymed limerick is a master's playfulness, a joke, a by-product of skill, not something to found a new era upon. Extreme experiment pushes so far out into the air that it breaks off and falls. New growth enlarges and endures nearer the trunk of the tree, and even the green tips of boughs draw life from the trunk.

The reader of this is not a poet unless he has continuously been transposing remarks on art, manners, television, music, and sculpture into comments on writing poetry. I would not talk at such length about children's TV programs, sheet-iron statuary, or abstractionist painting, except that I believe all art is the poet's school. It seems to me that the painter, maturing through many pictures or perhaps reaching a not very impressive limit, exposes himself, as if mercilessly, and most instructively, to the eye of the poet. Failures of skill, dullness of style, and meanness of vision are rudely revealed in the graphic and plastic and structural arts. Poets would be swift, I believe, to reject their equivalents in a poem, once these characteristics have been seen in other media.

It is impossible that the poet can move a hundred feet from where he is or live through an hour without learning something about style. It is everywhere. It shows forth in the existence, growth, and behavior of everything. The poet needs only to discriminate between the live and the dead—which is to say the furthering, the lawful, the excellent, and the false, the excrescent, the disharmonious—to find the elements he will shape into his style. It is simple to do this and requires only ruthless effort, and only for a lifetime. It is not achieved through the unrhymed limerick.

As poet, then, where should the poet begin? He should begin by mastering the five-stress iambic line.

Iambic pentameter is the name given to the line in English poetry that has ten syllables in it, with the accent coming on two, four, six, eight, and ten. Iambic pentameter is the great line in the English language. It was not chosen as the great line; the English language made it the great line. Since Chaucer it has been the body and substance of our major poetry. Of it have been made *The Canterbury Tales,* the plays of Shakespeare, the satires of Pope, the odes of Keats, the soliloquies, sonnets, lyrics, narratives, and contemplations of Frost, Wordsworth, Hardy, Gray, Donne, Yeats, and of companies more. They did not choose the line; they made it what it is and can be. The masters have always been heard, freely and clearly, each in his own voice, in the five-stress English line.

Far from cramping anyone, it has given everyone the scope and power for works of the greatest length and the most profound subjects. John Milton's craft with the five-stress line might be education enough for any poet. One excellent study of Milton's prosody is that by Robert Bridges, and another is Ernest Sprott's. But no matter who writes in this line, his own style will be evident. It can be handled so that the poet's tone, the pitch of his nervous energy, his peculiar vocabulary, and the rush and halt of his emotion will be wholly alive in it. It can be as much his own as his handwriting, or his stride.

Mastery of the five-stress iambic line is where the poet's training begins. Whether or not the poet has it in him to become a better, a very good, and at last a great poet, is another matter. But for one who asks where to begin the work, in what fundamental discipline to perfect himself, the iambic pentameter line is the best answer.

Here are some single lines of iambic pentameter, chosen for their differences one from another, and the individuality of each, as examples of immediate identity of style though all conform to the one measure:

Bow down the walls of the ferned and foxy woods.—Dylan Thomas

A Being darkly wise, and rudely great.—Alexander Pope
Supple and turbulent, a ring of men.—Wallace Stevens
Who are these coming to the sacrifice?—John Keats
My true-love hath my heart, and I have his.—Sir Philip Sidney
In sleep, a king; but waking, no such matter.—William Shakespeare
Now fades the glimmering landscape on the sight.—Thomas Gray
And left the vivid air signed with their honor.—Stephen Spender
And death shall be no more; Death, thou shalt die.—John Donne
That looked unchristian but be that as it may.—John Crowe Ransom
They are all gone into the world of light!—Henry Vaughan
Assail'd, fight, taken, stabb'd, bleed, fall, and die.—John Donne
The army of unalterable law.—George Meredith
The ceremony of innocence is drowned.—William Butler Yeats
At the round earth's imagined corners, blow.—John Donne
And peace proclaims olives of endless age.—William Shakespeare
The poetry of earth is never dead.—John Keats
O chestnut tree, great rooted blossomer.—William Butler Yeats
To make us wish that we were in his place.—E. A. Robinson
Where the heel-headed dogfish barks its nose.—Robert Lowell

Great Paul, great pail of sound, still dip and draw.—
Richard Wilbur
In winter he comes back to us. I'm done.—Robert Frost
Let us be prodigal, as heaven is.—Conrad Aiken
For a rainbow footing it nor he for his bones risen.—G. M.
Hopkins
Someone had better be prepared for rage.—Robert Frost
Whirled all about—dense, multitudinous, cold.—John
Masefield
Tomorrow to fresh woods and pastures new.—John Milton
Through gold-moth-haunted beds of pickerel-flower.—
R. W. Emerson
Having shook disaster till the fruit fell down.—Edna St. V.
Millay
Mountainous, woman not breaks and will bend.—John
Berryman
That I have had my world as in my tyme.—Geoffrey
Chaucer

Reading slowly, and re-reading these lines, gives me a physical pleasure, partly through the ear, as the surprises come in the beat and in the length or brevity and the weight of the single words, and partly through the body's muscles, as the line moves itself standing still. The pleasure is all in the variation from the norm, and the reminders of the norm. The norm is a monotonous one-*two,* three-*four,* five-*six,* seven-*eight,* nine-*ten,* rarely to be used, but always near the beginning, to establish it, and occasionally in the poem. All the rest is that variation which is the poet himself, his style.

But in choosing these lines for variation's sake, I have also chosen each one for its wholeness of sense, and in some instances lost the certainty of a normal rhythm because the context is missing. Most of the lines are made with the simpler variations. A foot is reversed, or an extra light syllable is added, or a heavy accent doubled. What the ear at first questions—as to what has become of the metronomic one-*two,* three-*four,* five-*six,* seven-*eight,* nine-*ten*—can be located by counting the five beats with the five fingers. More poets check their own first drafts of poems in iambic pentameter than might admit it, with finger tips on table-top, and there is just as good reason for a reader to educate himself by doing the same thing. If one were to count the five beats in the foregoing lines, he would soon become aware of the shifts in placement, and adept at shifting with them, yet never lose the feel of the regular ground-beat. Even so, out of context, one is not fully prepared for some of the extremes in variation. The poet would not have written such lines singly, but only after he had accustomed the reader's ear to the meaning's movement forward through lines normal or nearly so.

The third line, for instance, "Supple and turbulent, a ring of men," which is from Wallace Stevens' "Sunday Morning," begins the seventh of eight fifteen-line stanzas of unrhymed iambic pentameter. Each stanza is a consideration of a possible worship, other than church-going. The sixth stanza ends with

> DEATH is the MOTHer of BEAUty, MYStiCAL,
> WithIN whose BURNing BOSom WE deVISE
> Our EARTHly MOTHers WAITing, SLEEPlessLY.
>
> Supple and turbulent, a ring of men
> Shall chant in orgy on a summer morn
> Their boisterous devotion to the sun,

and I have hammered out the beat of the last three lines of the sixth stanza in capitals, and run on into the first three lines of the next stanza, without the hammer. The ear has been hearing the beat so steadily that it hears

SUPPle and TURBuLENT, a RING of MEN

with some extra weight on TURB as indicated, because the likelihood, in reading this line by itself, would be to give it four beats only, and slide rapidly through the three syllables in the middle,

SUPPle and TURBulent, a RING of MEN.

In both readings, one could claim he makes turbulent *sound* turbulent, full of twist and roll and effort. But if one has been reading the whole poem, he has the ground-beat going steadily, and easily balances a strong TURB with a LENT strong enough to mark the beat. The iambic rhythm runs insistently through lines, sentences, stanzas, and pages. On this lattice the variations climb like a vine, and a reader needs a passage of poetry of some length in order to perceive the pattern of the flowering.

The twelfth line quoted is the third from last in John Donne's "Elegie XVI, On His Mistris," in a passage asking her to keep their secret, and though she dream of him, not reveal it in a nightmare of his death. Donne creates a terror in dream, with all its mounting outcry, almost to a shriek and diminishing in a wail. But do not thus prophesy my death, he says, unless Jove's judgment is that my happiness till now is all I deserve. This is an instance where the whole context is necessary; without it the climax has no support, and a correct accenting is impossible.

When I am gone, dreame me some happinesse,
Nor let thy lookes our long hid love confesse,
Nor praise, nor dispraise me, nor blesse nor curse
Openly loves force, nor in bed fright thy Nurse
With midnights startings, crying out, oh, oh

> Nurse, o my love is slaine, I saw him goe
> O'r the white Alpes alone; I saw him I,
> Assail'd, fight, taken, stabb'd, bleed, fall, and die.
> Augure me better chance, except dread Jove
> Thinke it enough for me to 'have had thy love.

The accenting given the line under discussion seems inevitably, because of the increasing breathless haste and nightmare terror, to be:

> asSAIL'D, fight, TAken, STABB'd, bleed, FALL, and DIE.

The only light syllables in the line, the as- of assail'd, the *-en* of taken, and the word *and,* determine three of the heavy stresses, on the closest accompanying syllables, and these heavy stresses determine the remaining two. Perhaps one could race roughly through the line, gasping each word with equal if hurried breath, and not take any longer to say the line than it has taken to say the preceding lines. And in fact it must be hurried, gasped, but the steady iambic beat has been set in motion earlier, and this line must conform, and can be read so that it does. Then the two closing lines return to a quieter, more obvious rhythm, and we find we were not so far away from it. Or we were no further than a brief imagined bad dream away from it.

In another of John Donne's poems, his magnificent "Holy Sonnet XIV," we must read, in each of three successive lines, three emphatic words together, and although these sequences are not as crowded as the sequence of seven emphatic words in the preceding poem, nevertheless they are not easy. Again the ground-beat gives us the pace, and again the meaning and tone help us.

> BATer my HEART, three PERson'd GOD; for, YOU
> As YET but KNOCKE, breathe, SHINE, and SEEKE to MEND;

That I may RISE, and STAND, o'er THROW me, and BEND
Your FORCE, to BREATHE, blowe, BURN, and MAKE me
NEW.

The twentieth quoted line is from Robert Lowell's "The Quaker Graveyard at Nantucket." The long poem is not wholly in iambic pentameter, though predominantly so, and the nearest lines are clearly so. One way of describing the variation of this line from the norm is to say that it contains ten syllables, as it should, but that the five heavy and the five light accents are wrenched out of position, yet balanced out in the whole. The wrenching comes in "heel-headed dogfish," which has three heavy beats, I think simply to give weight and actual blunt thrust to the nudging of the body by the fish.

Its open staring eyes
Were lustreless dead-lights
Or cabin-windows on a stranded hulk
Heavy with sand. We weight the body, close
Its eyes and heave it seaward whence it came,
Where the HEEL-HEADed DOGfish BARKS its NOSE
On Ahab's void and forehead; and the name
Is blocked in yellow chalk.

The line by Gerard Manley Hopkins, the twenty-fourth of those quoted, is the last line of a sonnet, "The Caged Skylark." One's first impression is that the line contains too many syllables to be iambic pentameter, and it does, having fourteen instead of ten. A natural reading accents it thus:

For a RAINbow FOOTing it nor HE for his BONES RISen,

and one asks by what rule there can be several unaccented syllables between the accents, and how two accents may come together at the end. Hopkins made his own rules. Or rather, he made his own name for something he said was used in the Elizabethan age, and is now returning to English poetry. This he called sprung rhythm. When the joints of a frame are loosened, and it is no longer rigid, we call it sprung. Hopkins loosened the rigid frame of iambic pentameter and allowed the use of from one to four, and even more, unaccented syllables between beats. He said, "Sprung Rhythm is the most natural of things. For (1) it is the rhythm of common speech and of written prose, when rhythm is perceived in them. (2) It is the rhythm of all but the most monotonously regular music, so that in the words of choruses and refrains and in songs written closely to music it arises. (3) It is found in nursery rhymes, weather saws, and so on; because, however these may have been made once in running rhythm, [Hopkins' word for common English rhythm without extreme variations] the terminations having dropped off by the change of language, the stresses come together and so the rhythm is sprung. (4) It arises in common verse when reversed or counterpointed, for the same reason."

The line from John Donne's elegy being more easily accountable when in its context, so the Hopkins line is more natural in its place in the poem. But with Hopkins, this was a principle of composition, and he said, "Remark also that it is natural in Sprung Rhythm for the lines to be *rove over,* that is, for the scanning of each line immediately to take up that of the one before, so that if the first has one or more syllables at its end, the other must have so many the less at its beginning; and in fact the scanning runs on without break from the beginning, say, of a stanza to the end and all the stanza is one long strain, though written in lines asunder."

This obviously makes it unuseful to quote Hopkins in single lines, although I feel that the rainbow line can be read alone. However, no poet writes lines to be quoted singly. Lines are part of a poem, and the poem is the whole. What Hopkins says of poems in sprung rhythm, that in fact the scanning runs on without break from the beginning, and that all the stanza is one long strain (of music), though written in lines printed and counted separately, is true of any well-made poem.

The sonnet itself says that man's spirit is a skylark sometimes caged, sometimes needing rest, but springing from the flesh to soar, and leaving the flesh as lightly below as the soft meadow from which a rainbow seems to arch.

NOT that the SWEET-fowl, SONG-fowl, NEEDS no REST—
Why, HEAR him, HEAR him BABble and DROP DOWN to
 his nest,
 But his OWN NEST, WILD NEST, no PRIson.
MAN's spirit will be FLESH-BOUND when FOUND at
 BEST,
But UNCUMbered: MEAdow-down is NOT disTRESSED
 For a RAINbow FOOTing it nor HE for his BONES RISen.

"The young man knows the rules, but the old man knows the exceptions," said Oliver Wendell Holmes, Sr., in one of his medical essays. It may be true of medicine—of course it is, as it is in every profession, art, and skill—but in poetic style it is the essence. The beginner is the young poet, and the experienced one is the old poet; it is not a matter of calendar years. The rule is the absolutely regular iambic pentameter, ten syllables with the beat on the even syllables. The exceptions are the line that starts on the beat and shifts back, the line that has eleven or more syllables, the line that has its crest of feeling in the middle or near the end, the line that sounds like talk, the line that reverberates like a great bell, and more without end. Most of the variations are so often used that they have been given names, as any rulebook tells. We have seen examples of some of them in the pages preceding. But there are qualities of springiness, or standing flat, and of a voice yearning, proclaiming, insisting, that can be identified only with the name of the poet who wrote them and many like them—the Miltonic line, the Robinsonian, the John Berryman or Robert Lowell line. When we must name the poet, we are acknowledging a style.

It remains to point out that one of the characteristics of the iambic pentameter line is a slight pause somewhere within the dipping swing from first to tenth syllable. This makes two dips. The point between is called the caesura, or cut. Because of the necessities of our grammar, it occurs even without a poet's planning it, but it can be planned, and should be. The ten-syllable line provides space enough for a verb, a noun, an adjective, and minor parts of speech —room enough, that is, to say something. But it is too long a line for saying it in one breath, and the caesura is the necessary taking of a breath, and hence a division of phrases. Since the five-beat line will always have its caesura, the writer will learn to avoid the monotony of having it always come at the same place. In lines one to ten of those quoted, the caesura comes successively after the word "walls" in the first, "wise" in the second, and after "turbulent," "coming," "heart," "king," "landscape," "air," "more," and "unchristian." Marks of punctuation often come naturally at the caesura, but not always. The test of a poet's skill in this matter is of course to note all the way down a page of iambic pentameter the constant shift from left to right. It is a test one should make of a page of his own writing, though the experienced poet knows what he will find.

Once the poet has mastered the five-beat line, its extension in a sentence, and its mounting structure in a paragraph, he can write rhymed stanzas in it, four-and-three-beat lines, rhymed at his own invention and by the book, and every sort of combination. The craftsman's pleasure in shortening to the four-beat line is equalled only by the stretch of power he feels in writing the five-beat line again in the next poem. Instinct tells him which line-length to use for different emotions and subjects. Instinct? It is made up of taste, a sense of design, some memory of other poems, and some selfish pleasure. It is another of those matters Oliver Wendell Holmes was thinking of.

Imagery is as personal in a line of his poetry, as inescapably part of a poet's style, as his body movement or his sound-making. The time comes, as I have said, after the poet is young in the art and before he is old, when a reader will say to him, "I came across a poem the other day that I knew was yours, as soon as I read it, and even without your name on it." One of the clues is speech-rhythm of lines, and another one is imagery. The poet learns to move freely, and as himself, in iambics, throwing his unmistakable shadow up on the permanent trellis or framework of a vertical stanza-scheme and horizontal syllable-count. But the details of the picture he casts will be images of the kinds of things he, and no one else, has seen, imagined, and remembered. Image means the things seen, the objects in a poem having names. The named objects may be autobiographical, the accumulation of the senses and memory, and they may also be chosen as symbols, but even then they are likely to be personal.

Dr. Caroline Spurgeon's book, *Shakespeare's Imagery,* is a tabulation of all the objects named in Shakespeare's plays and a comparison of them with the imagery of his contemporaries. It disposes forever of a doubtful identity. The writer (Shakespeare) who mentioned scores of times the horse, his harness, his smell, is not the writer (Bacon) who mentions a horse once, as a simile for something else.

How much Shakespeare knew of domestic life, nature, shipping, the law, mythology, can be counted and his knowledge shown in charts. At the least, the chart is as unlike Marlowe or Jonson as any two people are unlike in appearance. The poet cannot conceal himself: His imagery shows what he is and is not. If the Spurgeon book is used for nothing else, it proves this one point, and endlessly fascinating as its chapters and tabulations are, this point is enough here. The categories Dr. Spurgeon uses for Shakespeare's imagery are general enough to be applied to any modern poet, with additions for modern life. The application to oneself is the use that interests us.

If the writer has enough poems, anything more than fifty, he or a devoted and methodical friend could make an image-count, and produce a table showing exactly what the poet is. The poet's awareness of colors, of sound, and the other senses, would show. The degree of his physical activity would show, and his special knowledges—of geology or sailing or children or God or climate. Color-blindness would show, as it did, to my surprise, in an analysis of a book by a friend of mine. Then I recalled being with the man and having to warn him about the traffic lights. The imagery of outline and mass seemed to compensate for the lack of color imagery in his book. I'm afraid that if this poet tried to increase color-imagery in his poetry, that would show, too, as being forced. But it seems to me that we can learn which of the senses we are not making much use of, and, assuming we possess them all, perhaps we can consciously increase imagery. Imagery-count can also be a warning of the over-use of one kind of image. But the poet need not go all through this. He ought to be able to do it for himself simply because he ought always to be on guard against a poverty of image and active in the search for new imagery.

The poet always has usable imagery ready, near the top of his mind; he brings up from deeper in his consciousness imagery he has stored there. His fullest use of it is his major preoccupation. Insofar as the poet is abundantly an image-making, image-summoning, image-speaking writer, he is a poet of rich, powerful style. There are provisions, of course. It is not enough to be well-supplied, if there is no skill in using the materials, and it is not enough to be elaborately skillful with poor materials. It is not enough to be both well-supplied and skillful, if the poet has no convictions, philosophy, or vision. And the poet cannot be very different from the man he was born. The margin of freedom is small, but there is a margin, and in this area the poet can improve what he is. The poet can deliberately work to enrich his imagery and, by unremitting effort of mind and will, perfect his skill in using his imagery. He has this freedom. This is where he is a poet or will never be a poet.

Yeats is a poet's poet, because he never forgot the act itself of writing, and often wrote about the making of poems. His poems, essays, and autobiographies, in reflected combination, are great texts of our time. Donald Stauffer says, "The acceptance of life in all its variety may be bewildering, and for a long time the young poet trod the road of the chameleon. But the choices became clearer, the tentative speculations fell gradually into patterns, and Yeats emerged with a confidence in himself, or in his creative imagination, which may best be called his courage. He emerged with beliefs (because he found that they squared with his experience) in aristocracy, desire, individuality, custom, and ceremony, wholeness through oppositions, and immortality." The point is not what the beliefs were, but that he emerged with them. "How shall such a faith be cast into the forms of art? Through symbols."

Stauffer's book on Yeats, *The Golden Nightingale,* is a study of Yeats's forming and control of such metaphors as the tree, the dance, the mummy, the flame, the fountain.

That is what Yeats did. Why take any example but the best?—a most Yeatsian comment. But the poet must go through the time of considering every sort of example and every kind of poet's history of growth. He comes eventually, and only after endurances and aggressions hardly to be foreseen, to be himself, the product of much example chosen and re-combined, always to the confirmation of what he could become. If only the poet could always use all the imagery that lies near the top of his mind, no day would be long enough for the poems he must write. So he dies a little every day, or lives enough to feel that he has not quite died, measured by how much he has written that day, how much he has been open enough to, to name at the instant. We agonize to learn how to be open enough, to name a thing. Of course, this naming does not happen every day, but it is possible to make it happen more often than it was happening to us a year ago.

This is the closest secret of all the mysteries of the art. But it is secret because we but barely know it; we cannot explicitly tell what we do not yet understand. Explicitly we can only say what it is *like,* not what it really *is.* If the poet recognizes this feeling, these days when he feeds on anything, and everything goes into a poem, then he knows. The imagery that comes up from deeper in the memory or subconscious may be startled up by accidental reminder or stimulated by deliberate effort. As one's age increases the infinite storage in memory and the subconscious, it is possible to understand a little how and when this deep source breaks through and flows. At the least, we can be always watching. After a time, we know some of the stimuli that work for us—the bodily condition, the season, the state of the active mind, or perhaps music or frustration or making love. Poetry is not a part-time but a more than full-time life. No one conducts his whole living to the one end of poetry and then blurs in the crowd. He is distinct, he has the name of a poet. He has style.

PART TWO

A Great Quickness

When W. H. Auden was invited to be Professor of Poetry at Oxford University, he kept the ancient custom of preparing and delivering an Inaugural Lecture. The full text was published by the University, as he gave it on June 11, 1956. Auden was autobiographical in part, and the section in which he talked about his own earliest examples and efforts is presented here. He names Thomas Hardy as his first Master, of all the libraries offered to the young reader and writer, and this proof of a beginning poet's master is included for that fact's sake.

VI

Making, Knowing, and Judging

BY W. H. AUDEN

A beginner's efforts cannot be called bad or imitative. They are imaginary. A bad poem has this or that fault which can be pointed out; an imitative poem is a recognizable imitation of this or that poem, this or that poet. But about an imaginary poem no criticism can be made since it is an imitation of poetry-in-general. Never again will a poet feel so inspired, so certain of genius, as he feels in these first days as his pencil flies across the page. Yet something is being learned even now. As he scribbles on he is beginning to get the habit of noticing metrical quantities, to see that any two-syllable word in isolation must be either a *ti-tum,* a *tum-ti,* or, occasionally, a *tum-tum,* but that when associated with other words it can sometimes become a *ti-ti;* when he discovers a rhyme he had not thought of before, he stores it away in his memory, a habit which an Italian poet may not need to acquire but which an English poet will find useful.

And, though as yet he can only scribble, he has started reading real poems for pleasure and on purpose. Many things can be said against anthologies, but for an adolescent to whom even the names of most of the poets are unknown, a good one can be an invaluable instructor. I had the extraordinary good fortune to be presented one Christmas with the De La Mare anthology, *Come Hither*. This had, for my purposes, two great virtues. Firstly, its good taste. Reading it today, I find very few poems which I should have omitted and none which I think it bad taste to admire. Secondly, its catholic taste. Given the youthful audience for which it was designed, there were certain kinds of poetry which it did not represent, but within those limits the variety was extraordinary. Particularly valuable was its lack of literary class-consciousness, its juxtaposition on terms of equality of unofficial poetry, such as counting-out rhymes, and official poetry such as the odes of Keats. It taught me at the start that poetry does not have to be great or even serious to be good, and that one does not have to be ashamed of moods in which one feels no desire whatsoever to read *The Divine Comedy* and a great desire to read

> When other ladies to the shades go down,
> Still Flavia, Chloris, Celia stay in town.
> These Ghosts of Beauty ling'ring there abide,
> And haunt the places where their Honour died.
>
> Alexander Pope

Matthew Arnold's notion of Touchstones by which to measure all poems has always struck me as a doubtful one, likely to turn readers into snobs and to ruin talented poets by tempting them to imitate what is beyond their powers.

A poet who wishes to improve himself should certainly

keep good company, but for his profit as well as his comfort the company should not be too far above his station. It is by no means clear that the poetry which influenced Shakespeare's development most fruitfully was the greatest poetry with which he was acquainted. Even for readers, when one thinks of the attention that a great poem demands, there is something frivolous about the notion of spending every day with one. Masterpieces should be kept for High Holidays of the Spirit.

I am not trying to defend the aesthetic heresy that one subject is no more important than any other, or that a poem has no subject or that there is no difference between a great poem and a good one—a heresy which seems to me contrary to human feeling and common sense—but I can understand why it exists. Nothing is worse than a bad poem which was intended to be great.

So a would-be poet begins to learn that poetry is more various than he imagined and that he can like and dislike different poems for different reasons. His Censor, however, has still not yet been born. Before the poet can give birth to him, he has to pretend to be somebody else; he has to get a literary transference upon some poet in particular.

If poetry were in great public demand, so that there were over-worked professional poets, I can imagine a system under which an established poet would take on a small number of apprentices who would begin by changing his blotting paper, advance to typing his manuscripts and end up by ghost-writing poems for him which he was too busy to start or finish. The apprentices might really learn something, for, knowing that he would get the blame as well as the credit for their work, the Master would be extremely choosey about his apprentices and do his best to teach them all he knew.

In fact, of course, a would-be poet serves his apprenticeship in a library. This has its advantages. Though the Master is deaf and dumb and gives neither instruction nor criticism, the apprentice can choose any Master he likes, living or dead, the Master is available at any hour of the day or night, lessons are all for free, and his passionate admiration of his Master will ensure that he work hard to please him.

To please means to imitate and it is impossible to do a recognizable imitation of a poet without attending to every detail of his diction, rhythms and habits of sensibility. In imitating his Master, the apprentice acquires a Censor, for he learns that, no matter how he finds it, by inspiration, by potluck or after hours of laborious search, there is only one word or rhythm or form that is the *right* one. The right one is still not the *real* one, for the apprentice is ventriloquizing but he has got away from poetry-in-general; he is learning how a poem is written. Later in life, incidentally, he will realize how important is the art of imitation, for he will not infrequently be called upon to imitate himself.

My first Master was Thomas Hardy, and I think I was very lucky in my choice. He was a good poet, perhaps a great one, but not *too* good. Much as I loved him, even I could see that his diction was often clumsy and forced and that a lot of his poems were plain bad. This gave me hope where a flawless poet might have made me despair. He was modern without being too modern. His world and sensibility were close enough to mine—curiously enough his face bore a striking resemblance to my father's—so that, in imitating him, I was being led towards, not away from myself, but they were not so close as to obliterate my identity. If I looked through his spectacles, at least I was conscious of a certain eye-strain. Lastly, his metrical variety, his fondness for complicated stanza forms, were an invaluable training in the craft of making. I am also thankful that my first Master did not write in free verse or I might then have been tempted to believe that free verse is easier to write than stricter forms, whereas I know it is infinitely more difficult.

When three young American poets, Donald Hall, Robert Pack, and Louis Simpson, made the anthology called *The New Poets of England and America,* with an upper age-limit of forty for the contributors, they allowed one most notable exception by asking Robert Frost, more than twice that age, to write a preface. His prose is scarce, but a good many times longer than the number of words in any piece he writes. He thinks all poets have struck their note long before forty, and are as good and lyric by then as they will ever be. Maturity is not the poet's object, he says. But before Frost has finished, we more than suspect he is not talking about years, but about staying young as poet while mental age increases. Better to season slowly outdoors than mature too quickly indoors; that is, within school doors, he says, leaving the problem still open at both ends.

VII

Maturity No Object

BY ROBERT FROST

Maturity is no object except perhaps in education where you might think from all the talk that the aim and end of everything was to get sophisticated before educated. Shakespeare says it is the right virtue of the medlar to be rotten before it is ripe. Overdevelop the social conscience and make us all social meddlers. But I digress before I begin. My theme is not education, but poetry and how young one has to be or stay to make it. And it is not schools in general I reflect on, only bad schools which something should be done about before they get much larger. My excuse is that school and poetry come so near being one thing. Poetry has been a great concern of school all down the ages. A large part of reading in school always has been and still is poetry; and it is but an extension from the metaphors of poetry out into all thinking, scientific and philosophic. In fact, the poet and scholar have so much in common and live together so naturally that it is easy to make too much of a mystery about where they part company. Their material seems the same—perhaps differs a little in being differently come by and differently held in play. Thoroughness is the danger of the scholar, dredging to the dregs. He works on assignment and self-assignment with some sense of the value of what he is getting when he is getting it. He is perhaps too avid of knowledge. The poet's instinct is to shun or shed more knowledge than he can swing or sing. His most available knowledge is acquired unconsciously. Something warns him dogged determination however profound can only result in doggerel. His danger is rhyming trivia. His depth is the lightsome blue depth of the air.

But I suppose the special distinction I was going to invest the poet with, that is, making no object of maturity, was a mistake. It certainly belongs as much to the composer, the musician, the general, and, I'm told, the mathematician and the scientist. And it probably belongs to the scholar. Be that as it may, all poets I have ever heard of struck their note long before forty, the deadline for contributions to this book. The statistics are all in favor of their being as good and lyric as they will ever be. They may have ceased to be poets by the time appreciation catches up with them, as Matthew Arnold complains somewhere. (I don't have to say exactly where because I'm not a scholar.) I have personal reasons to trust that they may go phasing on into being as good poets in their later mental ages. For my country's sake I might wish one or two of them an old age of epic writing. A good epic would grace our history. Landor has set an example in prolonging the lyric out of all bounds.

Maturity will come. We mature. But the point is that it is at best irrelevant. Young poetry is the breath of parted lips. For the spirit to survive, the mouth must find out how to firm and not harden. I saw it in two faces in the same drawing room—one youth in Greek sculpture, the other manhood in modern painting. They were both noble. The man was no better than the boy nor worse because he was older. The poets of this group, many of them my friends and already known to many of us, need live to write no better, need only wait to be better known for what they have written.

The reader is more on trial here than they are. He is given his chance to see if he can tell all by himself without critical instruction the difference between the poets who wrote because they thought it would be a good idea to write and those who couldn't help writing out of a strong weakness for the muse, as for an elopement with her. There should be some way to tell that, just as there is to tell the excitement of the morning from the autointoxication of midnight. Any distinction between maturity and immaturity is not worth making unless as a precaution. If school is going to proclaim a policy of maturing boys and girls, ultimately it might become necessary for us to stay away from school or at least play hooky a good deal to season slowly out of doors rather than in an oven or in a tanning vat. And that seems too bad; for so many of us like school and want to go there.

As I often say, a thousand, two thousand, colleges, town and gown together in the little town they make, give us the best audiences for poetry ever had in all this world. I am in on the ambition that this book will get to them—heart and mind.

Richard Eberhart responds with seriousness to such a question as might be asked anyone who writes poetry, and he provides an answer in three parts, useful for hurling in teeth. Why not write prose, which we understand? Why do you say it in verse? Because it is easier for me, he says, an obviously unsatisfactory reply. Because it is natural for him to do so, he says next, an answer from the strength of humility, and it might be left there, by some. Then he says, Because it is power; and his final paragraphs blaze with it. This essay appeared on the second page of the New York *Times Book Review*. Eberhart, a poet and teacher, is author of *Great Praises, Burr Oaks, Reading the Spirit,* and other collections of poems.

VIII

Why I Say It in Verse

BY RICHARD EBERHART

When asked "why I write in verse," I have a ready answer: "Because that is easier for me." Maybe I should demonstrate by writing this article in meter. Prose, however, is better for explanation. We shall see that poetry is supreme for suggestiveness.

One writes in verse because one should give oneself to a delirium of joy, which inheres between vowels, where is the ultimate mystery of language, as being the fluid river or sea pent between rigidities or monumental masses of consonants, and is an exercise of music.

Because one does not know how many summers are left to one's life, although one felt this more fiercely, perhaps, at twenty to thirty, poetry is a great quickness over prose.

Because poetry entertains the nuances of our frailty and leads the mind between rational essences to those other electrifying essences which blaze in the most secret hour, the strangest fashions, the primordial and fiercest individuations, known to every man, unarticulated unless poetry prize them in the specific and bring them forth in happy forms.

Because prose makes you lazy but poetry makes you bright.

Because, to say the same thing over in a thousand possible, invented ways, poetry leaps to the ultimate, in an ultimate concentration of essence, and stands for the purpose of man, needing, needless to say, not the justification of this apology, whereas prose, in its log-footed measurement and dogged stance, tells us only what we knew before: poetry suggests an infinite more, a new-made best.

If you would contemplate, while time departs from you, one line so seemingly simple as "My love is like a red, red rose," you might be better rewarded than if you read a thousand pages of expository prose on any subject. What will they expose?

The simple likeness of love to a rose will offer a basic enchantment. It is only a rose-jump to, "To be or not to be, that is the question." And a quick turn to, "Brightness falls from the air." Or thrust toward any profound poetic statement you may love.

In these the concentration is so great that they may ramify in the mind. They put you in love with life. You become part of something beyond you. You become identified with eternal relationships. A sweet religious essence may fill you, for if you think only an hour on some vague possibility of a religious nature, you will be refreshed; if you require the specific, in any cogitation, the result will be the same, if the take-off is poetry and you are contemplative.

The poetry of the line goes over into the supreme poetry of life, of every hour, of every act, of every gesture. Thus you become a part of every man; you lose your oddity. You mate with the changeless. You may do this more efficiently and more naturally through reading poetry than through reading prose. The struggle of the poet may be painful. The reader's pleasure may be relatively painless.

Nevertheless, I consider it an assault on perhaps ununderstandable compulsions to try to state why I write in verse instead of in prose. Synaptic verisimilitude? Prose and verse are the husband and wife of letters. If they have been separated, they come together again. They acknowledge an instinctive dependence. Yet each has its own individuality.

So in a sense the problem is idle, while the problems are universal! I write in verse because it is natural for me to do so. The heaviest prose, the greatest novel, may try to say what Blake uttered in "O Rose, thou art sick!"

Poetry is more challenging to me than prose. In its concentration and refinement there are greater chances for error than in the longer measures of exposition, description and narration usual to prose. Subtlety of mind is enjoined to side-step these errors natural to man; sinuosity of intellect is invited to the tireless game of controlling error (or allowing it to sprout in interesting ways) in the invention of a possible total esthetic satisfaction. Poetry has infinite resource and time-defying propensities.

One reads prose for knowledge, poetry for power. Power is the sense of insight, not in the sense of practical good, although this is not necessarily excluded. It is the powerful, useless, time-defying, God-inciting and Godward-looking nature of poetry, its truth enhancement, in which there is the greater possibility and which makes one obeisant to this primitive and exalted mode.

The best poetry should not be finally understood lest we know too much and might as well have read of the matter in prose. The best poetry should evoke suggestions which please and satisfy but do not exhaust themselves on the hardness of intellect. It is too easy to be intellectually too hard.

One can never be too sensitive, on the other hand, to the mysteries of poetry, which may entice and satisfy the soul, itself a mystery which the rational mind is always trying to destroy.

Wallace Stevens kept a book of his own proverbs, which he called "Adagia," concerning man, art, God, the mind, and especially poetry. It is included by Samuel French Morse in *Opus Posthumous,* the poems, essays, and other manuscripts unpublished at Stevens's death. Morse says, "The right metaphor in the right place achieves a temporary illusion of wholeness . . . a good proverb has this same kind of inexhaustibility and finality; its perennial rightness and freshness is its truth." For Stevens, his proverbs were *materia poetica,* not aphorisms to be left by themselves, but a first step in thought, later to be used, and sometimes unchanged, in his poems and essays. To call attention to this preparatory contemplation as an excellent discipline for any poet, the comments concerning poetry have been selected.

Adagia

BY WALLACE STEVENS

To give a sense of the freshness or vividness of life is a valid purpose for poetry. A didactic purpose justifies itself in the mind of the teacher; a philosophical purpose justifies itself in the mind of the philosopher. It is not that one purpose is as justifiable as another but that some purposes are pure, others impure. Seek those purposes that are purely the purposes of the pure poet.

The poet makes silk dresses out of worms.

Merit in poets is as boring as merit in people.

Authors are actors, books are theaters.

An attractive view: The aspects of earth of interest to a poet are the casual ones, as light or color, images.

It is life that we are trying to get in poetry.

After one has abandoned a belief in God, poetry is that essence which takes its place as life's redemption.

Art, broadly, is the form of life or the sound or color of life. Considered as form (in the abstract) it is often indistinguishable from life itself.

The poet seems to confer his identity on the reader. It is easiest to recognize this when listening to music—I mean this sort of thing: the transference.

Accuracy of observation is the equivalent of accuracy of thinking.

A poem is a meteor.

The collecting of poetry from one's experience as one goes along is not the same thing as merely writing poetry.

A grandiose subject is not an assurance of a grandiose effect but, most likely, of the opposite.

A new meaning is the equivalent of a new word.

Poetry is not personal.

Poetry is a means of redemption.

Poetry is a form of melancholia. Or rather, in melancholy, it is one of the *"aultres choses solatieuses."*

The poem reveals itself only to the ignorant man.

To a large extent, the problems of poets are the problems of painters, and poets must often turn to the literature of painting for a discussion of their own problems.

Weather is a sense of nature. Poetry is a sense.

In poetry at least the imagination must not detach itself from reality.

Not all objects are equal. The vice of imagism was that it did not recognize this.

The poet must put the same degree of intentness into his poetry as, for example, the traveler into his adventure, the painter into his painting.

All poetry is experimental poetry.

The bare image and the image as a symbol are the contrast: the image without meaning and the image as meaning. When the image is used to suggest something else, it is secondary. Poetry as an imaginative thing consists of more than lies on the surface.

One has a sensibility range beyond which nothing really exists for one. And in each this is different.

In poetry, you must love the words, the ideas and the images and rhythms with all your capacity to love anything at all.

The purpose of poetry is to make life complete in itself.

Consider: I. That the whole world is material for poetry; II. That there is not a specifically poetic material.

One reads poetry with one's nerves.

The poet is the intermediary between people and the world in which they live and also, between people as between themselves; but not between people and some other world.

Sentimentality is a failure of feeling.

Poetry is not the same thing as the imagination taken alone. Nothing is itself taken alone. Things are because of interrelations or interactions.

Intolerance respecting other people's religion is toleration itself in comparison with intolerance respecting other people's art.

Poetry is a poetic conception, however expressed. A poem is poetry expressed in words. But in a poem there is a poetry of words. Obviously, a poem may consist of several poetries.

The exposition of a theory of poetry involves a comparison with other theories and the analysis of all.

Ethics are no more a part of poetry than they are of painting.

The poet feels *abundantly* the poetry of everything.

It is the explanations of things that we make to ourselves that disclose our character: The subjects of one's poems are the symbols of one's self or of one's selves.

Poetry has to be something more than a conception of the mind. It has to be a revelation of nature. Conceptions are artificial. Perceptions are essential.

A poem should be part of one's sense of life.

To read a poem should be an experience, like experiencing an act.

Money is a kind of poetry.

Poetry is an effort of a dissatisfied man to find satisfaction through words, occasionally of the dissatisfied thinker to find satisfaction through his emotions.

It is not every day that the world arranges itself in a poem.

The thing said must be the poem not the language used in saying it. At its best the poem consists of both elements.

A poet looks at the world as a man looks at a woman.

To have nothing to say and to say it in a tragic manner is not the same thing as to have something to say.

The poem is a nature created by the poet.

I don't think we should insist that the poet is normal or, for that matter, that anybody is.

Poetry is a purging of the world's poverty and change and evil and death. It is a present perfecting, a satisfaction in the irremediable poverty of life.

Poetry is the scholar's art.

To study and to understand the fictive world is the function of the poet.

The tongue is an eye.

God is a symbol for something that can as well take other forms, as, for example, the form of high poetry.

When the mind is like a hall in which thought is like a voice speaking, the voice is always that of someone else.

There must be something of the peasant in every poet.

The body is the great poem.

It is necessary to any originality to have the courage to be an amateur.

Life is the elimination of what is dead.

The fundamental difficulty in any art is the problem of the normal.

The poet must not adapt his experience to that of the philosopher.

Description is an element, like air or water.

The poet comes to words as nature comes to dry sticks.

We have made too much of life. A journal of life is rarely a journal of happiness.

Poetry sometimes crowns the search for happiness. It is itself a search for happiness.

Poetry must resist the intelligence almost successfully.

A change of style is a change of subject.

Ignorance is one of the sources of poetry.

The poet represents the mind in the act of defending us against itself.

On the bearing of the poet: 1. The prestige of the poet is part of the prestige of poetry. 2. The prestige of poetry is essential to the prestige of the poet.

Every poem is a poem within a poem: the poem of the idea within the poems of the words.

One cannot spend one's time in being modern when there are so many more important things to be.

I have no life except in poetry. No doubt that would be true if my whole life was free for poetry.

The world of the poet depends on the world that he has contemplated.

Poetry is a health.

Poetry is great only as it exploits great ideas or, what is the same thing, great feelings.

Imagination applied to the whole world is vapid in comparison to imagination applied to a detail.

Poetry is a response to the daily necessity of getting the world right.

A poem should stimulate some sense of living and of being alive.

A poem need not have a meaning and like most things in nature often does not have.

Newness (not novelty) may be the highest individual value in poetry. Even in the meretricious sense of newness a new poetry has value.

The essential fault of surrealism is that it invents without discovering. To make a clam play an accordion is to invent, not to discover. The observation of the unconscious, so far as it can be observed, should reveal things of which we have previously been unconscious, not the familiar things of which we have been conscious plus imagination.

The theory of poetry is the life of poetry.

Poetry is (and should be) for the poet a source of pleasure and satisfaction, not a source of honors.

Gaiety in poetry is a precious characteristic but it should be a characteristic of diction.

The degrees of metaphor. The absolute object slightly turned is a metaphor of the object.

Success as the result of industry is a peasant ideal.

Suppose any man whose spirit has survived had consulted his contemporaries as to what to do, or what to think, or what music to write, and so on.

All serious poets hope to renew the language, and some also succeed in systematizing the renewal, as Hopkins did in his preface to his poems. William Carlos Williams felt powerfully that the American language has a line-length or measure, not to be described by any terms before used. It is more flexible, more like speech, he often said. His readers and hearers know he used such a measure, though he had not described it with complete satisfaction to himself. When John C. Thirlwall edited Dr. Williams's letters, published in 1957, he included one, written to him and perhaps at his request, in which the poet got the idea stated.

A New Measure

A LETTER FROM WILLIAM CARLOS WILLIAMS TO JOHN C. THIRLWALL, JAN. 13, 1955.

Dear Jack,

Of recent years I have become more and more aware of a basic change that has come over the way in which our poems must be made. I say "must be made," because it is part of our present situation in the world that when we perceive an alternative to our actions which enlarges the field which they occupy, we feel inevitably impelled to give them the head to go where they are called. We cannot conceive of a world any more without the miracles which astronomy and physics have presented to us. And in aesthetics, the construction of a poem, we shall find ourselves equally bound.

There are leads, when we become aware of them, which

point the way to the approaching changes, undoubtedly unwelcome, that have been latent for centuries. The tendency of the race is to resist change violently. At the same time the new presses to be recognized. Which is the most conservative? That which drives us to keep the old or that which seeks a place for us in some slowly, or at times, as in the present, some rapidly evolving new? Certain it is that we have no voice in the matter; we cannot refuse to go forward when the opportunity offers itself. Not to do so is the end of us.

Open to us is only a choice in aesthetic matters of what we prefer; the perfection of a Homeric line (which, by the way, we cannot any longer properly pronounce) or, say, a stanza from one of Villon's ballads. But that is not at all a choice, since all men are agreed that each in its own category is perfection. But when availability for human expression is broached, the structure of the poetic line itself enters the field. That is where aesthetics is mated with physics, to broaden the view.

What word will you employ to bring more meaning to your chosen text? That is the question which must open more avenues to your mind or fail to interest it.

The mind always tries to break out of confinement. It has tried every sort of interest which presents itself, even to a flight to the moon. But the only thing which will finally interest it must be its own intrinsic nature. In itself it must find devices which will permit it to survive—physical transportation to another planet will not help, for it will still be the same mind which has not been relieved by the movement.

But in the arts, the art of the poem, lie resources which when we become aware of their existence make it possible for us to liberate ourselves, or so I believe and think, with reason I hope, can be made plain to anyone who will read.

We are no longer children; it is in the mind, not on the moon, we must find our relief.

The first thing you learn when you begin to learn anything about this earth is that you are eternally barred save for the report of your senses from knowing anything about it. Measure serves for us as the key: we can measure between objects; therefore, we know that they exist. Poetry began with measure, it began with the dance, whose divisions we have all but forgotten but are still known as measures. Measures they were, and we still speak of their minuter elements as feet.

If the measure by which the poem is to be recognized has at present been lost, it is only lost in the confusion which at present surrounds our lives. We don't, any more, know how to measure the lines and therefore have convinced ourselves that they can't be measured.

So what can we do but retreat to some "standard" which we have known in the past and say to ourselves, Beyond this standard you shall not go! That we do not know how to go beyond this standard practice or may not want to go beyond it for conservative reasons is humanly possible. Whole reaches of knowledge with the forms which attach to them, the academies and schools which are frozen into complex pattern, impress our minds and our emotions until we defend them even with our lives, fill the field.

We have our measures of English verse from *Beowulf* to the present, and all the polite prejudices that stem from them but—in spite of their beauty none offers release from our dilemma. A new measure or way of measuring the line is beyond our thoughts.

The first thing that was necessary before we could look beyond the stalemate which had been created by the classic measure was to break it apart. That would be, under our ordinary understanding of the term, to destroy it. That was accomplished (I am speaking of the classically accepted measure) by Walt Whitman. That he had no clear conception of what he had done is beside the point. A break had been made. He apparently thought that the break was toward some objective known as "freedom" and not, as was actually the case, toward a more *ample* measure.

If the measurement itself is confined, every dimension of the verse and all implications touching it suffer confinement and generate pressures within our lives which will blow it and us apart. It is no matter that we are dealing with a comparatively unnoticed part of the field of our experience, the field of poetics, the result to our minds will be drastic. You cannot break through old customs, in verse or social organization, without drastically changing the whole concept and also the structure of our lives all along the line.

That is merely and magnificently the birth of a new measure supplanting the old—something we hardly hoped to dare.

The realization of what can come about in any of the fields of human interest we must be ready to accept. It may seem presumptive to state that such an apparently minor activity as a movement in verse construction could be an indication of Einstein's discoveries in the relativity of our measurements of physical matter, but such is the fact.

Witlessly, but taking his cue out of the air, Whitman was in his so-called free verse only initiating a new measure. It is to the line, the ancient poetic line, that we have to look for what is to come next. The unit of which the line has in the past been constructed no longer in our minds is permitted to exist. That is the thing which makes poems as they still continue to be written obsolete. A new measure has supplanted the old!

That the foot can no longer be measured as it was formerly but only relatively makes a basic alteration necessary in our plans for it. But measure we must have, as long as we are impelled to know complexities of the world about our ears. The verse I can envisage, a measure infinitely truer and more subtle than that of the past, comes much closer in its construction to modern concepts of reality.

Sincerely yours
S/Bill

This defense of poets first asks an alarming question because just such a question has been asked. Stephen Spender, the English poet and editor, wrote the essay for the New York *Times Book Review*'s second page. His answer can save souls: The greater the insistence on total conformity, the more we need the poets, the preservers of individuality. He speaks of the serious non-seriousness of poetry, in which the subject or theme is the serious thing, and the form of the poem is the game, or non-serious. "Poetry," he says, "insists on the individual nature of experience, and the element of play in life."

Can't We Do Without the Poets?

BY STEPHEN SPENDER

Poets and critics have long speculated—if only idly—as to the use and necessity of poetry. Are poets the "unacknowledged legislators of mankind," as Shelley claimed, or should they be excluded from the Republic, as Plato postulated? Or is poetry a kind of game not to be taken too seriously—perhaps not seriously at all, and certainly not with solemnity—as Eliot and Auden seem sometimes to indicate?

To the shrewd reader it may appear that there is something suspect about disclaimers made with such authority. For may not a game, conducted on the level of the highest thought throughout the ages, after all be the most significant activity in life? May not Eliot and Auden be laughing at our seriousness? Perhaps Eliot's concept of poetry as play may, paradoxically, be more serious than Shelley's vision of a poem as a kind of City-State of the Social Intellect: a simulacrum of a perfect society which will act as a kind of constructive explosion transforming human institutions instead of destroying them.

Certainly there is a poetry written within the shadow of towering institutions, and yet unshadowed by public thought, which seems to state a truth within whose still greater shadow those institutions seem to lie, as the lines:

> Golden boys and girls all must,
> Like chimney sweepers, come to dust.

The poets are responsibles who nevertheless have divided responsibility which can even assert itself as responsibility to nothing but their art. Religion, tradition, morality, patriotism, socialism can all claim with justice that their theses have been woven into tapestries of words by poets. Quite true. Who can deny that Shakespeare, Milton, and Wordsworth dramatized a concept of the English character which still helps win English wars?

Yet, at the moment, when patriotism is going full blast, Falstaff is discerned lugging the guts of Harry Hotspur off the battlefield, Wordsworth's inspiration seems fused with a French love affair which in turn was inspired by the French Revolution, though his patriotism was directed against France; and Blake pointed out that in depicting Satan, Milton was "of the devil's party without knowing it." And yet it would be untrue to say that Shakespeare and Wordsworth were unpatriotic, Milton a satanist.

The truth is that if they had a vision of England and of heaven their responsibility was toward their vision and not to the British monarchy and the Protestant Church. In their own minds, the distinction between vision and fact may not have been clear, but the test of their poetry is their fidelity to the vision and their willingness to deride or betray the fact when it disturbed the vision.

Poets can inspire political parties, but they are bad party men. It is always a bad time for poets when the social or religious cause they have inspired and propagated comes into power. In our century the Russian poets certainly discovered this, and even in Socialist England the poets who discerned the real glory in the equality of man are discouraged by the drudgery of socialism, which, while really fulfilling many of the ideals of a juster society, tends to reduce all values to a common multiple. You may be sure that if Shelley had lived long enough for one of his poems to affect legislation, the poet's inspiration would have been damned by the new law.

The difference between the poet and the proselytizer is that the advocate of a realistic program of action tries to maintain a consistency between his program and reality. The program has to be related to facts, shown to be consistent with an interpretation of history. Poetry, however, cannot be responsible to the logic of theories and events, and attempts to make it so are fatal to the poetry. Poetry is responsible to the logic of poetry, which is partly the poet's fidelity to those sequences of imagery which are the thought processes of the imagination, partly his power to develop imagery and metaphor correctly, and partly his observation of the (often unwritten) rules of technique.

The fact that poets write in meter and perhaps also in rhyme illustrates the divided loyalty of poetry. Balzac in his famous introduction to Stendhal's *The Charterhouse of Parma* criticizes the poets (even Racine) because they often have to substitute an image or an ornament for a fact, in order to find a rhyme. Some other critic, however, has pointed out that often a poet's best inspirations come from the search for a correct rhyme, which forces his thought into an unexpected channel. So that a poet might be described as someone who in writing about one thing is often impelled, by the exigencies of the form he seeks to achieve, to write about something else.

Does this not suggest the serious non-seriousness of poetry? The subject, the theme, is serious in the way that philosophy or scientific description is. The form is non-serious in the way that a game such as a crossword puzzle is. Yet the precision of logic or science is brought to bear just as much on the non-serious as the serious element. And is it not this conflict between a serious and a non-serious purpose, fused within the same work, precisely that which raises great poetry to the level where even tragedy seems a game of the gods?

Does not the contradiction also embody a very important truth about life: that life has important aims, acted out within the parentheses of death? The art which above all others has the appearance of creating immortal works is most conscious of the passage of time and the certainty of extinction.

We are moving into a world governed by know-besters. In all countries governments discover a little more every day about the best way in which citizens should have their money, time and lives spent by officials. Owing to the mess the world is in—which has to be got out of—individuals have to admit, nearly everywhere, that the government probably does know best. We are scarcely aware at present of the tremendous effect that this shift of emphasis from individual intuition to expert advice and ordering is having on art.

The poet (and for him read also the creative artist) feels that he is living in a world governed by generalized rules too impersonal and perhaps also too indisputable to be material for his art. At the same time, personal values which he clutches at are either insignificant (escapism is the word coined to express this) or they lead him rapidly back into a position which challenges society, and which, therefore, itself depends on generalized rules. In the 1950's having "personal values" either means very little or it means that I object to being conscripted into the Army or to paying my income tax or (if I am a European) to currency regulations which inhibit my freedom to travel. These attitudes, though, lead in turn to pacifism and perhaps anarchism (such as the views of Mr. Herbert Read).

So it seems—in Europe, at all events—as if every individual is caught in a social or anti-social web, which means that he no longer feels himself to be an individual. Everything but the purely "escapist" is forced into having official views or subversive ones. And the few poets who do not seem affected by this situation—T. S. Eliot and Edith Sitwell in England, for examples—seem like survivors from another age.

No wonder that these subversive conformists, those responsible irresponsibles who are the poets, seem to lead existences poised on a margin which is rapidly being narrowed, as the official view of what an individual has to do comes more and more nearly to coincide with a necessity which the individual—however unwillingly—grows to accept: unless, indeed, he is forced into a revolt which itself implies another kind of system. Everything in life seems to have become public and serious, and the non-serious seems to be the unnecessary.

The poet who is a legislator has become unthinkable in modern society, and the individualist in revolt *pour épater le bourgeois* is a mere survival from a time when the bourgeois himself was an individualist, head of a family shocked by the spectacle of a rebellious son. The "know-besters" of today are not impressed by rebels, they merely note a bad mark against them in their little black books. There remains one concept of the function of poetry—discussed usually only to be dismissed—which seems to me to be useful in our time. That is Matthew Arnold's definition: "Poetry is a criticism of life." At all events, I can see various ways in which poetry can be a criticism of various contemporary phenomena.

First, poetry is a criticism of language. Poetry is concrete, personal and exact. We live in a time when language tends to be used in ways that are abstract, generalized, impersonal and inaccurate. Logical positivism and semanticism are philosophic and dictionary revolts against the misuse of language, but poetry by dealing with contemporary experiences, values, situations and aims, and expressing these in its own language of the logic of the imagination measures the distance between the standardized values of our world expressed in official language and their values as personal experience.

Second, the insistence on the nonseriousness of the poetic game is just as much a contemporary way of asserting poetry as a "criticism of life" as was Shelley's attempt to legislate through poetry. The officialized view of the necessity-dominated world of today is that lives are or should be completely serious; that is to say, they be entirely absorbed into social aims which are really aims of using power in order to remove supposed evils from the world and to improve conditions.

Whether or not one accepts the programs of action laid down by governments, it is surely necessary to challenge the current heresy that generalized social aims into which all lives are conscripted are life for all people or any one person, except, possibly, a bureaucrat. Every line of true poetry, by insisting on the individual nature of experience and on the element of play in life, challenges this point of view. And here it becomes extremely important that there should be a contemporary poetry. For, if there were none, past poetry might recede into being a museum of examples having no relation to contemporary conditions.

This brings me to my last point. We are living in a time which above all challenges the concept of the individual. The reaction from the commercial individualism of the last century has gone so far that in this century we have seen political movements based on the idea that the individual has no reality except as an object mirroring and acting out the conflicts of society. Poetry is a lifeline attaching us to an individualism of men before the nineteenth century. Poetry witnesses that the individual is not just the individualist exploiter. That there should be a rebirth of a pious and sacrosanct concept of the individual as millions of single lives, which are in some sense beyond the good and evil workings of society, is most important, for there can be no sane and unfanatical politics without this. Here the serious non-seriousness of poetry witnesses to a truth which may not legislate, but which still could save our souls.

Poets learn some of the matters of their craft by overhearing, and Marianne Moore on her own sentence structure makes some of the best overhearing, for the acute listener, that there could be. The rarity of a poet talking at all on this simplest most profound matter is no more surprising than her directness. Her prose style is stirring example. Instantly, in this essay, we are caught up and swept by her "lion's leap" till we feel capable of it, too. She keeps nothing back; that would be "disobliging," and one feels alone with her, the only one in the world she wishes to talk to. Few poets can talk like this, about their own principles for writing. This essay is complete here, and comes from *Predilections,* her book of literary essays.

XII

Feeling and Precision *from* Predilections

BY MARIANNE MOORE

Feeling at its deepest—as we all have reason to know—tends to be inarticulate. If it does manage to be articulate, it is likely to seem overcondensed, so that the author is resisted as being enigmatic or disobliging or arrogant.

One of New York's more painstaking magazines asked me, at the suggestion of a contributor, to analyze my sentence structure, and my instinctive reply might have seemed dictatorial: you don't devise a rhythm, the rhythm is the person, and the sentence but a radiograph of personality. The following principles, however, are aids to composition by which I try, myself, to be guided: if a long sentence with dependent clauses seems obscure, one can break it into shorter units by imagining into what phrases it would fall as conversation; in the second place, expanded explanation tends to spoil the lion's leap—an awkwardness which is surely brought home to one in conversation; and in the third place, we must be as clear as our natural reticence allows us to be.

William Carlos Williams, commenting on his poem "The Red Wheelbarrow," said, "The rhythm, though no more than a fragment, denotes a certain unquenchable exaltation"; and Wallace Stevens, referring to poetry under the metaphor of the lion, says, "It can kill a man." Yet the lion's leap would be mitigated almost to harmlessness if the lion were clawless, so precision is both impact and exactitude, as with surgery; and also in music, the conductor's signal, as I am reminded by a friend, which "begins far back of the beat, so that you don't see when the down beat comes. To have started such a long distance ahead makes it possible to be exact. Whereas you can't be exact by being restrained." When writing with maximum impact, the writer seems under compulsion to set down an unbearable accuracy; and in connection with precision as we see it in metaphor, I think of Gerard Hopkins and his description of the dark center in the eye of a peacock feather as "the colour of the grape where the flag is turned back"; also his saying about some lambs he had seen frolicking in a field, "It was as though it was the ground that tossed them"; at all events, precision is a thing of the imagination; and it is a matter of diction, of diction that is virile because galvanized against inertia. In Louis Ginsberg's poem, "Command of the Dead," the final stanza reads:

> And so they live in all our works
> And sinew us to victory.
> We see them when we most are gay;
> We feel them when we most are free.

The natural order for the two mosts would be

> We see them when we are most gay;
> We feel them when we are most free

but that would mean, being at our gayest makes us think of them, and being free makes us feel them—gross inaccuracy since these "mosts" are the essence of compassion.

"Fighting Faith Saves the World," an inadvertent ambiguity, as a title for a review of *Journey Among Warriors* by Eve Curie, seems to mean, fight faith and the world is saved; whereas to say, a fighting faith saves the world, would safeguard the meaning.

Explicitness being the enemy of brevity, an instance of difficult descriptive matter accurately presented is that passage in the Book of Daniel (X:9,10,11) where the writer says: "Then was I in a deep sleep on my face, and my face toward the ground. And, behold, an hand touched me, which set me upon my knees and upon the palms of my hands. And I stood trembling." Think what *we* might have done with the problem if we had been asked to describe how someone was wakened and, gradually turning over, got up off the ground.

Instinctively, we employ antithesis as an aid to precision, and in Arthur Waley's translation from the Chinese one notices the many paired meanings—"left and right"; "waking and sleeping"; "one embroiders with silk, an inch a day; of plain sewing one can do more than five feet." Anyone with contemporary pride thinks of W. H. Auden in connection with antithesis, as in "The Double Man" (the *New Year Letter*) he says of the devil:

> For, torn between conflicting needs,
> He's doomed to fail if he succeeds,
>
> . . .
>
> If love has been annihilated
> There's only hate left to be hated.

Nor can we forget Socrates' answer: "I would rather die having spoken in my manner than speak in your manner and live." And there is that very dainty instance of antithesis in Thomas Watson's and William Byrd's madrigal, "A Gratification unto Master John Case":

> Let Enuy barke against the starres,
> Let Folly sayle which way she please,
> with him I wish my dayes to spend. . . .
> whose quil hath stoode fayre Musickes frend,
> chief end to peace, chief port of ease.

When we think we don't like art it is because it is artificial art. "Mere technical display," as Plato says, "is a beastly noise"—in contrast with art, which is "a spiritual magnetism" or "fascination" or "conjuring of the soul."

Voltaire objected to those who said in enigmas what others had said naturally, and we agree; yet we must have the courage of our peculiarities. What would become of Ogden Nash, his benign vocabulary and fearless rhymes, if he wrote only in accordance with the principles set forth by our manuals of composition?

> I love the Baby Giant Panda,
> I'd welcome one to my veranda.
> I never worry, wondering maybe

Whether it isn't Giant Baby;
I leave such matters to the scientists—
The Giant Baby—and Baby Giantists.
I simply want a veranda, and a
Giant Baby Giant Panda.

This, it seems to me, is not so far removed from George Wither's motto: "I grow and wither both together."

Feeling has departed from anything that has on it the touch of affectation, and William Rose Benét, in his preface to the *Collected Poems of Ford Madox Ford,* says: "Whether or not there is such a thing as poetic afflatus there are certain moments that must be seized upon, when more precise language than at any other time is ready to hand for the expression of spontaneous feeling." My own fondness for the unaccented rhyme derives, I think, from an instinctive effort to ensure naturalness. Even elate and fearsome rightness like Shakespeare's is only preserved from the offense of being 'poetic' by his well-nested effects of helpless naturalness.

Chaucer and Henryson, it seems to me, are the perfection of naturalness in their apparently artless art of conveying emotion intact. In "Orpheus and Eurydice," Henryson tells how Tantalus stood in a flood that rose "aboif his chin"; yet

quhen he gaipit thair wald no drop cum In;

. . .

Thus gat he nocht his thirst [to slake] no[r] mend.

Befoir his face ane naple hang also,
fast at his mowth upoun a twynid [threid],
quhen he gaipit, It rollit to and fro,
and fled, as it refusit him to feid.
Quhen orpheus thus saw him suffir neid,

> he tuk his harp and fast on it can clink;
> The wattir stud, and tantalus gat a drink.

One notices the wholesomeness of the uncapitalized beginnings of lines, and the gusto of invention, with climax proceeding out of climax, which is the mark of feeling.

We call a climax a device, but is it not the natural result of strong feeling? It is, moreover, a pyramid that can rest either on its point or on its base, witty anticlimax being one of Ludwig Bemelmans' best enticements, as when he says of the twelve little girls, in his story *Madeline:*

> They smiled at the good
> and frowned at the bad
> and sometimes they were very sad.

Intentional anticlimax as a department of surprise is a subject by itself; indeed, an art, "bearing," as Longinus says, "the stamp of vehement emotion like a ship before a veering wind," both as content and as sound; but especially as sound, in the use of which the poet becomes a kind of hypnotist—recalling Kenneth Burke's statement that "the hypnotist has a way out and a way in."

Concealed rhyme and the interiorized climax usually please me better than the open rhyme and the insisted-on climax, and we can readily understand Dr. Johnson's objection to rigmarole, in his takeoff on the ballad:

> I put my hat upon my head,
> And went into the Strand,
> And there I saw another man,
> With his hat in his hand.

"Weak rhythm" of that kind "enables an audience to foresee the ending and keep time with their feet," disapproved by Longinus, has its subtle opposite in E. E. Cummings' lines about Gravenstein apples—"wall" and "fall," "round," "sound," and "ground," worked into a hastening tempo:

> But over a (see just
> over this) wall
> the red and the round
> (they're Gravensteins) fall
> with a kind of a blind
> big sound on the ground

And the intensity of Henry Trece's "Prayer in Time of War" so shapes the lines that it scarcely occurs to one to notice whether they are rhymed or not:

> Black Angel, come you down! Oh Purge of God,
> By shroud of pestilence make pure the mind,
> Strike dead the running panther of desire
> That in despair the poem put on wings,
> That letting out the viper from the veins
> Man rock the mountain with his two bare hands!

With regard to unwarinesses that defeat precision, excess is the common substitute for energy. We have it in our semi-academic, too conscious adverbs—awfully, terribly, frightfully, infinitely, tremendously; in the word "stunning," the phrase "knows his Aristotle," or his Picasso, or whatever it may be; whereas we have a contrastingly energetic usefulness in John Crowe Ransom's "particularistic," where he says T. S. Eliot "is the most particularistic critic that English poetry and English criticism have met with." Similarly with Dr. Johnson's "encomiastick," in the statement that Dryden's account of Shakespeare "may stand as a perpetual model of encomiastick criticism."

It is curious to see how we have ruined the word "fearful" as meaning full of fear. Thomas Nashe says of his compatriot Barnes—quoting Campion—"hee bragd when he was in France, he slue ten men, when (fearful cowbaby), he never heard a piece shot off but he fell on his face."

One recalls, as a pleasing antidote to jargon, Wyndham Lewis's magazine, *The Tyro,* which defined a tyro as "an elementary person, an elemental usually known in journalism as the veriesttyro." "Very," when it doesn't mean true, is a word from which we are rightly estranged, though there are times when it seems necessary to the illusion of conversation or to steady the rhythm; and a child's overstatement of surprise upon receiving a gift—a playhouse—seems valuable, like foreign-language idiom—"This is the most glorious and terrific thing that ever came into this house"; but Sir Francis Bacon was probably right when he said, "Hyperbole is comely only in love."

I have an objection to the word "and" as a connective between adjectives—"He is a crude and intolerant thinker." But note the use of "and" as an ornament in the sonnet (66) in which Shakespeare is enumerating the many things of which he is tired:

> And art made tongue-tied by authority,
> And folly (doctor-like) controlling skill,
> And simple truth miscall'd simplicity,
> And captive good attending captain ill.

Defending Plato against the charge of "allegorical bombast" in his eulogy of man's anatomy and the provision whereby the heart "might throb against a yielding surface and get no damage," Longinus asks, "Which is the better, in poetry and in prose, . . . grandeur with a few flaws or mediocrity that is impeccable?" And unmistakably Ezra Pound's instinct against preciosity is part of his instinct for precision and accounts for his "freedom of motion" in saying what he has to say "like a bolt from a catapult"—not that the catapult is to us invariably a messenger of comfort. One of his best accuracies, it seems to me, is the word "general" in the sentence in which he praises "the general effect" of Ford Madox Ford's poem "On Heaven," avoiding the temptation to be spuriously specific; and although Henry James was probably so susceptible to emotion as to be obliged to seem unemotional, it is a kind of painter's accuracy for Ezra Pound to say of him as a writer, "Emotions to Henry James were more or less things that other people had, that one didn't go into."

Fear of insufficiency is synonymous with insufficiency, and fear of incorrectness makes for rigidity. Indeed, any concern about how well one's work is going to be received seems to mildew effectiveness. T. S. Eliot attributes Bishop Andrewes' precision to "the pure motive," and the fact that when he "takes a word and derives the world from it, . . . he is wholly in his subject, unaware of anything else." Mr. McBride, in the New York *Sun,* once said of Rembrandt and his etching "The Three Crosses": "It was as though Rembrandt was talking to himself, without any expectation that the print would be seen or understood by others. He saw these things and so testified." This same rapt quality we have in Bach's *Art of the Fugue*—his intensively private soliloquizing continuity that ends, "Behold I Stand before Thy Throne." We feel it in the titles of some of his works, even in translation, "Behold from Heaven to Earth I Come."

Professor Maritain, when lecturing on scholasticism and immortality, spoke of those suffering in concentration camps, "unseen by any star, unheard by any ear," and the almost terrifying solicitude with which he spoke made one know that belief is stronger even than the struggle to survive. And what he said so unconsciously was poetry. So art is but an expression of our needs; is feeling, modified by the writer's moral and technical insights.

The fifteen chosen by John Ciardi for his *Mid-Century American Poets* were each asked to select representative poems, and to write an introduction to them. Ciardi, rightly assuming that fifteen more or less uniformly useful introductions was an unlikelihood, set up a guiding questionnaire on attitudes toward the problems of writing. It suggested twelve responses to such topics as the oral quality of a poem; the audience of a poem; the function of overtone; imagery; rhyme; structure of the total poem; and so on. It invited the poets to answer it, abuse it, add to it, or reject it, but somehow to help a reader to a more immediate response to the poems. The result was an extraordinary and valuable book, for the poems and the introductions. We were happy choosing among our poems, and terrified to have to write about our writing; the divergences are a study in themselves. Wilbur's obliging partial acceptance of the conditions is one of the best self-examinations in the book: firm, practical, honest, and individual, a valuable insight.

XIII

The Genie in the Bottle

BY RICHARD WILBUR

Before answering the present questionnaire, I should like to say that I have certain reservations about it. For one thing, I think artists do well not to talk too much about art, their natural language being that of their media, and not that of abstract analysis. A writer who talks too much of writing runs the risk of becoming a Literary Figure. For another thing, I mistrust most "statements of principles" by artists, since they are necessarily in the nature of apologia. Works of art can almost never be truthfully described as applications of principles. They are not coerced into being by rational principles, but spring from imagination, a condition of spontaneous psychic unity. Asked to produce his "principles," the average artist (fearful of being thought frivolous if he declares that he has none) studies his best work of the past for whatever consistencies he can find. From this *post facto* enquiry, which another might have made as well as he, the artist derives a list of constants in his performance, which he then formulates as "principles." This self-codification may in some cases be harmless; but there is a danger in it, particularly for younger artists. The drawing up of an aesthetic Deuteronomy, the committing himself to a set of "working principles," is very likely to be a hindrance to a younger artist, if he has any taste for consistency. It may very well dissuade him from experiments he ought to make, and if so would prove a bad thing to have done.

These reservations of mine may serve to explain why some of my answers to the questionnaire below are a trifle short and oblique, why I have omitted several topics altogether, and why in certain cases I have re-phrased the questions to harmonize with my answers.

[Mr. Ciardi had said, "As nearly as you are able to systematize your own attitudes toward the technical problems of your own writing, what working principles (or rejection of principle) guide your attitude toward: 1. The oral quality of the poem? (Is it meant to be read aloud?)" Mr. Wilbur re-phrased it:]

1. *Is the poem meant to be read aloud?*

Any poem written by a man or woman with an ear profits by being read aloud. But we are a long way now from the times of oral epic, scops, and ballad singers. Many modern poems take a bit more doing than one can manage in the course of a single hearing; the ear cannot gulp down in two minutes what the eye was meant to drink in at leisure. This is not to say that there is no pleasure to be got from partial comprehension: a good audience can respond to Yeats' "I saw a staring virgin stand" without a preparatory lecture on the *Vision*. But I find on the whole that I most enjoy hearing modern poems with which I am already familiar. In such cases there are no problems of discontinuous comprehension, and I can concentrate on how well the reader supplies the patterns of sound and emphasis, and the prevailing emotional tone.

It is said that there are more public poetry-readings these days than ever before, and that they are better than ever attended. If so, this is an opportunity for American poets to furnish the poetry public with a sharper awareness of that part of the meaning of a poem which is carried by the sound. Most poetry at present is not of course heard with the ear, but seen with the eye and heard, if at all, in the inner ear. The inner ear is that part of the memory which stores the sound of words. The keenness of a reader's inner ear depends somewhat on his natural sensitivity to sound, but also on what kinds of sound he has heard. I strongly suspect that Americans in general are now suffering from degeneration of the inner ear, owing to the unpopularity or decline of many forms of heightened utterance (sermon, oration, declamation, recitation, soliloquy) and the taming and flattening of our daily speech.

Like all poets who value sound, I want the sounds in my poetry to be heard, and I am always grateful for the opportunity to read aloud. If, however, poets are to be of any use in regenerating the public's inner ear, they are going to have to study recitation. With several striking exceptions, our poets (myself included) read in such a way as to convince their audiences that "Heard melodies are sweet, but those unheard/Are sweeter."

["The audience of the poem? (To whom is it addressed? How "difficult" may a poem be? When is it "difficult"?), asked Mr. Ciardi. Mr. Wilbur asked himself:]

2. *To whom is the poem addressed? How difficult may a poem be?*

A poem is addressed to the Muse. It is one function of the Muse to cover up the fact that poems are not addressed to anybody in particular. During the act of writing, the poem is an effort to express a knowledge imperfectly felt, to articulate relationships not quite seen, to make or discover some pattern in the world. It is a conflict with disorder, not a message from one person to another. Once the poem is written, and published, however, it belongs to anyone who will take it, and the more the better.

I am sure that in all poets there is a deep need to communicate. But a poet by his nature has to see and say things in his own way. Though the wish to communicate may be one desire which prompts the poet to write, the experience of writing cannot include any calculations as to the public intelligibility of what is written. While writing, the poet is singlemindedly pursuing a glimpsed perfection of utterance, and he is the only person to whom the poem *must* be clear. If the poet is something of a human being, and has talent, his poem's being clear to him is a near-guarantee that it will be clear to some, if not all others.

The question of difficulty does not much interest me, really. I think there are many justifications for poetry's being difficult at present. On the other hand, I do not feel that all poetry *must* be difficult at present, or that the man who writes readily-understood poetry is criminally opposing the *Zeitgeist*. The League for Sanity in Poetry to the contrary, I think that among our good poets "wilful obscurity" is extremely uncommon. Those who attempt to arouse public opinion against difficulty in poetry are appealing, I think, to the laziness and uneasy pride of a half-educated and excessively comfortable middle class, whose intelligences have so long been flattered by all our great entertainment media that they cannot associate pleasure with effort, and therefore receive any demand for spiritual exertion as a calculated insult.

It seems to me that there are two ways of thinking about universality. A poem may be said to be universal when it is *for* everybody; it may also be called universal when it is *about* everybody. In these incoherent times, to try for the first kind of universality is generally to become a literary whore. Provisionally—that is, until the arrival of the millennium—I think we had better cling to the second criterion. A poem is not the less universal for being incomprehensible to some; so long as it deals humanly with some human experience, so that the imaginative order it contrives may enrich another, it may be said to be *about* everybody—and that is the only kind of universality we can sensibly desire. "To believe your own thought, to believe that what is true for you in your private heart is true for all men" seems to me no less possible now than in Emerson's time. The poetry of those who so believe, however difficult it may be, is never guilty of solipsism.

["The language of the poem? (Its idiom. Any special theories of diction?)" This was shortened by Mr. Wilbur to read:]

3. *What is your attitude toward the language of the poem?*

I have no special theory of diction, but I am strongly in favor of the greatest possible catholicity in the choice of words. Some of the poets of our older poetic generation accomplished, before and after the first world war, a necessary subversion of the poetic diction of their predecessors. Since then their imitators have been so slavish as to establish in current verse several recognizable *argots*. The Auden school of the 30's, which gave poetic language a refreshing infusion of slang and technical terminology, has also been aped quite enough now. In an age of separation and specialization, poets can serve the public sensibility by making continual recombinations of all our many modes of speech—by trying incessantly to counterfeit a general language. If this is to be done, we must hope that no particular combination will be allowed to harden into a poetic dialect.

The borrowing of words from other tongues should not be condemned as mere elegance. Self-confident cultures like the Elizabethan have always very cavalierly taken whatever they needed from foreign languages; and the Elizabethans pronounced their borrowings as they chose. Whenever a foreign tongue can supply us some word more exact or more suggestive than those at hand, I think we may profitably do the same.

["The function of overtone?" was Mr. Ciardi's next question, but here Mr. Wilbur substituted another:]

4. *Do you have anything to say about allusion?*

I think the point should be made that one does not, merely by referring to the dying god or what not, evoke a legitimate emotional response. The value of the reference must in every case be proven. I think it possible that the basic aesthetic mistake in *Finnegan's Wake* is what one might call, in the language of the new critics, "the fallacy of mere reference." This is not of course to say that references must be *explained* in poetry. Artistic economy won't allow it. But it should be the use of the reference, and not its inherent prestige, which demands response.

["Levels of meaning?" asked Mr. Ciardi, as his next suggestion, and Mr. Wilbur somewhat obliquely, as he says, put it in his way:]

5. *What is your attitude toward irony and paradox?*

There should be no flight from irony and paradox in writing poetry, rather an insistence on them. They are often the source, I think, of what richness and honesty we may sense in a poem. But "the corruption of the best is the worst," and it is unfortunately the case that these devices, which when honorably handled are the best means of telling the whole truth, can also be the slickest tools for saying nothing at all. Putting reverse English on one's words, uttering apparent contradictions and oxymorons—these can make for the stark, condensed presentation of divided feelings and irreconcilable facts. But when irony and paradox are employed as a compositional *tic,* when they are used as a means to simultaneous assertion and retraction, when they produce only a brilliant surface of mock-logic, then what one has is the current version of "pure poetry"—a highly camouflaged way of being *vox et praeterea nihil.*

In a poem which makes proper use of irony and paradox, the materials will be grandly polarized, and the contradictions made sharp. In a poem which makes cheating use of these devices, one will discover on analysis only a dispersion of flashy short-circuits, and one will end by feeling like poor Alice, when she and the Red Queen had flown so fast to get nowhere.

I dwell so much on this matter because I think that current critical enthusiasm for the ironic has led us to be somewhat uncritical of the perverse and the deviously aimless. For some time now, the ideal conception of the modern poet has been that of a deeply divided man—so much so that when Mr. Eliot turned to the writing of meditative-religious poetry, some complained of him as a lost leader who had "taken the easy way out." The complexity of the age still appears to demand a corresponding complexity in the poet: he is expected to refine our awareness of contradictions, rather than to resolve them, and whenever he approaches a synthesis of modern experience, through faith, politics or what have you, we seem to prefer him at all costs to eschew serenity. I think it true that any simplicity of understanding is very likely, in 1950, to be fraudulent, and I imagine we may rightly persist in demanding that our ideal poet be as divided as honesty requires. But we need not extend our admiration from the divided man to the shattered man and the liquefied man. The poet ought not to be divided and re-divided to the point of disappearance, and our respect for irony should not betray us into a toleration of the "pure poetry" of intricate aboulia and evasion.

["Subject matter? (Any predilections? Restrictions?)" was the guide given by Mr. Ciardi as his sixth question, and Mr. Wilbur put it:]

6. *What is your attitude toward subject-matter?*

Ideally, the "subject-matter" of poetry should be limitless. For the individual poet, however, limitation in subject-matter seems often to be a condition of power. A jack-of-all-subjects is likely to be master of none. As for bigness and smallness in subject-matter, I do not sympathize with the cultural historian who finds a poem "serious" and "significant" because it mentions the atomic bomb. Scope and assimilative power are highly to be respected, but there are other values in poetry, and Milton and Herrick have an equal loftiness in my private Pantheon.

It does not upset me to hear poetry paraphrased and its "subject-matter" stated. But I don't usually care for the sort of poem which too readily submits to paraphrase. A poem ought not to be fissionable. It ought to be impossible satisfactorily to separate "ideas" from their poetic "embodiment." When this can be done to a poem, it is a sign that the poem began with a prose "idea"—i.e., began wrongly—and that the writer was not a poet but a phrase-maker.

["Imagery?" asked Mr. Ciardi, perhaps bluntly, since Mr. Wilbur inquired of himself graciously:]

7. *Do you have anything to say about imagery?*

I think it a great vice to convey everything by imagery, particularly if the imagery is not interrelated. There ought to be areas of statement. But the statement should not equal and abolish the "objects" in the poem, as Arnold's does in *Rugby Chapel.* All those rocks and cataracts gone in a puff of piety! The statement should have obliquity, and congruence to the imagery, as Marianne Moore's does—not vitiating the objects, but rather finding in them another and ideal dimension.

["Symbolism?" says Mr. Ciardi, as his eighth question, and Mr. Wilbur does not wish to say anything about it. "Of rhyme and its function in the poem?" is Mr. Ciardi's next, and Mr. Wilbur asks:]

8. *What about rhyme?*

Aside from its obvious value in the finished poem as a part of poetic form and as a heightener of language, rhyme seems to me an invaluable aid in composition. It creates difficulties which the utterance must surmount by increased resourcefulness. It also helps by liberally suggesting arbitrary connections of which the mind may take advantage if it likes. For example, if one has to rhyme with *tide,* a great number of rhyme-words at once come to mind (ride, bide, shied, confide, Akenside, etc.) Most of these, in combination with *tide,* will probably suggest nothing apropos, but one of them may reveal precisely what one wanted to say. If none of them does, *tide* must be dispensed with. Rhyme, austerely used, may be a stimulus to discovery and a stretcher of the attention.

["Of line length and of the function of the line-end (if any) in guiding the reading of the poem?" was Mr. Ciardi's tenth, and this is also ignored. But the eleventh by Mr. Ciardi, "Of the structure of the total poem. (Formal? Free? What makes its unity?)" is accepted by Mr. Wilbur:]

9. *What is your attitude toward the structure of the total poem?*

As my friend Pierre Schneider has observed, some writers think of art as a window, and some think of it as a door. If art is a window, then the poem is something intermediate in character, limited, synecdochic, a partial vision of a part of the world. It is the means of a dynamic relation between the eye within and the world without. If art is conceived to be a door, then that dynamic relation is destroyed. The artist no longer perceives a wall between him and the world; the world becomes an extension of himself, and is deprived of its reality. The poet's words cease to be a means of liaison with the world; they take the place of the world. This is bad aesthetics—and incidentally, bad morals.

The use of strict poetic forms, traditional or invented, is like the use of framing and composition in painting: both serve to limit the work of art, and to declare its artificiality: they say, "This is not the world, but a pattern imposed upon the world or found in it; this is a partial and provisional attempt to establish relations between things."

There are other less metaphysical reasons for preferring strictness of form: the fact, for example, that subtle variation is unrecognizable without the pre-existence of a norm; or the fact that form, in slowing and complicating the writing-process, calls out the poet's full talents, and thereby insures a greater care and cleverness in the choice and disposition of words. In general, I would say that limitation makes for power: the strength of the genie comes of his being confined in a bottle.

In the great collection of poets' manuscripts and workbooks made for the Lockwood Memorial Library at the University of Buffalo by Charles D. Abbott, are several versions of "Missa Vocis," a poem by R. P. Blackmur. These and the worksheets of poems by other poets were studied in 1947 by Donald Stauffer, professor of English at Princeton. He contributed an essay, "Genesis, or The Poet As Maker," to Mr. Abbott's book, *Poets at Work*. The Blackmur poem is shown in moments of the most intense coming-into-being that is possible, that point when the poem, literally in the heat of composition, changes itself into something other and finer than the writer had expected. Mr. Stauffer has first, in his longer paper, examined a poem by A. E. Housman, "I hoed and trenched and weeded," to find out which of four stanzas was written a year after the first three, and revised thirteen times; he thinks it was the third. He then goes on to a closer study of a poem in manuscript by the American poet.

XIV

Genesis, or the Poet as Maker

BY DONALD A. STAUFFER

Let us set against Housman's poem, in some detail, one which exists in various versions in the Lockwood Library —the "Missa Vocis" by Richard P. Blackmur. The two provide a neat comparison, not only because they fall into formal four-part balanced structures, but also because their common subject is the use and permanence of poetry. Blackmur's is harder to grasp. What light, let us ask, does the composition of a poem throw upon its meaning and its beauty? What difficulties in a finished poem may be explained, what pointless ambiguities dispelled, what purposeful ambiguities sharpened, by references found in its earlier states? Naturally, no one should claim that the study of all versions will necessarily make any and every poem crystal-clear. Words do not behave in such fashion, even when poets use them.

Here, then, as it appears in its published version in Blackmur's volume, *The Second World,* is:

MISSA VOCIS

Priest-mannerly the mind,
that president mask,
gives dogsight to the new blind,
priest-mannerly unknowing
what mastering ear-task
keeps the great churn going.

O unmannerable heart,
monk-dancer, be still,
be leashless, apart:
the sounding, the growing
unabettable will
sets the great churn going.

Lie chidden, lie dark,
in the reserved deep
lie prone, lie stark:
the unprayable flowing,
the vast sluiceage of sleep,
sets the great churn going.

In the wringing of new sound,
chance flowering to choice,
old words in full round
in-breathing, thrall-throwing;
the mass of new voice
keeps the great churn going.

A reader is struck first of all, I suppose, by unusual words that seem to contain much meat—such words as "priest-mannerly," "dogsight," "unmannerable," or "sluice-age." Yet in trying to tie their meanings into the poem precisely, he is soon struck also by the notable repetitions and contrasts that organize the poem and give definitions to many of its words. Take "priest-mannerly." The first line defines "mind" in the form of a simple equation. If the mind is a priest, it is also a mask, a mask with the modifying adjective or noun-adjective "president." It is further associated with the blind, to whom it cannot give the best kind of sight (though dog-lovers may not agree). The mind, moreover, does not know true mastery. To aid in its definition in this poem, the priest-mind is set in opposition to the monk-dancer, the heart, with the further contrast of "mannerly" with "unmannerable." The religious imagery of the first two stanzas colors the last two, so that prayers (or rather, their absence) occur in the third stanza; while "the *mass* of new voice" is given its primary meaning of the sacrament (which might not otherwise be apparent, since it is not the most frequent meaning of the word), not only through the title but through the imagery that permeates and organizes the poem.

Similarly, the poem-in-itself may be used to explain, or give further and better meanings to, other words which it contains. That puzzling "dogsight," which at first I took to be connected with a dog's sense of smell, is made clearer by the word "leashless" in the corresponding point of the next stanza. Now the reader may conjure up a Seeing Eye dog—or, if he cares about consistency in imagery, perhaps a blind beggar with his dog before some cathedral. The "ear-task" ("Doth God exact day labor, light denied?") fills with more meaning as one comes to the sound, the words, the mass, the voice, the ringing, of the final stanza.

Indeed, the poem as it stands is so closely woven that one feels confident that not one of its effects is an accident.

Even the simple words do not seem single in meaning. "Round" in the last stanza is not only the full perfection of a circle but a round of singing. It is more than coincidence that the "sound" of the fourth stanza has its harbinger in the "sounding" of the second stanza. And though the "wringing" of new sound may mean primarily the strenuous process in harmonizing the "Sphere-born harmonious sisters, Voice and Verse," it may also suggest a joyous ringing chime of bells. (Housman, by the way, uses this pun of wring-ring even more demonstrably.) Are we now becoming too impossibly refined if we point out that the negative "un-"s of the first three stanzas change to "in-" in the final section, not in the sense of negation but of self-sufficiency? Mr. Blackmur, in his desire to express the ineluctable, unabettable, unknowable infinite, has used in other poems these mysterious negatives in "un-" and "in-" until they have become almost a trademark for his writing. It is hardly without significance that they drop out in the final positive section. Note, too, the single word that changes in the powerful refrain. Almost purely by formal means—by the balance thoughout between sight and sound, between negatives and positives, between the changed refrains—a logical structure could be set up for the poem; a negative statement, or rebuttal, or unsatisfactory hypothesis, is established in the first stanza; the next two stanzas fix a groundwork and speculate concerning origins; the final stanza states positively that art, not intellect—and art based on emotion and instinct—preserves, shall we say, the life of the spirit. In view of the extreme conscious symmetry of the poem, evident even in the controlled alliteration, one might dare to speculate that the adjective "what *mas*tering ear-task" sets going at the start a query which is answered by an echoing assertion in the same foot of the stanza in the last section: "the *mass* of new voice."

But this is exactly the type of criticism which many people impatiently dismiss as finical and overnice. The critic, they maintain, is outdoing Arachne, spinning webs out of himself which the poem itself cannot possibly support. Well, let us see. Let us turn to Mr. Blackmur's own actual earlier versions. We have so far applied the pure-aesthetic technique of asking the poem to explain itself within its own self-contained limits. Let us now apply historical criticism—but historical criticism which few could consider irrelevant, since it will use solely the materials which the poet himself used in bringing his finished work into shape. And here, in six successive versions, one may watch in fascination as chance flowers into choice.

That fine alliterative opposition of chance and choice, so frequent in the poetry of William Butler Yeats, seems only one of the deliberate compliments which Blackmur pays to the Irish poet. One might profitably compare the structure of "Missa Vocis" with that of Yeats's four-stanzaed "Sailing to Byzantium." Moreover, the use of a vigorous refrain in homely language is reminiscent of Yeats's later poems. I shall have occasion later to mention again how sympathy with another poet, no less than the desire to describe faithfully the subject at hand, may mold a poem. Here one wonders if the faintly medieval ecclesiastic imagery may not be one of Yeats's many responsibilities. And as for "monk-dancer"—neglecting the old *sursum corda* idea of "My heart leaps up"—may it not have been dictated in part by Yeats's repeated symbol of the dancer? The "monk" half of it obviously ties in with the priest and the mass in imagery; I wish my own unmannerable heart did not also call up, because of "dogsight" and "leashless," the idea of a monkey dancing on a string. The other versions do not help to make "monk-dancer" clearer, except the very first, where we have, instead, the much more flat "old traveler."

The sixth and final version gives the poem as it was published. The fifth version makes some definite commitments on parts which earlier had troubled Mr. Blackmur. There is an erasure of "hindsight" in place of "dogsight" —the only version in which that word is questioned—but since it is an erasure, perhaps we had better not play with it, except to use it as ghostly support for our earlier suspicion that dogsight is not a good thing. But in this fifth version, to finish up with canine matters, Blackmur settles on the certain and balanced:

Lie chidden, lie dark.

This had begun as "Lie doggo be dark," and had persisted doggedly through later versions until the artist's sense that the whole is greater than the part led Blackmur to abandon a bad pun and rescue harmony in diction. Nevertheless, that almost catastrophic persistence of "doggo" through so many trials may help in understanding the vast sluiceage of sleep in the reserved deep—two lines that hold steady throughout.

A similar well-balanced line—"in-breathing, thrall-throwing"—comes to rest in the fifth version. The fourth had wavered between "in-breathed" and "in-breathing," each of which was an alternative for "breathed deep" in the second and third versions. This line took much work. That it was well worth the effort is obvious from its original form—"breathless tiptoeing"—which is so innocuous as almost to be deadly. The "breathless" is crossed out in favor of "flowering," and we can learn something of the working of a poet's mind from the way in which that fine word "flowering" was not discarded, even though it proved useless where first introduced, but was inserted instead in the line which read originally "Chance *deepening to* choice."

Version four considers altering the earlier "lie plumb" to "lie prone." Here again, the earlier and ultimately abandoned word "plumb" helps in interpreting the reserved deep and the vast sluiceage of sleep. This version also first invents the line "In the wringing of new sound." If it had seemed unwarranted at first reading to detect as overtone here the ringing of church bells, our speculation is now given more confidence when we see the original of this line:

The whole church of new sound.

Versions two and three merely play with punctuation, spelling, and compounds, and incorporate second-thoughts that are already suggested in the margin of the first (and only manuscript) version, which is easily the most interesting, and in which the poem, even at such an early stage, encounters forks in the trail and always takes the path toward sharper, fresher imagery and toward unity. Thus, the very first word of the first line—"Most mannerly the mind"—has "Priest" as an emendation in the margin, which increases the consistency and vividness of the imagery, and at the same time trades too much *rum-rum-ruf* on the letter "m" for a more powerful binding alliteration between "priest" and "president" in the next line.

Most revealing are some jottings that float free at the right-hand top of the page. Are these not the true germs of the poem?

only the voice
keeps the great churn going
sluiceage of sleep
only the flowing

One cluster of marginal words that has nothing to do with the poem will make any of us who scribble verses self-conscious: "none" "atone" "moan" "drone" "tone" "stone" "alone." This is journeyman stuff, fit matter for the rhyming dictionary; it is mentioned here merely because it does call our attention to the rhyme words or sounds which Blackmur actually decided upon, to his care in choosing solid monosyllables, to their fine contrasts in adjacent lines, and their equally fine correspondences over larger areas, so that in rhyme as well as in thought stanzas one and four are allied, as are two and three. And never (except possibly in "thrall-throwing"?) does the poet's thought seem enslaved to his powerful, exact, and rewarding rhyme.

If any doubt remains that such painstaking revisions are worth the candle, I suggest that you compare the finished version with this earliest form:

Most mannerly the mind,
that president mask,
makes dogsight the new blind.
Most mannerly unknowing
what mastering task
keeps the great churn going

O unmannerable heart,
old traveler, be still,
be leashless, apart:
the sounding, the growing
unabettable will
sets the great churn going

Lie doggo be dark
in the reserved deep
lie plumb, lie stark:
the unprayable flowing

the vast sluiceage of sleep
sets the great churn going

The whole church of sound
chance deepening to choice
old words in full round
breathless tiptoeing:
the mass of new voice
keeps the great churn going

What is the sum of all these minute considerations? First, that a work of art may have extremely small beginnings—in this instance merely the persistent refrain of the great churn, plus a few tied-in images of sound and of liquidity which the churn itself might suggest. Second, at least to judge from Blackmur's rougher notes, that a poem may develop by giving a kind of metaphysical skeleton to its initial inspiration—working it out, perhaps, as mental propositions in a triple or quadruple division (here, finally: mind, heart/will, the unconscious, voice). Third, that a poem may be sketched as a whole, including weak, padded lines that must later be changed, but also including phrases that are already finished and characteristic—in Blackmur's case the startling adjectives and nouns, the "great churn" itself, the "sluiceage of sleep," "mannerly," "dogsight," "leashless," as well as the magisterial and ominously abstract "unknowing," "unmannerable," "unabettable," and "unprayable." Fourth—and this comes with the sense of discovery—that at some point in composition a spark may flash that will illuminate the whole; a sudden insight may develop into a nervous system that brings the whole body alive. In this poem the spark sprang from the religious imagery. It is not present in the seed-kernel, "only the voice keeps the great churn going." In the original draft the *liquid* imagery which the churn may have initiated is developed only in the third stanza and is expanded in no later versions. The *sound* imagery, dominated by the voice, never expands through the entire poem. And in the sketch as first set down there is no religious imagery until "unprayable" late in the third stanza. But at some moment, somehow, something clicks, and it all becomes clear. Before the draft is put aside, we have in the last stanza "The whole *church* of new sound"; "only the voice" has become "the *mass* of new voice" at the end; the same title in Latin, *"Missa Vocis,"* has been added at the beginning; and in the margins as afterthoughts appear the mannerly *priest* and the dancer *monk*. Now the poem is so ecclesiastically colored throughout that Blackmur can change the first line of the last stanza to "In the wringing of new sound" and still leave the whole church in it by implication.

And finally among these conclusions: that the progress of the artist in creation is always toward greater purity, intensity, and unity—in short, toward greater significance. The changes are small, but their cumulative effect should furnish an impressive lesson that the control and the form that make daydreams into art are not the results of happy accidents but of happy contrivings. Chance flowers into choice only when it is carefully tended.

PART THREE

The Poet's Work

XV

The Poet's Words

The poet's work is to find words for the sense of life which he learns more and more surely to recognize in himself. Some people need to build ships, fences, or footstools. Some people need to dance or have children or play games of strength and speed. Some need to act or paint; some to fight or sell; or collect facts, books, or money. They express as they may the sense of life that demands expression. A good poet (the streets are full of bad poets) probably finds deep enduring pleasure, too, in doing some of these things, because he is really different from other men in but one way. That difference is his use of words to satisfy his continuous creative needs.

At first the poet will delight in all words, any words that grow on the page, thinking that they represent his sense of life. When the young poet recovers from blind reverence for his own words bcause they are his words and therefore sacred, then he begins to grow. If he is not one whose merely healthy energy at one passing age releases itself in writing and then moves on to other things, he will become profoundly uncomfortable about all the words he has written, and this will grow to still darker dissatisfaction. Midnight vows and muttered curses at the heaviness of his hand on paper will slowly, though he does not know it, lighten the dark and ease the hurt. He will wish to write only the best words, the words his ear chooses, the words his unique and secret pulse requires. He teaches himself discrimination in words, alert more and more, as he grows, for the sound of the just, the right, the only word to express his feeling and thought. At this stage of his labors (lonely, angry, happy, proud, miserable), he admires the pace and color of the words of other poets. He imitates them, though he desires a style all his own. But out of this long workmanship, he is bringing a new combination of the best he knows beyond his own page, the best he himself has done, and best he knows he will do. Suddenly he learns from some articulate reader that he has created a new style, recognizable and approved. Then the poet knows that his work, to which no one but himself has yet given time and foresight and courage, has been successful. He begins to believe that it will be possible to record his world, within and around him, and his sense of the life of it.

In trying to explain what primitive men might have felt about the man of words, we now please ourselves with imagining the tribes, fearful of wordy magic, murmuring uneasily at the first poet's imitation of real action. But it must have begun that way. The art of poetry lies in imitation by words and in the pleasure of play with words, in its first age. Of all man's imitations the dance is perhaps the most deeply and simply instinctive. A dumb man can dance, or make his hands and face dance the story out. The dance, too, had a pattern which could be remembered and repeated. But when there was language, words could be made to move in imitation of that action, with the exact posture, the same swiftness, the same satisfaction in rhythm. At last, when the words themselves came to have such rolling reverberations of meaning, such ghostly genealogies of memory, such Saturn-rings of light around them, all the dance was in the words. Poetry had become words. The words had become life.

Now with our tens of thousands of words we may, as John Donne said, "knocke, breathe, shine, and seeke to mend." We may, as he prayed, batter the heart. Donne himself, "in whose words there is such height of figures, such peregrinations to fetch remote and precious metaphors," knew how to storm the imagination with thundering phrases and strange devices of the language. His vehement and tragic mind must have found great though brief content, writing sermons in the dean's study at St. Paul's. It was not wholly a churchly delight, either, not only a pastor's anxiety to teach his congregation, that fetched words onto paper like those of his Christmas evening service in 1624. He spoke then of God's bounty. "If some King of the earth," he wrote, "have so large an extent of Dominion, in North, and South, as that he hath Winter and Summer together in his Dominions, so large an extent East and West, as that he hath day and night together in his Dominions, much more hath God mercy and judgement together: He brought light out of darknesse, not out of a lesser light; he can bring thy Summer out of Winter, though thou have no Spring; though in the wayes of fortune, or understanding, or conscience, thou have been benighted till now, wintred and frozen, clouded and eclypsed, damped and benummed, smothered and stupified till now, now God comes to thee, not as in the dawning of the day, not as in the bud of the spring, but as the Sun at noon to illustrate all shadows, as the sheaves in harvest, to fill all penuries, all occasions invite his mercies, and all times are his seasons."

These rolling, mounting Elizabethan cadences are probably some of the most satisfying public words a poet ever prepared and delivered. We may not doubt that Donne's passionate sincerity impelled them. But we may be sure that he gloried, as a lyric poet passed from the weather of his youth to the more threatening weather of middle age, in these sheer cataracts and cascades, this surf, this rising gale and stormy sky of language for its own sake.

No satisfaction, for the poet, equals the satisfaction of springing at last the obstinate words into the stubborn line. No matter how clearly drawn his system of thought, no matter how extravagant his emotion, still the poet warms to the word. Still he smiles alone as a carver will at some cut that makes of skill and luck and inspiration a new shape in the world. The dangers are very great. Words will diminish and die, or change to offend the ears of another generation. Some overtone harmonized with whatever honest cunning may in the course of time turn all the rest to discord. The rewards are also great. Words may outlive generations of men and come enriched to the newest readers of all time. The poet has an almost medical sense for healthy words that have the seeds of poems in them. To work in words, knowing their present excellence and foreknowing their immortality, is itself an enduring satisfaction. And there is the harder, more actual life in words, when the writer stands up on his feet and builds, and we see it and hear it; as Carlyle said, "Wonderful it is with what cutting words, now and then, he severs asunder the confusion; shears it down, were it furlongs deep, into the true center of the matter; and there not only hits the nail on the head, but with crushing force smites it home, and buries it."

It is said, and romantically said, that language was once upon a time all poetry, pure in its symbolism, and strong and exact, and that the ages have dulled and blackened it.

But it is nonsense to suppose that a current language cannot become, through art, worthy of and part of the great tradition. We like to mourn, saying that the freedom, brevity, vigor, and resonance of the Elizabethans was superior to anything we write now. But where could the great tradition be, if it were living at all, and not be here and now? We may or we may not accept the language of the age; what we must not accept of any age are the counterfeit, the shoddy, the ill-nourished words. There is a strong chance that a word will endure further because it has already lasted. But this is the sort of word that has gathered association, not the word that with much handling has blurred and begun to crumble. Every language and every age has both kinds. The poet's labor is one of discrimination.

John Donne, for his towering sermons and the black hammer of his mind that beat and shaped them upward; and Shakespeare for the bright, trembling flow and flight of his imagery; and Montaigne, and Carlyle, for their different passionate reasons, would have waked to the words of Gerard Manley Hopkins. Hopkins has brought with his new vivid shapes and sounds more astonishment and envious despair to the minds of later poets than any writer. It was Hopkins who wrote "the widow-making unchilding unfathering deeps." It was Hopkins who wrought this tremendous hyphenation to describe the falcon "in his riding of the rolling level underneath him steady air"; who said he woke later than moonrise "in the white and the walk of the morning"; who called ancient Oxford "towery city and branchy between towers; cuckoo-echoing, bell-swarmèd, lark-charmèd, rook-racked, river-rounded." He did what any poet would wish to do. With the work of his mind he stretched language to reach up to and enclose new sights, wider thoughts, more vivid experience. He was a poet who worked slowly, writing little (or rejecting much), and testing his words through silent years, till he could join them to create his sense of the world.

When the words have been put together, and words so plain in themselves matched to make phrases like "this goodly frame, the earth . . . this majestic roof fretted with golden fire" or "else a great Prince in prison lies" or "I also bear a bell-branch full of ease," then falls that inexplicable radiance on the page, and round the room where the page is read, that is called poetry. It has taken more than words to do this, to be sure. There was an urgency in the poet that brimmed, and he could not help it; it overflowed, and he was glad. The nature of that urgency may be decided in another place by other more painstaking, methodical probers and examiners. We can be sure only that unless that surge of wonder, that intolerable beating of wings in the poet's mind, had found the right words, we never should have cared. There is poetry in words, much blood in words, but there is a thing that moves behind them, a spirit that puts them on like a garment and wears them, filling the infinite possibilities of their drapery with a body that lives and moves, goes up and down to delight us with its grace and stir us with its vigor.

Grant Me But Decent Words

Then there arose a masterless man, one who had taken no part in the action of his fellows, who had no special virtue, but who was afflicted—that is the phrase—with the magic of the necessary word. He saw, he told, he described the merits of the notable deed in such a fashion, we are assured, that the words "became alive and walked up and down in the hearts of all his hearers."

Rudyard Kipling
A Book of Words

Poetry is words. It is a certain way of using words, so that they take on a vitality which they have in no other use of them. Every significance which words can carry in speech or prose is intensified in poetry—quality of sound, shades of meaning, symbolic importance—but as well as this sharpening of value, there is a creation of new values, which belong to the poetic use of words alone. They work with a secret potency, they take on a new personality. They may not be distinguished or unusual, at all; indeed, they can be of the barest simplicity. But their choice and ordering seem inevitable; they create a harmony, a security, a conviction.

Elizabeth Drew
Discovering Poetry

It is the spirit that quickeneth; the flesh profiteth nothing: the words that I speak unto you, they are spirit, and they are life.

"St. John," VI. 63

He drew forth a phrase from his treasure and spoke it softly to himself:

—a day of dappled seaborne clouds—

The phrase and the day and the scene harmonized in a chord. Words. Was it their colours? He allowed them to glow and fade, hue after hue: sunrise gold, the russet and green of apple orchards, azure of waves, the gray-fringed fleece of clouds. No, it was not their colours: it was the poise and balance of the period itself. Did he then love the rhythmic rise and fall of words better than their association of legend and colour? Or was it that, being as weak of sight as he was shy of mind, he drew less pleasure from the reflection of the glowing sensible world through the prism of a language many-coloured and richly storied than from the contemplation of an inner world of individual emotions mirrored perfectly in a lucid supple periodic prose?

James Joyce
Portrait of the Artist as a Young Man

Poetry is a function of language, recording, vivifying, correcting word and idiom, like a purification of the bloodstreams of nations. As long as people are talking, exchanging new words and evolving a new idiom, poetry is an essential activity of life. If this function is not performed, language, literature, and hence, ultimately, humanity, suffer.

Stephen Spender
The Artistic Future of Poetry

Grant me, O ye powers which touch the tongue with eloquence in distress—whatever is my cast, Grant me but decent words to exclaim in, and I will give my nature way.

Lawrence Sterne

I would be willing to throw away everything else but that: enthusiasm tamed by metaphor. Let me rest the case there. I do not think anybody ever knows the discreet use of metaphor, his own or other people's, unless he has been properly educated in poetry.

Robert Frost
Education by Poetry

Communication is health; communication is truth; communication is happiness. To share is our duty; to go down boldly and bring to light those hidden thoughts which are most diseased; to conceal nothing; to pretend nothing; if we are ignorant to say so; if we love our friends to let them know it.

Virginia Woolf, "Montaigne"
The Common Reader

The written word
Should be clean as a bone,
Clear as light,
Firm as stone.
Two words are not
As good as one.

Anonymous

Verbs and words derived from verbs are of great importance. When you say that your object does something, rather than that it is something or like something else, you give it life and movement. Nouns stand for ideas, names and things. Each noun is a complete picture. Nouns and verbs are almost pure metal. Adjectives are cheaper ore; they have less strength of meaning, since they stand for just one aspect of a thing, one characteristic, and do not represent it in its entirety.

Marie Gilchrist
Writing Poetry

. . . words that have been
So nimble and so full of subtle flame
As if that everyone from whence they came
Had meant to put his whole wit in a jest
And had resolved to live a fool the rest
Of his dull life.

Francis Beaumont
"To Ben Jonson"

You must know that words like *charm* and *enchantment* will not do; the thought is of beauty as of something that can be physically kept and lost, and by physical things only, like keys; then the things must become *mundus muliebris*; and thirdly, they must not be very markedly old-fashioned. You will see that this limits the choice of words very much indeed.

Gerard Manley Hopkins, XCIII,
Letters to Robert Bridges

Ye knowe eek that in forme of speche is chaunge
Within a thousand yeer, and wordes tho
That hadden pris, now wonder nyce and straunge
Us thinketh hem, and yet thei spak hem so,
And sped as well in love as men now do.

Geoffrey Chaucer
Troilus and Criseyde

Nay all speech, even the commonest speech, has something of song in it; not a parish in the world but has its parish-accent;—the rhythm or tune to which the people there sing what they have to say! Accent is a kind of chanting; all men have accent of their own—though they notice only that of others.

Thomas Carlyle, "The Hero as Poet"
On Heroes, Hero-Worship, and the Heroic in History

Unspoken, a half-forgotten line flashed through his mind. Where had he read that, or heard it? Oxford, Carlisle, The Highlands, Avignon? "We are lost, Queen Honour—" How did it go? ". . . Queen Honour is the deathless—" Who said that? How could he have forgotten? ". . . a battered rascal guard still closes round her."

Eugene Manlove Rhodes
The Trusty Knave

Into this wild ocean of words Shakespeare plunged head over heels, and disported himself in it with a wild dolphin joy. He collected words from everywhere, from rustic speech and dialect (he no doubt spoke the Warwickshire dialect all his life), from Chaucer and the old books, from translators of the classics, from lawyers and grave theologians, from travelled young gallants. He was, moreover, perhaps the greatest word-creator the world has ever known, and has probably added more new words to our vocabulary than all the other English poets put together. He made up his language as he went along—"crashing," as he has been described, "through the forest of words like a thunderbolt, crushing them out of shape if they don't fit in, melting moods and tenses, and leaving people to gape at the transformation."

Logan Pearsall Smith
On Reading Shakespeare

Hands, do what you're bid:
Bring the balloon of the mind
That bellies and drags in the wind
Into its narrow shed.

William Butler Yeats, "The Balloon of the Mind"
The Wild Swans at Coole

When Coleridge composed—in a dream, as he alleged—

In Xanadu did Kubla Khan
  A stately pleasure-dome decree,
Where Alph, the sacred river, ran
Through caverns measureless to man,
  Down to a sunless sea

was he aware that, as Stevenson showed later on, he was runing hard, all through, a certain chord or group of letters—KANDLSR, the first being built on a kind of framework of KANDL, the second on KDLSR, the third on all the letters of the chord, the fourth on KANSLR, and the fifth on NDLS? Did he chop and change words in his dream, perhaps using at first the word "sombre" in the third line, and then saying, "No, I must work in that K and D," and so substituting the word "sacred?"

We may well doubt that. Quite as probably he just kept turning each line over and over in his mind in some form which it took first, felt something gritty or obstructive here and there—perhaps in "sombre"— mused over possible alternative words, and feeling, when he tried "sacred," that the grit was gone, popped the word in, and there an end, without any consciousness of having stuck stoutly to the chord KANDLSR, and having escaped the seductions of the rival chord SMBR (which sounds like a useful dominant for an Ode to September). But there the strong consonantal skeleton is, however it came in.

C. E. Montague, "Easy Reading, Hard Writing"
A Writer's Notes on His Trade

To win the secret of words, to make a phrase that would murmur of summer and the bee, to summon the wind into a sentence, to conjure the odour of the night into the surge and fall and harmony of a line; this was the tale of the long evenings, of the candleflame white upon the paper and the eager pen.

Arthur Machen
The Hill of Dreams

No doubt the time will come when psychology will tell us exactly what does happen within our consciousness when a certain collection of words seizes upon us and sends a dazzle of glory rushing through our veins; or a haunting sweetness ringing in our ears; or brings a shock of surprised delight to our eyes; or kindles a glowing warmth about the heart; or brings us tears. At present we only know that when we read:

Lift up your heads, O ye gates, and be
lift up, ye everlasting doors: and
the King of Glory shall come in.

or

The horns of Elfland faintly blowing.

or

And hearken to the birds' love-learned song
The dewy leaves among.

or

And mighty poets in their misery dead.

or

Everyone suddenly burst out singing.

or

He is dead and gone, lady.

a certain sense of enchantment fastens upon many of us. Not, of course, upon everyone. There is always the examinee who paraphrased

Heard melodies are sweet, but those unheard
Are sweeter

as "it is nice to listen to music, but nicer not to." But for anyone who possesses a "sense of words," which is the same thing as the sense of poetry, a certain leaping of attention takes place, a brightening of the inward eye, a flame of response.

Elizabeth Drew
Discovering Poetry

. . . but his ears
Were filled with voices, filled with a sound of singing,
The wind's voice from the mountain; and his heart
Radiant in his breast was like a lamp . . .
And from that time his house was dark no more,
But housed an angel who was silent there,

Beating bright wings, yet moveless; and the light
Went forth from him; although he said no word.

Conrad Aiken, XXXIX
Preludes for Memnon

She waited. Her husband spoke. He was repeating something, and she knew it was poetry from the rhythm and the ring of exultation and melancholy in his voice.

Virginia Woolf
To the Lighthouse

But other men long after he is dead,
Seeing these hills, will catch their breath and stare:
As one who, reading in a book some word
That calls joy back, but can recall not where—
Only a crazy sweetness in the head—
Will stare at the black print till the page is blurred.

Archibald MacLeish, "Pony Rock"
Poems: 1924-1933

. . . something I cannot describe, but know to myself by the inadequate word *terrible pathos*—something of what you call temper in poetry: a right temper which goes to the point of the terrible: the terrible crystal.

Richard Watson Dixon, XXA
Correspondence with Gerard Manley Hopkins

Most rhythms are made up as much of disappointments and postponements and surprises and betrayals as of simple straightforward satisfactions.

I. A. Richards, "Rhythm and Metre"
Principles of Literary Criticism

What I have been after from the first, consciously and unconsciously, is tones of voice. I've wanted to write down certain brute throat noises so that no one could miss them in my sentences. I have been guilty of speaking sentences as a mere notation for indicating them. They have been my observation and my subject-matter.

Robert Frost
Notes on a lecture

The verse-rhythm of Donne's poetry is the natural and outward form of his mental temper . . . In Donne, the meaning, straining against the rhythm of the fore-established metre in the reader's mind, reproduces there the slow, tense emphasis of Donne's thought. The melodists, from Greene and Marlowe to Swinburne, are always in danger (if it is a danger) of lulling the mind to sleep with the music of the verse. The verse pattern is caught at once. . . . Donne's verse is never lyric in this sense. Instead he leaves you, line after line and phrase after phrase, in doubt of the pattern, or of how the line is to be fitted to the pattern, producing thereby a searching pause on almost every syllable—a sort of perpetual "hovering accent."

H. M. Belden
Donne's Prosody

You must evolve a set of counters or abstractions or allegories which will bear the inflection of the times without relying on the fashionable accent of the moment. . . . Not the well-rounded phrasemaking which is only the trade-mark of verse, but that untheatrical tone, that compelling pitch which cannot be defined and cannot be mistaken.

Louis Untermeyer, "Poets to Come!"
Play in Poetry

Before man came to blow it right
The wind once blew itself untaught,

And did its loudest day and night
  In any rough place where it caught.
Man came to tell it what was wrong:
  It hadn't found the place to blow;
It blew too hard—the aim was song.
  And listen—how it ought to go!
He took a little in his mouth,
  And held it long enough for north
To be converted into south,
  And then by measure blew it forth.
By measure. It was word and note,
  The wind the wind had meant to be—
A little through the lips and throat.
  The aim was song—the wind could see.

Robert Frost, "The Aim Was Song"
New Hampshire

Wonderful it is with what cutting words, now and then, he severs asunder the confusion; shears it down, were it furlongs deep, into the true center of the matter; and there not only hits the nail on the head, but with crushing force smites it home, and buries it.

Thomas Carlyle
Sartor Resartus

If we cannot say why we capitulate thus, we may at least try to fix and describe the sensations that visit us while the charm is at work.

For one thing, we are deeply excited. We are shaken or lifted out of our ordinary state of consciousness. Many of our faculties are, for the moment, enhanced. We feel keener perceptions coming into action within us. We are given the use of more than our normal stock of penetrative sympathy: we feel that we can enter into people's feelings, and understand the quality of their lives better than ever before.

Another effect of the drug is that, while it is acting strongly, the whole adventure of mankind upon the earth gains, in our sight, a new momentousness, precariousness, and beauty. The new and higher scale of power in ourselves seems to be challenged by an equal increase in the size of the objects on which it is exercised. Living becomes a grander affair than we had ever thought.

A third effect on the mind is a powerful sense—authentic or illusory—of being in the presence of extraordinary possibilities. You feel as if new doors of understanding and delight were beginning to open around you. Some sort of mysterious liberation or empowerment seems to be approaching. You are assured, in an unaccountable way, that wonderful enlightenments, still unreceived, are on their way to you, like new stars that are nearing the point in space at which they will come within range of our sight.

These sensations may not be defined or measured as closely as doctors measure a patient's temperature, his pulse, and his blood pressure. And yet they are worth describing, if only because you will find that you are also describing something else by the way. The nearer you get to saying just what you feel, when under the spell of great writing, the nearer you are, too, to defining the state of mind and heart in which great things are written.

C. E. Montague, "The Last Question of All"
A Writer's Notes on His Trade

Shakespeare does not confine himself, like many poets, only to visual images; he makes use of impressions from the other senses, the senses of smell and hearing; and seems to have been especially fond of images of reverberating sound, trumpets and horns and the baying of hounds from afar. Motor images, as they are called, sensations of effort, strain, movement, of rushing winds or horses, are frequent in his poetry, and also of the sea ("surge" is a favorite word with Shakespeare) and of the flow of rivers, as in one of his most splendid images, of the Pontic sea.

Logan Pearsall Smith
On Reading Shakespeare

. . . for freedom, for brevity, and for vigour, Elizabethan is superior to modern English. Many of the words employed by Shakespeare and his contemporaries were the recent inventions of the age; hence, they are used with a freshness and an exactness to which we are strangers. Again, the spoken English so far predominated over the grammatical English that it materially influenced the rhythm of the verse, the construction of the sentence, and sometimes the spelling of the words. Hence sprung an artless and unlaboured harmony which seems the natural heritage of the Elizabethan poets, whereas such harmony as is attained by modern authors frequently betrays a painful excess of art. Lastly, the use of some few still remaining inflections (the subjunctive in particular), the lingering sense of many other inflections that had passed away leaving behind something of the old versatility and audacity in the arrangement of the sentence, the stern subordination of grammar to terseness and clearness, and the consequent directness and naturalness of expression, all conspire to give a liveliness and wakefulness to Shakesperian English which are wanting in the grammatical monotony of the present day. We may perhaps claim some superiority in completeness and perspicuity for modern English, but if we were to appeal on this ground to the shade of Shakespeare in the words of Antonio in *The Tempest*—

Do you not hear us speak?

we might fairly be crushed with the reply of Sebastian—

I do; and surely
It is a sleepy language.

E. A. Abbott, "Introduction"
A Shakesperian Grammar

Marlowe was a master of resonance. There are here and there tender passages for a subdued voice in his writings, but for the most part his lines demand "mouthing" by a good actor, they call for the setting of the stage, they are rhetoric shot through with poetry. Back of the sonority lies violence of passion demanding an outlet in strong words. Marlowe is the swashbuckling Elizabethan, dynamic with the longing for infinite power, as in *Tamburlaine*; or for endless riches, as in the *Jew of Malta*; or for all knowledge, as in *Dr. Faustus*.

M. J. Herzburg, "Marlowe's Mighty Line"
Word Study

. . . in whose words there is such a height of figures, such peregrinations to fetch remote and precious metaphors, such curtains of allegories, such third heavens of hyperboles.

John Donne
Sermons

The reader of Milton must always be on his duty: he is surrounded with sense; it rises in every line; every word is to the purpose. There are no lazy intervals; all has been considered, and demands and merits observation. If this be called obscurity, let it be remembered that it is such obscurity as is a compliment to the reader; not that vicious obscurity which proceeds from a muddled head.

Samuel Taylor Coleridge
Lectures on Shakespeare

An Elizabethan drama was, as Coleridge perceived in one of the flashes of his dark lantern, "something between a recitation and a representation;" it was built, as a later critic put it, "upon the vigor and beauty of speech. We may suppose that at its best the mere speaking of the plays was a very brilliant thing, comparable to *bel canto* or a pianist's virtuosity."

We do it wrong, being so majestical,
To offer it the show of violence;
For it is, as the air, invulnerable,
And our vain blows malicious mockery.

Death, that hath sucked the honey of thy breath,
Hath had no power yet upon thy beauty:
Thou art not conquered; beauty's ensign yet
Is crimson in thy lips and in thy cheeks,
And death's pale flag is not advancèd there.

Speeches like these were recited to audiences who loved fine language as we love music, and who by no means cared, as we care, for the consistency of character. Plangent declamation, or passages made splendid by this overplus of diction, this fine-broken starlight of fine words, was what they liked.

Logan Pearsall Smith
On Reading Shakespeare

Yet even the greatest writers are affected by the intoxication of mere words in the artistry of language. Shakespeare is, constantly, and not content with "making the green one red," he needs must at the same time "the multitudinous seas incarnadine." It is conspicuous in Keats . . . and often, as in "The Eve of St. Agnes," where he seemed to be concerned with beautiful things, he was really concerned with beautiful words. . . . I recall how Verlaine would sometimes repeat in varying tones some rather unfamiliar word, rolling it round and round in his mouth, sucking it like a sweetmeat, licking the sound into the shape that pleased him; some people may perhaps have found a little bizarre the single words ("Green," for example) which he sometimes made the title of a song, but if they adopt the preliminary Verlainian process they may understand how he had fitted such words to music and meaning.

Havelock Ellis, "The Art of Writing"
The Dance of Life

Therein lay the manliness of the Elizabethans, they wrote because they enjoyed it: why the sheer villainy of their handwriting shows what fun they had, the words tumbling down in such golden-burning heat they halted not to mend and correct their scrawls and quill-forks.

Christopher Morley
Inward Ho!

Theirs, too, is the word-coining genius, as if thought plunged into a sea of words and came up dripping.

Virginia Woolf, "Notes on An Elizabethan Play"
The Common Reader

The Holy Ghost is an eloquent Author, a vehement, and an abundant Author, but yet not luxuriant; he is a far from penurious, but as far from a superfluous style too.

John Donne
Sermons

"When *I* use a word," Humpty Dumpty said, in rather a scornful tone, "it means just what I choose it to mean—neither more nor less."

"The question is," said Alice, "whether you *can* make the words mean so many different things."

"The question is," said Humpty Dumpty, "which is to be master—that's all."

Lewis Carroll
Through the Looking Glass

As we go back in history, language becomes more picturesque, until its infancy, when it is all poetry; or all spiritual facts are found represented by natural symbols. The same symbols are found to make the original elements of all languages. It has moreover been observed, that the idioms of all languages approach each other in passages of the greatest eloquence and power. And as this is the first language, so it is the last.

Ralph Waldo Emerson, "Nature"
The Conduct of Life

In all languages the creation and use of echoic and symbolic words seems to have been on the increase in historical times. If to this we add the selective processes through which words which have only secondarily acquired symbolical value survive at the cost of less adequate expressions, or less adequate forms of the same words, and subsequently give rise to a host of derivatives, then we may say that languages in the course of time grow richer and richer in symbolic words.

Otto Jespersen
Language

Every word which is used to express a moral or intellectual fact, if traced to its root, is found to be borrowed from some material appearance. Right means straight; wrong means twisted. Spirit primarily means wind; transgression, the crossing of a line, supercilious, the raising of an eyebrow. We say the heart to express emotion, the head to denote thought; and thought and emotion are words borrowed from sensible things, and now appropriated to spiritual nature. Most of the process by which this transformation is made, is hidden from us in the remote time when language was framed; but the same tendency may be observed daily in children. Children and savages use only nouns or names of things, which they convert into verbs, and apply to analogous mental acts.

Ralph Waldo Emerson, "Nature"
The Conduct of Life

Under the dream of that stupendous night,
With furious brain, and heart absurdly stout,
I dared to cry my difference to the height;
My way, my love, and words I thought about.

At first my words were sparks that blotted out.
Then miles above a storm of music grew,
And the sky changed, light bloomed, and I heard shout
The echoing arches where the sun comes through.

White daylight broke around the airy shores:
My mind pressed hard at every boundary,
Opening taller and more distant doors—
And I had always known how this would be!

John Holmes, "For the Poet's Birthday"
Address to the Living

The magic of literature lies in words, and not in any man. Witness, a thousand excellent, strenuous words can leave us quite cold or put us to sleep, whereas a bare half-hundred words breathed upon by some man in his agony, or in his exultation, or in his idleness, ten generations ago, can still lead whole nations into and out of captivity, can open to us the doors of the three worlds, or stir us so intolerably that we can scarcely abide to look at our own souls.

Rudyard Kipling
A Book of Words

But the finer the poet, the fuller and richer will be the value of his words and the necessary response of the reader. It is not only their surface, but their whole content and substance which has to be savoured; their sound in the ear and their taste and feel in the mouth; a sense of their plasticity and density; their coloring from the past; their echoes and associations; their disposal and manipulation in the poem itself, and all the modifications of their significance which arise from that. It is amazing how a single word can make a whole poem by an isolation of it in a special use which brings a throb of unexpected discovery.

Elizabeth Drew
Discovering Poetry

It was a field that was almost virgin. For Science, according to Victorian ideas, as a subject for Poetry, had been almost completely taboo. Poetry must be "poetical" (in the bad old sense of that really impossible word): but all these new things—the inventions of science and scientific processes and scientific terminology—were exactly the reverse. They were "practical." They were too new to have acquired even a suspicion of glamour. Consequently if a poet touched them at all, he must do so with the utmost circumspection. Think, for instance, of Tennyson's difficulties in the "Princess":

A dozen angry models jetted steam:
A petty railway ran: a fire-balloon
Rose gem-like up before the dusky grives
And dropt a fairy parachute and past:
And there thro' twenty posts of telegraph
They flashed a saucy message to and fro
Between the mimic stations; so that sport
Went hand in hand with Science . . .

It has a monstrous archness. Subject and expression are not fused and interfused. They go uneasily together. But turn to a modern poet, who accepts all the component parts of modern life as natural and therefore stuff out of which poetry is to be made:

After the first powerful plain manifesto
The black statement of pistons, without more fuss
But gliding like a queen, she leaves the station.

Beyond the town there lies the open country
Where, gathering speed, she acquires mystery,
The luminous self-possession of ships on ocean.
It is now she begins to sing—at first quite low
Then loud, and at last with a jazzy madness—
The song of her whistle screaming at curves,
Of deafening tunnels, brakes, innumerable bolts,
And always light, aerial, underneath
Goes the elate metre of her wheels.

(Stephen Spender)

Here all the material, the awkward facts, the embarrassing new things of the new world have been unconditionally accepted and absorbed. And therefore, it comes out a homogeneous whole, naturally and inevitably transmuted into poetry.

Martin Gilkes
A Key to Modern English Poetry

Peculiar, not far-fetched; natural, but not obvious; delicate, not affected; dignified, not swelling; fiery, but not mad; rich in imagery, but not loaded with it—in short, a union of harmony and good sense, of perspicuity and conciseness. Thought is the body of such an ode, enthusiasm the soul, and imagery the drapery.

Samuel Taylor Coleridge
Anima Poetae

XVI

The Poet's Knowledge

The poet who is an artist makes it the work of his lifetime to find the inner rhythm which makes him different from all men, and to perfect the transmission of that rhythm to them. His difficulties and triumphs, failures and explanations of them, his allies, his enemies, and, above all, his actual skill in performance, are what the poet meditates most after he has come of age in his art. It is one thing to see the glories of the world with an eye that magnifies them to the spirit; it is another to control that change. By whatever name we call them, both things are necessary for the poet's purpose; understanding of both is necessary to the readers of poetry.

The labor a poet performs in making poetry is endless, difficult, lonely, and, when rightly concluded, more deeply satisfying than any other work. Unless, as he sometimes suspects, that work is architecture. What is he trying to do, that he is willing to endure some public neglect and much private bafflement for the sake of scattered victories? Is he trying to establish communication across the loneliness that separates man and man? Is he trying to discover some time-resisting substance that will contain his soul and so let him live forever? Is he crying round the town for the world to know some news of beauty he is too generous to keep to himself? Is he consecrating himself to the art of doing these things, unselfishly, yet thoughtless of others? A little of all, and all of none. Most of the time he is simply trying to get the thing right that he is doing. In a world where many men have no work to do, or hate the work they must do to live, the poet is happy. He has his work. To say he is devoted to the high cause of truth is true, but he does not speak in that exalted language; ministers do not talk of God at lunch. The nature of poetry makes it possible to speak of him thus, perhaps, but of his own work as an artist the poet would say that he is trying to do the job right as he sees it, for its own sake.

Manipulation of the word in the line scarcely has an end, and while he has it to do he is happy. It fills all his conscious mind, and he brings to his problem part of an answer from every experience. Not that he seeks experience for the answer, but he gives himself to it. He knows how durable a satisfaction lies hard in the hand, actual with weight, when every excursion returns him to some unfinished work with words. He is free of the shadow of boredom. He has light on the long task of stripping away from his own spirit, as much as from the half-made poem, all the husks that hide its outline, until the form stands forth. The very concentration of this work sometimes creates its own share of the perfected poem. The ultimate degree of heat needed to melt the heart and mind into active skill comes at the moment of making, and not until then; he writes better than he knows how. Otherwise it is struggle. Hazlitt says it is not like painting, where the painter contends only with nature. But for a while, before the words find their perfect order, when it seems as though they will with one more right epithet or rhyme be done, there is a feeling that the air is full of infinite possibility.

But writing poetry is a contention with inner man as well as with outer world, and there is always more to learn about not being defeated.

The poet's teachers are the poets alive before him and with him. But after a certain apprenticeship, he must teach himself or stop learning. When he is a young man, he is curious about poets as people: where did they grow up and go to school? what accident got their first poems into print? who helped them and what delayed them? were they married or not, and were they happy so? were they sick or well, and who were their friends, and where did they sit to talk?—no question is too trivial. The answers to all of them are patiently fitted like parts of a picture puzzle into a map, which will with suitable coloring and alterations of boundaries become a chart of his own career.

At first it is of importance for the poet to know that Coleridge walked the hills with William and Dorothy Wordsworth, or that Browning had to steal his wife from her father, or that Yeats was active and influential in politics. There must be significance for the poet in the facts that Hopkins became a priest; that Robert Frost refused to finish a college course; that T. S. Eliot, born in St. Louis, lives a royalist, a classicist, and an Anglican in London. From such facts the poet learns, because he compares with such circumstances the writing these men did then and later. He sees that to be a poet is infinitely more than to write and publish a volume. It is a way of life, and a way with life.

As a poet perfects his own geography, he is more concerned with actual poetry. As he succeeds a little here with his lines, and fails much elsewhere, he learns to estimate the integrities and urgencies that lie behind the volume of collected works, or the volume of life and letters over which he pores. He comes to realize a standard below which he himself may not fall, and conceives some ultimate to which he vows to lift that standard; he is driven with desire to taste the satisfaction in achievement he has read about. From then on he must be his own teacher. Whether his books are read and remembered or not is his responsibility now to himself. If he puts his self-knowledge and the limit of his craftsmanship and the best of his human understanding into them, he will accept the result.

It is the sum of what he teaches himself that determines his quality, which in turn foretells the result. In the midst of external activity, he may, like Yeats rehearsing a play, perceive suddenly that "tragedy must always be a drowning and breaking of the dykes that separate man from man," and from that time on be able to write tragedy. Or like George Moore, he may gradually come to place the capacity for revision of the written page above all virtues. He may learn Mozart's lesson that "when I am feeling well and in good humor, thoughts come in swarms and with marvelous ease," or that that may not be at all his condition for getting things done. Analogies may teach him, if he has the eye for them, like the one Hazlitt drew between the writer and the Indian juggler of knives. Or because of the poet's knowledge of poetry of the past, he may discover that a contemporary has by adapting or accepting or exaggerating old methods fashioned a new one.

Failure teaches him that all failure in the arts may possibly be mended in the next attempt. Praise teaches him how imperfectly he has transmitted himself, so unpredictable and often so absurd praise is. All pronouncements on style by artists of his own generation, of those years ago, help him shape the idea of his own, for he knows that his style must be his own or nothing. He learns, by experiences he would hardly care to tell, what medicine cures or eases for him the old unwillingness to make the imaginative effort. The weather of his mind, he knows, is an affair of low pressure areas and sudden storms, which he must learn to predict with unfailing accuracy. He watches the least stirring of leaves that indicates a rising wind, and he knows what planets draw his tides. He supports the findings of an almost instrumental skill in this kind of self-knowledge with an old native wisdom of intuition and shrewd speculation. Time concerns him, that he may not waste it. No waking day is ever quite long enough. But eventually he learns whether he must hurry with his life and writing or not. He feels his own sense of time mysteriously regulating his days. He comes to trust that sense, for it will tell him when to wait, when to act, and it tells him that life will be as long as he requires for his work. At last he learns what all great artists know, each in his kind, to hold to a single ruthless purpose, and that purpose poetry.

The object of this unwearying study is to write poetry that will represent a poet's peculiar inner rhythms, so confirmed and set free that it will speak, original and significant, in the poetry of his age. And who will know whether or not he has succeeded? He will know. That is his greatest satisfaction, even though he may have found readers who have been pleased and changed by poetry he has written. He knows, too, that other poets will know. He has learned to value most the praise of equals, and next the confidence of living men. "The oration is to the orator," said Whitman, "the acting is to the actor and actress, not to the audience." The poet values response of other poets because as artists they understand not only the finished thing, but the rigors of devotion to the art.

In spite of much example to the contrary, the poet learns that not all the artistry in the world avails unless his life as a human being is fulfilled and integrated. No man, whatever his purpose, can give himself to it wholly if he has made wrong commitments, and wastes time and strength in anxiety over them, finding them unendurable and inescapable. The great artist could not squander his life; lesser artists reveal themselves by doing so. Just as the poet searches everywhere and all the time for more knowledge of his task as poet, he will apply himself to strengthening his position as man, citizen, husband, and father. Beneath the surface of life lies a pattern of order. No one can ignore its shape once it has been revealed, and no one, without partial but continuous harm, may live contrary to its direction and harmony. A man cannot be a good artist and a bad citizen, a strong poet and a weak human being, or if he is, the strain and twisting show.

The artist who is a poet has enemies and allies, some within himself and some, the least important, outside himself. The indifferent, the stubborn, the wilfully blind never cease reproducing themselves, and they are the enemies of art, dangerous whether passive or active. But the temptation to publish what will satisfy nearly everyone, and not, in his own heart, himself, is the poet's more immediate danger. Time is always a potential enemy. In merciless and unforeseen ways, time destroys all but the best and the most honest poetry. Victory over the temptation to haste can conquer both indifference and time.

Sudden inspiration, completing the poem, is a treacherous friend, for it glosses the surface with what seems to be the light of poetry. But the light fades and the workmanship loosens in its joints, and the poem that creation without toil had fashioned falls apart. The waste of emptiness may threaten, but here, as Ben Jonson says, "the mind is like a bow, the stronger by being unbent." Infertile hours are not failure or defeat, but a part of the process of writing, a process that has, like green things growing, spaces of rest. Danger may come from an excess of loyalty to some one method or poet or audience; to some habit or party or subject, till proportion is destroyed. The complex pull of affections, duties, or pleasures in life as a plain citizen may also distort artistry. Since these things go very deep, one or another is sometimes the most corruptive enemy of all, having place and power within and without. It is an expensive but important chapter in the poet's history that tells how he learned to adjust his poetic to his private life, and both to his life in public. It is a story of unfailing renewal of an exact balance among the three.

Allies in the poet's self-preservation are his self-respect as an artist, the attraction of the goal still before him, and the height of his old vows. In composition, his allies serve with vital allegiance, but not always with their presence when it is most fervently asked. Health and peace of mind are his allies, too; or lacking them, the drive of such a necessity from within that the writing gets done—but this is costly. Knowledge of life and of all poetry are obviously a loyal part. Mastery of his creative powers is something he has learned slowly and thoroughly, and can usually summon to the endeavour, and control. But the support of the unconscious mind, while powerful, is unpredictable. In the crisis a memory of things he had forgotten may rush in, and a knowledge of things he never learned.

Neither in defeat nor in achievement is the poet unattended. Enemies and allies serve or threaten, and he learns that he does not live to himself. He must look before and after along the road he has been sent, and keep his lantern lighted at his belt, no matter how many others shine from the darkness ahead of him or come winking alone behind.

What every artist knows is that his work is never done. So long as he is conscious (and the poet is known for his supreme consciousness), he is bound to life and art, and has been pulling the knot tighter all the time. The poet and life and art go three together, and the poet is the one least willing to part company. If with all his pondering and practice of craftsmanship, his untiring adjustment of the necessities of writing to the necessities of living, and his accompaniment by enemy and ally to the blank white paper, he writes at last ten living lines, does he then retire clutching laurel? He knows better than anyone that he does not. In the next poem he may write twelve lines as good or better, and even if it is only five more, he is willing (he cannot help himself) to try until then—and a little further.

The Great and Golden Rule

She remembered, all of a sudden as if she had found a treasure, that she had her work. In a flash she saw her picture, and thought, Yes, I shall put the tree further in the middle; then I shall avoid that awkward space. That's what I shall do. She took up the salt-cellar and put it down again on a flower in the pattern in the table-cloth, so as to remind herself to move the tree.

Virginia Woolf
To the Lighthouse

In the one case, the colours seem breathed on the canvas as by magic, the work and wonder of a moment: in the other, they seem inlaid in the body of the work, and as if it took the artist years of unremitting labour, and of delightful never-ending progress to perfection. Who would ever wish to come to the close of such works—not to dwell on them, to return to them, to be wedded to them at the last?

William Hazlitt, "On the Pleasure of Painting"
Table Talk

Fly to thy talent! To thy charm!
Thy nest, thine hive, thy sheltering arm!
Who can to sing,
There let him flee;
This is, naught else is, certainty.

James Stephens
Strict Joy

Assimilation and Selection: When a subject begins to ripen in a poet's mind, the process can be compared with the expanding of a cell whose walls gradually become thin and porous and develop, we might say, a thousand, or a hundred thousand, mouths. Everything which comes in contact with a cell so altered can and must serve to nourish it. If it finds something unsuitable, it closes up or hastily withdraws; on the other hand it swallows, digests, and assimilates anything which can be made of use to it. And just as such a cell absorbs everything which can contribute to its nourishment, growth, and completion, so a poet's subject draws on all his experiences, knowledge, and emotions for likely material, rejecting and expelling the unadaptable, and continuing gradually to expand until it finally seems to form the entire content of the poet's mind —yes, the poet's mind itself seems transformed into his subject.

Arthur Schnitzler
"Work and Echo"

Can you doubt that the reason why Shakespeare knew every sound and syllable in the language and could do exactly what he liked with grammar and syntax, was that Hamlet, Falstaff, and Cleopatra rushed him into this knowledge; that the lords, officers, dependents and murderers and common soldiers of the plays insisted that he should say exactly what they felt in words expressing their feelings? It was they who taught him to write, not the begetter of the Sonnets. So that if you want to satisfy all those senses that rise in a swarm whenever we drop a poem among them—the reason, the imagination, the eyes, the ears, the palms of the hands and the soles of the feet, not to mention a million more that the psychologists have yet to name, you will do well to embark upon a long poem in which people as unlike yourself as possible talk at the tops of their voices. And for heaven's sake, publish nothing before you are thirty.

Virginia Woolf
Letter to a Young Poet

Nothing goes by luck in composition. It allows of no tricks. The best you can write will be the best you are. Every sentence is the result of a long probation. The author's character is read from title-page to end. Of this he never corrects the proofs.

Henry David Thoreau
Journals

That pre-existent vision does not exist at all. It only comes into existence while the technical and physical work of painting or writing goes on. To what may end by being a masterpiece an artist may come at first with a mind empty and stone-cold. It may be that "another commonplace model to paint!" was all that Raphael thought as he began the Sistine Madonna. Suppose it is so. Well, he gets out his tackle and starts. In a little while the mere feel of the brush in his hand begins to excite him; the cold engine of his mind is warmed a little; it inclines to move; there kindles in him a faint spark of curiosity about the being who is before him; the quickened mind enlivens the hand, and the brush moves more featly; eagerness is growing in all the employed faculties of the man; images, thoughts, memories, sympathies crowd in upon him till he wonders at himself, with a kind of alarm mixed with delight—will he ever be able to keep himself up to this pitch, he is now so much above par, so strangely endowed, for while it may last, with spiritual insight and also with an unwonted dexterity of hand.

C. E. Montague, "The Blessing of Adam"
A Writer's Notes on His Trade

What actually happens in a writer's mind when he gets through fiddling and fuming and sits down to tackle the job must always remain a secret between himself and his Demon. The preliminary horrors and shufflings are a valid part of the human comedy. There are innumerable ways of postponing. Some sit on the floor and begin dusting the books on the lower shelves, where they usually find *The Pentecost of Calamity* or *The Cradle of the Deep* and re-read it entire. Others get into pajamas and trim their toe-nails, or lock themselves into an office building with a bottle of Bisquit Dubouché. Homer Croy has remarked that his form of trifling is tinkering with his typewriter. "I have the best-cleaned typewriter in the world," he says, rather ashamed.

Christopher Morley
"The Folder"

Every day, every day, my Guide says to me,
Are you ready?
And I say to my Guide, I am ready.
And my Guide says, March.

Anonymous

Poems consciously composed may reach a very high plane, but never so high a one as poems subconsciously composed. It may be said that Keats wrote "The Triumph of Bacchus"; but that "The Hymn to Pan" wrote itself. I am not taking into consideration corrections made after the heat of composition is over, because, strange as it may seem, they have almost nothing to do with whether the original draft is done subconsciously or not. A common reason for them is that the subconscious mind dictates too fast for the poet to follow; again, the connection between the subconscious and the conscious minds may break, here and there, leaving holes which the poet must fill as best he can.

Amy Lowell
John Keats

It is as if the imagination, seeking for expression, had found both verb and substantive at one rush, had begun to say them almost at once, and had separated them only because the intellect had reduced the original unity into divided but related sounds.

Charles Williams
Introduction to *Poems of Gerard Manley Hopkins*

Everybody cannot be expected to like my pieces. Moreover, the oddness may make them repulsive at first sight and yet Lang may have liked them on second reading. Indeed, when, on somebody returning me the Eurydice, I opened and read some lines, as one commonly reads whether verse or prose, with the eyes, so to say, only, it struck me aghast with a kind of raw nakedness and unmitigated violence I was unprepared for: but take breath and read it with the ears, as I always wish to read, and my verse becomes all right.

Gerard Manley Hopkins, LIX
Letters to Robert Bridges

If you work in a storm of atoms and seconds, if your highest joy is "life; London; this moment in June" and your deepest mystery "here is one room; there is another," then how can you construct your human beings so that each shall be not a movable monument but an abiding home, how can you build between them any permanent roads of love and hate?

E. M. Forster, "The Early Novels of Virginia Woolf"
Abinger Harvest

Water color is swift and immediate in its expression of the artist's emotion. The worst fault of beginners is the desire to copy nature slavishly. Before you touch color to paper, you should consider composition and selection carefully. Define the shapes. Plan your light and dark masses. Then (1) lay in the dark masses, with a full brush. "Only in this manner can you secure a rich bloom." The dark masses can be made vibrant by flushing rich colors together. Add last the color required to dominate the mass. (2) After establishing the dark colors, develop the middle plan. Keep white and brilliances to the last. Area of white paper held in reserve "is a safety hold on the picture." (3) The final vital stage is to express your highlights: sunshine and shimmers. Sky; foreground; summing-up. If there is trouble in parts, lay it aside, or remove the offending parts by sponging. Purple is the only color difficult to remove. It stains and holds on like grim death. A water color must be painted without fear or favor, directly, lusciously, with a dripping flowing color. To falter is to fail.

George Ennis
Making Water Color

It comes back to me, the whole "job," as wonderfully amusing and delightfully difficult from the first; since amusement deeply abides, I think, in any artistic attempt, the basis and groundwork of which are conscious of a particular firmness. On that fine hard floor, the element of execution feels it may more or less consciously dance; in which case, puzzling questions, sharp obstacles, dangers of detail, may come up for it by the dozen without breaking its heart or shaking its nerve. It is the difficulty produced by the loose foundation or the vague scheme that breaks the heart—when a luckless fatuity has over-persuaded an author of the "saving" virtue of treatment.

Henry James
Preface to *The Awkward Age*

"The better part of godhead is design.
This is not theirs only, for I know mine,
And I project such worlds as need not yield
To this commanded April on the field.

And it is ample. For it satisfies
My royal blood even thus to exercise
The ancestral parts of my theogeny.
I am a god, though none attend to me."

And he watched, with large head resting in the sun,
The gods at play, and did not envy one.
He had his magic, too, and knew his power,
But was too tired to work it in that hour.

John Crowe Ransom, "Semi-Centennial"
Two Gentlemen in Bonds

A good scene should be, not a picture, but an image. Scene-designing is not what most people imagine it is—a branch of interior decorating. . . . Everything that is actual must undergo a strange metamorphosis, a kind of sea-change, before it can become truth in the theater. There is a curious mystery in this. You will remember the quotation from Hamlet:

> My father—methinks I see my father.
> O where, my lord?
> In my mind's eye, Horatio.

Robert Edmond Jones
Art in the Theater

The result of scribbling, the tale of perfect balance, all the elements of the tale understood, and an infinite number of minute adjustments perfectly made, the power of self-criticism fully at work, the shifting surface of word-values and color in full play, form and rhythmic flow of thought and mood marching forward with the sentences—these are things of a dream, of a dim far day toward which one goes knowing one can never arrive but infinitely glad to be on the road.

Sherwood Anderson
A Story-Teller's Story

No work of true genius dares want its appropriate form, neither indeed is there any danger of this. As it must not, so genius can not, be lawless: for it is even this that constitutes genius—the power of acting creatively under laws of its own origination.

Samuel Taylor Coleridge
Lectures on Shakespeare

To put all that is possible of one's idea into a form and compass that will contain and express it only by delicate adjustments and an exquisite chemistry, so that there will at the end be neither a drop of one's liquor left nor a hair's breadth of the rim of one's glass to spare—every artist will remember how often that sort of necessity has carried with it its particular inspiration.

Henry James
Preface to *The Tragic Muse*

But as air, melody, is what strikes me most of all in music and design in painting, so design, pattern, or what I am in the habit of calling inscape, is what I above all aim at in poetry. Now it is the virtue of design, pattern, or inscape to be distinctive, and it is the vice of distinctiveness to be queer.

Gerard Manley Hopkins, LIII
Letters to Robert Bridges

We sat together at one summer's end,
That beautiful mild woman, your close friend,
And you and I, and talked of poetry.
I said, "A line will take us hours maybe;
Yet if it does not seem a moment's thought,
Our stitching and unstitching has been naught."
. . . And thereupon
That beautiful mild woman for whose sake
There's many a one shall find out all heartache
On finding that her voice is sweet and low
Replied, "To be born woman is to know—
Although they do not talk of it at school—
That we must labour to be beautiful."

William Butler Yeats, "Adam's Curse"
In the Seven Woods

The great and golden rule of art, as well as of life, is this: That the more distinct, sharp, and wiry the bounding line, the more perfect the work of art: and the less keen and sharp, the greater is the evidence of weak imitation, plagiarism, and bungling. . . . How do we distinguish the oak from the beech, the horse from the ox, but by the bounding outline? How do we distinguish one face or countenance from another, but by the bounding line and its infinite inflections and movements? What is it that builds a house and plants a garden but the definite and the determinate? What is it that distinguishes honesty from knavery but the hard and wiry outline of rectitude and certainty in the actions and intentions? Leave out this line and you leave out life itself; all is chaos again, and the line of the Almighty must be drawn out upon it before man or beast can exist.

William Blake
"Prose Fragments"

All writers, all artists of any kind, in so far as they have had any philosophical or critical power, perhaps just in so far as they have been deliberate artists at all, have had some philosophy, some criticism of their art; and it has often been this philosophy, or this criticism, that has evoked their most startling inspiration, calling into outer life some portion of divine life, or of the buried reality, which could alone extinguish in the emotions what their philosophy or their criticism could extinguish in the intellect.

William Butler Yeats, "The Symbolism of Poetry"
Ideas of Good and Evil

There are two ways of becoming a writer. One, the cheaper, is to discover a formula; that is black magic; the other is to have the urge; that is white magic.

Carl Van Vechten
Peter Whiffle

Critics have observed that considerable writers fall into two classes—(1) those who start with their heads full of great thoughts, and are from the first occupied rather with the matter than with the manner of expressing it. (2) Those who begin with the love of expression and intent to be artists in words, and come through expression to profound thought.

A. Quiller-Couch, "The Popular Conception of a Poet"
Adventures in Criticism

There are four prime elements, as I look at it, in all writing, and a fifth which has to exist before good writing is possible.

This fifth element is, of course, the soil from which writing grows—a soil of the mind enriched by observation, experience, and abstract knowledge, rendered fertile by cultivation, and subject to a will to work it. Nothing comes from nothing; and to talk about the practice of writing apart from something to write about is a fallacy which has ruined many otherwise excellent rhetorics. I assume a warm and vigorous soil in this brief discussion of methods, only warning the beginning writer that, until he knows and feels, the fewer words he puts on paper the better for everybody—and, as a writer, he can never know and feel enough.

Henry S. Canby, "Style"
Designed for Reading

The one indispensable talent for creative art, whether of the theatre or literature or music or plastic representation, is the talent for experiencing.

Mary Austin
Everyman's Genius

It is not enough to have great thoughts before doing the work. The brush stroke at the moment of contact carries inevitably the exact state of being of the artist at the exact moment into the work, and there it is to be seen and read by those who can read such signs, and to be read later by the artist himself with perhaps some surprise, as a revelation of himself.

Robert Henri
The Art Spirit

Therefore, dive deep into thy bosom; learn the depth, extent, bias, and full forte of thy mind; contract full intimacy with the stranger within thee; excite and cherish every spark of intellectual light and heat, however smothered under former negligence, or scattered through the dull, dark mass of common thoughts; and collecting them into a body, let thy genius rise (if a genius thou hast) as the sun from chaos; and if I should then say, like an Indian, Worship it (though too bold) yet should I say little more than my second rule enjoins, (viz.) Reverence thyself.

Edward Young
"Conjectures on Original Composition"

I think what I am after is free meditation. I don't think anybody gets it when he's in anybody's company—only when his soul's alone. I do it when I wake up in the morning. . . . The person who has the freedom of his material is the person who puts two and two together, and the two and two are anywhere out of time and space, brought together.

Robert Frost
from notes on a lecture

Great things are done when men and mountains meet;
These are not done by jostling in the street.

William Blake
Ideas of Good and Evil

What is necessary to the free man, what is above all necessary to the free writer, is to consider without reference to his enemies the kind of world he himself would like to bring about. That world for all artists, for all men of spirit in a democratic world, the world in which a man is free to do his own work, the world in which a man may think as he pleases, the world in which a man may, with the complete responsibility of a mature individual, control his proper life.

Archibald MacLeish
Preface to *An American Manifesto*

Listen! I will be honest with you;
I do not offer the old smooth prizes, but offer rough new prizes;
These are the days that must happen to you:

You shall not heap up what is called riches,
You shall scatter with lavish hand all that you earn or achieve,
You but arrive at the city to which you were destined—you hardly settle yourself to satisfaction, before you are called by an irresistible urge to depart,
You shall be treated by the ironical smiles and mockings of those who remain behind you;
What beckonings of love you receive, you shall only answer with passionate kisses of parting,

You shall not allow the hold of those who spread their
reached hands toward you.

Walt Whitman, "Joy of the Road"
Leaves of Grass

It is beneath the dignity of poets, the dead and the living, to accept any praise but that true praise which is the confidence of living men.

Hugo von Hofmannsthal
"Der Dichter und diese Zeit"

Artists who do not love their art are more numerous, and more unhappy, than we think.

Logan Pearsall Smith
Afterthoughts

Now Intelligence is as much memory as perception; and for it there is always in the transformations it is watching something familiar which carries it back to what has already been witnessed, and forwards, expectantly, to something it may be going to witness. Hence, to Intelligence there is never mere repetition, just as there is never utter novelty.

Vernon Lee
Proteus, or the Future of Intelligence

To write on their plan, it was at least necessary to read and think. No man could be born a metaphysical poet, nor assume the dignity of a writer, by descriptions copied from descriptions, by imitations borrowed from imitations, by traditional imagery and hereditary similes, by readiness of style and volubility of syllables.

Samuel Johnson, "Abraham Cowley"
Lives of the Poets

You shall go to your run-out mountain farm,
Poor cast-away of commerce, and so live
That none shall ever see you come to market—
Not for a long time. Plant, breed, produce,
But what you raise or grow, why feed it out,
Eat it or plow it under where it stands
To build the soil. For what is more accursed
Than an impoverished soil pale and metallic?
What cries more to our kind for sympathy?
I'll make a compact with you, Meliboeus,
To match you deed for deed and plan for plan.
Friends crowd around me with their five year plans
That Soviet Russia has made fashionable.
You come to me and I'll unfold to you
A five year plan I call so, not because
It takes ten years or so to carry out,
Rather because it took five years at least
To think it out. Come close, let us conspire—
In self-restraint, if in restraint of trade.
You will go to your run-out mountain farm
And do what I command you. I take care
To command only what you meant to do
Anyway. That is my style of dictator.
Build soil. Turn the farm in upon itself
Until it can contain itself no more,
But sweating-full, drips wine and oil a little.
I will go to my run-out social mind
And be as unsocial with it as I can.
The thought I have, and my first impulse is
To take to market—I will turn it under.
The thought from that thought—I will turn it under.
And so on to the limit of my nature.

Robert Frost, "Build Soil"
A Further Range

The enemy has no definite name, though in a certain degree we all know him. He who puts the body before the spirit, the dead before the living: who makes things in order to sell them; who has forgotten that there is such a thing as truth, and measures the world by advertisement or by money; who daily defiles the beauty that surrounds him and makes vulgar the tragedy; whose innermost religion is the worship of the lie in his soul. The Philistine, the vulgarian, the great sophist, the passer of base coin for true, he is all about us, and worse, he has his outposts inside us, persecuting our peace, spoiling our sight, confusing our values, making a man's self seem greater than the race and the present things more important than the eternal. From him and from his influence we find our escape by means of the grammata into that calm world of theirs, where stridency and clamor are forgotten in the ancient stillness, where the strong iron is long since rusted, and the rocks of granite broken into dust, but the great things of the human spirit still shine like stars pointing man's way onward to the great triumph or the great tragedy; and even the little things, the beloved and tender and funny and familiar things, beckon across gulfs of death and change with a magic poignancy, the old things that our dead leaders and forefathers loved, *viva adhuc et desiderio pulcriora,* living still and more beautiful because of our longing.

Gilbert Murray
Religio Grammatici

I may say that the maker of the world exhausts his skill with each snowflake and dewdrop that he sends down. We think that the one mechanically coheres and that the other simply flows together and falls, but in truth they are the product of enthusiasm, the children of ecstasy, finished with the artist's utmost skill.

Henry David Thoreau
Journals

When I was young,
I had not given a penny for a song
Did not the poet sing it with such airs
That one believed he had a sword upstairs.

William Butler Yeats, "All Things Content Me"
The Green Helmet

To write this book well I must believe that it is my only novel and the last book I shall write. I wish to pour all into it without reserve.

André Gide
Journal

I feel assured I should write, for the mere yearning and fondness I have for the beautiful, even if my night's labors should be burnt every morning and no eye shine upon them.

John Keats
Letters

"Nice? It's the *only* thing," said the Water Rat solemnly, as he leant forward for his stroke. "Believe me, my young friend, there is *nothing*—absolutely nothing—half so much worth doing as simply messing about in boats. Simply messing," he went on dreamily, "messing—about —in—boats—"

Kenneth Grahame
The Wind in the Willows

When I am feeling well and in good humor, thoughts come in swarms and with marvelous ease. Once I catch my air, another comes soon to join it, according to the requirements of the whole composition. Then my mind kindles—the work grows—I keep hearing it and bring it out more and more clearly, and the composition ends by being completely executed in my mind, however long it may be.

Mozart
Letters

We but half express ourselves, and are ashamed of the divine idea which each of us represents. It may be safely trusted as proportionate and of good issues, so it be faithfully imparted, but God will not have his work made manifest by cowards. A man is relieved and gay when he has put his heart into his work and done his best, but what he has said or done otherwise shall give him no peace. It is a deliverance which does not deliver. In the attempt his genius deserts him; no muse befriends; no invention, no hope.

Ralph Waldo Emerson
"Self-Reliance"

The artist appeals to that part of our being which is not dependent on wisdom; to that in us which is a gift and not an acquisition—and, therefore, more permanently enduring. He speaks to our capacity for delight and wonder, to the sense of mystery surrounding our lives; to our sense of pity, and beauty, and pain.

Joseph Conrad
Preface to *The Nigger of the Narcissus*

Nothing is quite beautiful alone; nothing but is beautiful in the whole. A single object is only so far beautiful as it suggests this universal grace. The poet, the painter, the sculptor, the musician, the architect, seek each to concentrate this radiance of the world on one point, and each in his several work to satisfy the love of beauty which stimulates him to produce.

Ralph Waldo Emerson, "Nature"
The Conduct of Life

Whoever absorbs a work of art into himself goes through the same process as the artist who produced it—only he reverses the order of the process and increases its speed.

Friedrich Hebbel
Tagebücher

Then for the first time did it strike me that one cannot say anything about a woman. I noticed when they spoke of her, how much they left out, how they mentioned other things—surroundings, localities, objects—and described them up to a certain point where they stopped, stopped quietly, and, as it were, cautiously, just at the delicate outline, never retraced, which enclosed her.

Rainer Maria Rilke
The Notebook of Malte Laurids Brigge

Chekhov made a mistake in thinking that if he had more time he would have written more fully, described the rain, and the midwife and the doctor having tea. The truth is that one can get only so much into a story; there is always a sacrifice. One has to leave out what one knows and longs to use. Why? I haven't any idea, but there it is. It's always a kind of race to get in as much as one can before it disappears.

Katherine Mansfield
Journals

The surest thing there is is we are riders,
And though none too successful at it, guiders,
Through everything presented, land and tide
And now the very air, of what we ride.

What is this talked-of mystery of birth
But being mounted bareback on the earth?
We can just see the infant up astride,
His small fist buried in the bushy hide.

There is our wildest mount—a headless horse.
But though it runs unbridled off its course,
And all our blandishments would seem defied,
We have ideas yet that we haven't tried.

Robert Frost, "Riders"
West-Running Brook

I have observed some to make excuses that they cannot express themselves, and pretend to have their fancies full of a great many very fine things, which yet, for want of eloquence, they cannot bring out; a mere shift, and nothing else. Will you know what I think of it? I think they are nothing but shadows of some imperfect images and conceptions that they know not what to make of within, nor consequently how to bring out.

Montaigne, "Of the Education of Children"
Essays

One kind of criticism alone is worthy of respect. It says to the poet: This is what you willed to create, for this you were fated to will. It then proceeds to investigate the relation of the product to the producing will. All other criticism is of evil.

Friedrich Hebbel
Tagebücher

Danger is a good teacher, and makes apt scholars. So are disgrace, defeat, exposure to immediate scorn and laughter. There is no opportunity in such cases for self-delusion, no idling time away, no being off your guard (or you must take the consequences)—neither is there any room for humor or caprice or prejudice. If the Indian Juggler were to play tricks in throwing up the three case-knives, he would cut off his fingers. I can make a very bad antithesis without cutting off my fingers. The tact of style is more ambiguous than that of double-edged instruments.

William Hazlitt
"The Indian Jugglers"

He who goes against the fashion is himself its slave.

Logan Pearsall Smith
Afterthoughts

I am all for the man who, with an average audience before him, uses all means of persuasion—stories, laughter, tears, and but so much of music as he can discover on the wings of words. I would even avoid the conversation of lovers of music, who would draw us into the impersonal land of sound and color, and I would have no one write with a sonata in his memory.

William Butler Yeats, "The Musician and the Orator"
The Cutting of an Agate

"Your study seems to be a large room."

"No. Small. I prefer working in a small room. We have a family joke about it: 'In a small room thoughts grow great; in a great room thoughts grow small.' "

The question arose whether it was best to keep regular working hours.

"I know it is supposed to be a good rule," he conceded, "but I never could accomplish my best work that way. It is no doubt excellent for scientific men, but"—he quoted Goethe's dictum to Eckermann— " 'My counsel is to force nothing and rather to trifle and sleep away all unproductive days and hours, than on such days to compose something that will afterwards give no pleasure.' "

Lucien Price, "Portrait of Sibelius"
We Northmen

To write weekly, to write daily, to write shortly, to write for busy people catching trains in the morning or for tired people coming home in the evening, is a heartbreaking task for men who know good writing from bad. They do it, but instinctively draw out of harm's way anything precious that might be damaged by contact with the public, or anything sharp that might irritate its skin.

Virginia Woolf, "The Modern Essay"
The Common Reader

So far from the position holding true, that great wit (or genius, in our modern way of speaking) has a necessary alliance with insanity, the greatest wits, on the contrary, will ever be found to be the sanest writers. It is impossible for the mind to conceive a mad Shakespeare. The greatness of wit, by which the poetic talent is here chiefly understood, manifests itself in the admirable balance of all faculties. Madness is the disproportionate straining or excess of any one of them. . . . The ground of the mistake is, that men, finding in the raptures of the higher poetry a condition of exaltation to which they have no parallel in their own experience, besides the spurious resemblance of it in dreams and fevers, impute a state of dreaminess and fever to the poets. But the true poet dreams being awake. He is not possessed by his subject, but has dominion over it.

Charles Lamb, "The Sanity of True Genius"
Last Essays of Elia

People do not deserve to have good writing, they are so pleased with bad. In these sentences you show me, I can find no beauty, for I see death in every clause and every word. There is a fossil or a mummy character which pervades this book. I like gardens and nurseries. Give me initiative, spermatic, prophesying, man-making words.

Ralph Waldo Emerson
Journals

Thou wert never in more fair way to be cozened, than in this age, in poetry; wherein antics to run away from nature, and be afraid of her, is the only point of art that tickles the spectators. For they commend writers, as they do fencers or wrestlers; who, if they come in robustiously, and put for it with a great deal of violence, are received for the braver fellows. I deny not, but that these men, who always seek to do more than enough, may some time happen on something that is good, and great, but very seldom. I give thee this warning, that there is a great difference between these that utter all they can, however unfitly, and those that use election and a mean. For it is only the disease of the unskilful, to think rude things greater than polished; or scattered more numerous than composed.

Ben Jonson
The Alchemist

The mind is like a bow, the stronger by being unbent. But the temper in spirits is all, when to commend a man's wit, when to favor it. I have known a man vehement on both sides, that knew no mean, either to intermit his studies or call upon them again. When he hath set himself to writing, he would join night to day, press upon himself without release, not minding it till he fainted; and when he left off, resolve himself into all sports and looseness again, that it was almost a despair to draw him to his book; but once he got to it, he grew stronger and more earnest by the ease.

Ben Jonson
Timber: or Discoveries

My difficulty proceeds from the fact that, for each chapter, I must make a fresh start. Never profit from gathered momentum—such is the rule of my game.

André Gide
Journals

There never has been a story yet which has not backwatered at a state of semi-completion. It is a form of cowardice which overwhelms me, making me want to turn and run, making me wonder why I ever thought the idea was any good at all. To remember that this is a phase—not an irreparable state of mind—ought to help me to get over the mood quickly with each story.

Ruth Blodgett
Unpublished Notebooks

It is most wise not to worry too much about the intermissions (*temps d'arrêt*) in one's work. They air the subject and infuse it with life.

André Gide
Journals

Dec. 8. I thought and thought this morning but not to much avail. I can't think why, but my wit seems to be nearly deserting me when I want to get down to earth. I am all right—sky-high. And even in my brain, in my head, I can think and act and write wonders; but the moment I really try to put them down I fail miserably.

Katherine Mansfield
Journals

We are never satisfied with the maturity of those whom we have admired in boyhood; and, because we have seen their whole circle—even the most successful life is a segment—we remain to the end their harshest critics. One old school-fellow of mine will never believe that I have fulfilled the promise of some rough unscannable verses that I wrote before I was eighteen. Does any imaginative man find in maturity the admiration that his first half-inarticulate years roused in some little circle; and is not the first success the greatest?

William Butler Yeats, "The Trembling of the Veil"
Autobiographies

Not on sad Stygian shore, nor in clear sheen
Of far Elysian plain, shall we meet those
Among the dead whose pupils we have been,
Nor those great shades whom we have held as foes;

No meadow of asphodel our feet shall tread,
Nor shall we look each other in the face
To love or hate each other being dead,
Hoping some praise, or fearing some disgrace.

We shall not argue, saying, " 'Twas thus," or "thus,"
Our argument's whole drift we shall forget;
Who's right, who's wrong, 'twill all be one to us;
We shall not even know that we have met.

Yet meet we shall, and part, and meet again,
Where dead men meet, on lips of living men.

Samuel Butler
Notebooks

He could see, in a few pages, what Joyce was doing; it was thrilling, but it was something to consider by patient intuition, not to palaver and write papers about. There is no harm in reading any number of unimportant books for pastime, but the significant books must be taken cautiously. You don't want them to get in the way of what may perhaps be growing and brooding in yourself, taking its own time.

Christopher Morley
John Mistletoe

He punctuated after the manner of the seventeenth century and was always ready to spend an hour discussing the exact use of the colon. "One should use a colon where other people use a semi-colon, a semi-colon where other people use a comma," was, I think, but a condescension to my ignorance, for the matter was plainly beset with many difficulties.

William Butler Yeats, "The Tragic Veil"
Autobiographies

A good style in literature, if closely examined, will be seen to consist in a constant succession of tiny surprises.

Ford Madox Ford

Style is the man. Style, too, is autobiography. If the author withholds his face, we can learn something about him from the mask behind which he has chosen to conceal himself.

John Cournos

What I propose is to dispense with a style. Let us have style instead of a style. No one, as a matter of fact, gets rid of a certain gait, which, to the eye of the delicate observer, gives a family likeness to all his works. But let us carry our style next the skin instead of wearing it on our sleeve; let us bother about having good stuff to our coat rather than about putting smart patterns on it.

Jean Cocteau
Le Secret Professionel

I cannot grasp the contemporary notion that the traditional virtues of style are incompatible with a poetry of modern subject matter; it appears to rest on the fallacy of expressive form, the notion that the form of the poem should express the matter. This fallacy results in the writing of chaotic poetry about the traffic; of loose poetry about our sprawling nation; of semi-conscious poetry about our semi-conscious states. But the matter of poetry is and always has been chaotic; it is raw nature. To let the form of the poem succumb to its matter is and always will be the destruction of poetry and may be the destruction of intelligence. Poetry is form, its constituents are thought and feeling as they are embedded in language; and though form cannot be wholly reduced to principles, there are certain principles which it can not violate.

Yvor Winters
Before Disaster

In life, courtesy and self-possession, and in the arts, style, are the sensible impressions of the free mind, for both arise out of a deliberate shaping of all things, and from never being swept away, whatever the emotion, into confusion or dulness.

William Butler Yeats, "Poetry and Tradition"
The Cutting of an Agate

I believe in a wild profusion of imagery if need be, so that there be structure underneath and impressive cogency in what is said.

William Rose Benét
"Round About Parnassus"

And the unwillingness to make imaginative effort is the prime cause of almost all decay of art. It is the caterer, the man whose business it is to provide enjoyment with the very minimum of effort, who is in matters of art the real assassin.

Gilbert Murray
Religio Grammatici

But this I know: the writer who possesses the creative gift owns something of which he is not always master—something that, at times, strangely wills and works for itself. He may lay down rules and devise principles, and to rules and principles it will perhaps for years lie in subjection; and then, haply without any warning or revolt, there comes a time when it will no longer consent to "harrow the valleys, or be bound with a band in the furrow"—when "it laughs at the multitude of the city, and regards not the crying of the driver"—when, refusing absolutely to make ropes out of sea-sand any longer, it sets to work on statue-hewing, and you have a Pluto or a Jove, a Tisiphone or a Psyche, a Mermaid or a Madonna, as Fate or Inspiration direct. Be the work grim or glorious, dread or divine, you have little choice left but quiescent adoption. As for you—the nominal artist—your share in it has been to work passively under dictates you neither delivered nor could question—that would not be uttered at your prayer, not suppressed nor changed at your caprice. If the result be attractive, the World will praise you, who little deserve praise; if it be repulsive, the same World will blame you, who almost as little deserve blame.

Charlotte Brontë
Preface to *Wuthering Heights*

At least six distinctive senses of the word "imagination" are still current in critical discussion. . . .

(i) The reproduction of vivid images, usually visual images . . . is the commonest and least interesting thing which is referred to by imagination.

(ii) The use of figurative language is frequently all that is meant. People who naturally employ metaphor and simile, especially when it is of an unusual kind, are said to have imagination.

(iii) A narrower sense is that in which sympathetic reproducing of other people's states of mind, particularly their emotional states, is what is meant. "You haven't enough imagination," the dramatist says to the critic who thinks that his persons behave unnaturally.

(iv) Inventiveness, the bringing together of elements which are not ordinarily connected, is another sense. According to this, Edison is said to have possessed imagination, and any fantastic romance will show it in excelsis. Although this comes nearer to a sense in which value is implied, it is still too general. The lunatic will beat any of us at combining odd ideas.

(v) Next we have that kind of relevant connection of things ordinarily thought of as disparate which is exemplified in scientific imagination. This is the ordering of experience in definite ways and for a definite end or purpose, not necessarily deliberate and conscious, but limited to a given field of phenomena. The technical triumphs of the arts are instances of this kind of imagination.

(vi) "That synthetic and magical power, to which we have exclusively appropriated the name of imagination . . . reveals itself in the balance or reconciliation of opposite or discordant qualities . . . the sense of novelty and freshness, with old and familiar objects; a more than usual state of emotion, with more than usual order; judgment ever awake and self-possession with enthusiasm and feeling profound or vehement. . . . The sense of musical delight . . . with the power of reducing multitude into unity of effect, and modifying a series of thoughts by some one predominant thought or feeling."—Coleridge.

I. A. Richards, "The Imagination"
Principles of Literary Criticism

The more extensive your acquaintance is with the works of those who have excelled, the more extensive will be your powers of invention, and what may appear still more like a paradox, the more original will be your composition.

Sir Joshua Reynolds
Discourse to the Royal Academy

Experience is never limited, and it is never complete; it is an immense sensibility, a kind of huge spider web of the finest silken threads suspended in the chamber of consciousness, and catching every air-borne particle in its tissues. It is the very atmosphere of the mind; and when the mind is imaginative—much more when it happens to be that of a man of genius—it takes to itself the faintest hints of life, it converts the very pulse of the air into revelations.

Henry James, "The Art of Fiction"
Partial Portraits

It is to the inventive imagination that we look for deliverance from every other misfortune as from the desolation of a flat Hellenic perfection of style. . . . The true value is that peculiarity which gives an object a character by itself. . . . The imagination goes from one thing to another. Given many things of nearly totally divergent natures, but possessing one-thousandth part of a quality in common, provided that be new, distinguished, these things belong in an imaginative category and not in a gross natural array. . . . But the thing that stands eternally in the way of really good writing is always one: the virtual impossibility of lifting to the imagination those things which lie under the direct scrutiny of the senses, close to the nose.

By the brokenness of his composition the poet makes himself a master of a certain weapon which he could possess himself of in no other way. The speed of the emotions is sometimes such that . . . many matters are touched but not held, more often broken by the contact. . . . Thus a poem is tough by no quality it borrows from a logical recital of events nor from the events themselves but solely from the attenuated power which draws perhaps many broken things into a dance giving them thus full being.

William Carlos Williams
Kora in Hell

In every human being there is the artist, and whatever his activity, he has an equal chance with any to express the result of his growth and his contact with life . . . I don't believe any real artist cares whether what he does is "art" or not. Who, after all, knows what is art? I think the real artists are too busy with just being and growing and acting (on canvas or however) like themselves, to worry about the end. This end is what it will be. The object is intense living, fulfilment, the great happiness in creation.

Robert Henri
The Art Spirit

Art lives upon discussion, upon experiment, upon curiosity, upon variety of attempt, upon the exchange of views and the comparison of standpoints; and there is a presumption that those times when no one has anything particular to say about it, and has no reason to give for practice or preference, though they may be times of honor, are not times of development—are times, possibly, even of a little dullness.

Henry James, "The Art of Fiction"
Partial Portraits

Some may know what they seek in school and church,
And why they seek it there; for what I search
I must go measuring stone walls, perch on perch;

Sure that though not a star of death and birth,
So not to be compared, perhaps, in worth
To such resorts of life as Mars and Earth,

Though not, I say, a star of death and sin,
It yet has poles, and only needs a spin
To show its worldly nature and begin

To chafe and shuffle in my calloused palm
And run off in strange tangents with my arm
As fish do with the line in first alarm.

Such as it is, it promises the prize
Of the one world complete in any size
That I am like to compass, fool or wise.

Robert Frost, "Star in a Stone-Boat"
New Hampshire

When I was young, I painted as my nature compelled me to. Today I do so still, only then it seemed to give me more pleasure. Two uncompleted sketches did me more good then than all the recommendations of a whole academy. But one doesn't always stay young. What concerned me was gradually to acquire understanding of what I was doing. With every picture in which I freed myself I came nearer to myself.

Matisse
Notebooks

Time extracts various values from a painter's work. When these values are exhausted the pictures are forgotten, and the more a picture has to give, the greater it is.

Matisse
Notebooks

Life has at last been perfectly formed and measured to man's requirements; and in art man knows himself truly the master of his existence. It is this sense of mastery which gives man that raised and delighted consciousness of self which art provokes.

Lascelles Abercrombie
Study of Thomas Hardy

Of human activities, writing poetry is one of the least revolutionary. The states of being a rentier, a capitalist, contribute their bits to the revolution: they actively crumble. But the writing of a poem in itself solves the poem's problem. Separate poems are separate and complete and ideal worlds. . . . A work of art cannot reach out into everyday life and tell us whom to vote for and what kind of factories to build, because injunctions how to act in a world that has nothing to do with the poem destroy the poem's unity.

Stephen Spender
Poetry and Revolution

A great part of our racial knowledge of our lives and our earth and our destiny upon that earth has come in all ages from the intuitive and emotional perception of great poets. The poet works with those dimensions of invisibility which exist at the opposite extreme from the microscopic dimensions which concern the scientist. He works with the over-obvious, the too-apparent, the phenomena which men cannot see because they are so close the vision blurs, the phenomena which approach the seeing eye so near that they become sometimes the seeing eye itself. It is for this reason that the true perceptions of the poet have such an overwhelming and instantaneous feel of truth. They require no demonstration because they were always true. They were merely never "seen" before. The poet, with the adjustment of a phrase, with the contrast of an image, with the rhythm of a line, has fixed a focus which all the talk and all the staring of the world has been unable to fix before him.

Archibald MacLeish
"The Poetry of Karl Marx"

Man, as the savage first conceived him, man, as the mind of science still affirms, is not the center of the world he lives in, but merely one of her myriad products, more conscious than the rest and more perplexed. . . . He may cower before it like a savage, study it impartially for what it is, like the man of science; it remains in the end, as in the beginning, something alien and inhuman, often destructive of his hopes. But a third way is open. He may construct, within the world as it is, a pattern of the world as he would have it. This is the way of humanism, in philosophy, and in the arts.

Geoffrey Scott
The Architecture of Humanism

XVII

The Poet's Difficulties

The poet's difficulties are of two kinds, public and private, but it is the private difficulty which requires his unremitting care; his public problems are only an extension of it. Both rise from the nature of his position, from the inescapable fact that among men he is a poet, and must maintain himself in his place with honorable success. In neither predicament may he be caught off his guard. Since the spirit he is at such pains to discipline is the originator of his poems, the poet's work begins here, is carried on here all his life, and all but ends here. Only his written poems, his published books, are valid evidence of victory in the long, silent battle.

"A warlike, various, and tragical age is best to write of, but worst to write in," said Abraham Cowley. The poet is fortunate who feels that he has been born in the right age, at a time he would have chosen if he had the choice; and more than fortunate if he is right about it. The seventeenth century was warlike and various, but not tragical, and the poets lived in the full of their time. Their writing was their life, as lusty, proud, dangerous, and golden a literature as any poet could wish to be part of. The nineteenth century was in many ways tragical, and in some various; the social and intellectual changes were profound. The eighteenth century was none of these things. "Poetry did not rise spontaneously in their hearts, as true poetry should," said A. E. Housman, "and the result was that they wrote more verse. Either they had things to say, which is likely to be death to poetry; or they concentrated their attention upon form, which is fatal." But the second half of the twentieth century is all too surely a good age to write of, being terribly and undeniably warlike, various, and tragical; but a bad age to write in. This the poet makes it his business to understand. On this map of history, he must calculate his North, South, East, and West, and locate himself.

Always nearer than the shapes of history are the people who, though they do not know it, are making history, and who, though the poet does not know them, are his readers, his enemies, or his indifferent fellow men. Too much quivering indignation has been spent on the cruelty of those who neglect poets. Millions in every generation can live well without poetry, and do; a few thousands cannot live without it, and sometimes a few hundred may be won from the larger number to the smaller. But the poet who does not persuade his millions, or even his hundreds, should blame himself. He has, however, more immediate difficulties with enemies and readers, since both respond in positive ways to his existence. The poet must know that many people object to his existence on the ground that he is lazy, unmanly, and exclusive. They feel that no poet earns his living legitimately, because he does not do the sort of work that can be watched for real results. They are uneasy about his preoccupation with words and feelings, because that seems to them the business of women; what they remember is a time when women lived gently and in idleness, sewing, singing, reading books; not a manly life. And they violently object to the suggestion that they do not understand and could not appreciate, if it were explained, the fineness of the art of poetry. These three attitudes combine in the suspicion with which the poet is often regarded. It is an important part of the poet's work as poet to free himself of this suspicion, by refusing to confirm it in his actions, and by confidence in himself and his kind to keep himself unbewildered in his experience of it.

From the friendly part of the public, the poet will receive such payment in money as he ever gets from poetry; ordinarily it is very little. "Can you find some way of earning a decently liberal living," asks Arthur Davison Ficke of a young poet, "quite apart from your writing? Are you aware that poverty is a dark room, into which no sane man will voluntarily go? Do you know that the lovely fable of the poet's attic is a lie invented by rich people, and that lack of books and of diversion and of freedom is stunting to the soul?" And it is a hard but unavoidable fact that of twelve poets the last century called great, nine had the means to get a university education, and only one was not well-to-do. That one was John Keats. The son of an Athenian slave, said Sir Arthur Quiller-Couch, had as much hope as a poor poet in England of emancipation into that intellectual freedom of which great writings are born. But if the poet finds a "decently liberal living" aside from his poetry, and writes his poetry also, the friendly intentions of the public are still dangerous. The poet must teach himself never to propitiate the public for the sake of its praise, or for the sake of its good company, or for more of its money than another more rigorous poet gets. He must not deliberately be in style. If he makes the style, yet keeps his independence, he has his reward. But he may not say what people want to hear him say, unless his inner forces are in accord with the outer forces. It is the hardest lesson the artist learns, but from failure in it there is no recovery, no second chance.

It is clear that these relations with the world, so precariously maintained and so vital a condition of success, come from the poet's character, and derive from that character whatever healthy endurance they are to show. Not to be second-rate, is the poet's most private prayer. Not to be less than great in spirit, less than excellent in technique, less than adequate in energy for the completion of every poem undertaken. And although without help and against external odds this level has been achieved, there is no real necessity for such loneliness in self-discipline, for there are always excellent examples. The behavior of false poets, of whom there are five or ten times as many as there are true poets, will warn him in one direction. The less obvious behavior of the good poets will guide him in the other.

Self-study is constantly illuminated by the study of excellent example. That young poet works under a bright blessing who has a great living poet for friend, to whom he may now and then show his work, and with whom he may turn the many sides of thought to the light of day for examination. Literal apprenticeship, though right cases were rare, might be worth a revival. But the poet at work in self-perfection will learn from such sources however near or far. "His books are indeed a principal source," wrote Malcolm Cowley, "but there is also to be considered his career, the point from which it started, the direction in which it seems to be moving. There is his personality as revealed in chance interviews or caricatured in gossip; there are the values he assigns to other writers; and there is the value placed on himself by his younger colleagues."

From all this, the poet at the beginning of his career

chooses what he needs, and rejects what he knows is not good for him. Dramatic or amusing as it sometimes seems, the young poet will avoid displays of the artistic temperament, for he will learn that it is merely a way of describing everything that hinders the artist in producing. Wide acquaintanceship among literary men, though it comes as an inevitable and welcome reward for literary success, presents complex difficulties. Few poets are charitable to one another; the prize they are all after is too great, and the competition too ruthless, to make it safe to come unarmed and unready into such gatherings. Oscar Wilde once observed that the basis of literary friendship is mixing the poisoned bowl. And there are the dinners and the luncheons, the celebrations, the poetry groups of all kinds, with which society, though with eager good intention, cripples and silences the poet. He must be very shrewd in his choices and very patient in his refusals. He needs all his strength for poetry; he is extraordinarily generous if he can share it with the world in any other forms.

The time comes when the poet is in trouble of a sort that cannot be helped by his friends or his friendly public. It is difficult enough to write a poem—it is the one difficulty we may assume without discussion—but to have no poem to write is worst of all. Then only the strength the poet has cherished within can be called upon: his sincerity, his invention, his spiritual richness. Then he is thankful if he has not given part of himself away; and if he has, he is lost. Then the poets he admires do him no good. Then the meetings of poetry groups, the public readings, the luncheons to honor the visiting writer, are elaborate torture. It is the most private and the most desperate of the poet's difficulties, and an experience known to all men of imagination. It is against this time almost as much as for the bright, furious hours of creation that he has been preparing himself. "You know the Black Thought, gentlemen?" asked Rudyard Kipling. "It possesses some men in the dead of night; some when they are setting their palettes; some when they are stropping their razors; but only the very young, the very sound, the very single, are exempt."

Young the poet may always be, if he has taught himself to stay awake and stay alive, so that as his poetry grows it moves from vigor to new vigor. If he has resisted the enemy within and without, parrying even unsuspected difficulties with skill, then no one knows better than himself his soundness. His singleness is his secret. We may not invade that. But we can read the poems in his books.

No Royal Road

The notion that poetry, and sonnets in particular, are written only by the mild-mannered, and persons in precarious health, requires to be dispelled. As a fact, great poets are not only the sanest people in the world, but physically and temperamentally the toughest.

T. W. H. Crosland
The English Sonnet

Dear N——

It is a little hard to comply with your request and give you sensible advice on the subject. But I will try. Let me first ask you a series of questions.

Are you willing to work for many years without the slightest recognition? Are you strong enough to turn your back on all the cliques and schools of the hour, and devote yourself to principles of poetic composition that have not changed since the days of David the Psalmist? Would you rather write poetry than have all the kingdoms of the earth at your feet?

Are you strong enough to bear the dislike of the mob? Are you individual enough to go your own way, no matter what prudent counsel advises an opposite course?

Have you a real desire to explore the last depths of your emotions? Are you aware that those emotions are of no interest to anybody, except in so far as you give them beautiful and dignified expression?

Can you study endlessly the great masters of the past? Can you learn the lesson of their method—not merely of their manner—and borrow from them nothing except their power to express the passion of the individual heart? Can you refrain from copying them? Can you refrain from being "modern"?

Can you find some way of earning a decently liberal living, quite apart from your writing? Are you aware that poverty is a dark room, into which no sane man will voluntarily go? Do you know that the lovely fable of the poet's attic is a lie invented by rich people, and that lack of books and of diversion and of freedom is stunting to the soul? Are you prepared, I repeat, to earn a decent living quite apart from your poetry?

If you can honestly answer all these questions in the affirmative—then, I would say to you: "Go on! I wish you well! Maybe your great hopes will come true."

Arthur Davison Ficke
"Letter to a Poet"

Wanting to be a poet may be only an indication that you are afraid to take hold of life as most people live it. You may be using that ambition as a convenient lever to pry you loose from conditions of living that you hate, a piece of personal adornment to compensate for the fact that you do not seem especially desirable to others. In such cases, with a change of circumstances, your ambition to write will die. Another flaw in your purpose in life may lie in wanting to be a certain kind of person instead of wanting to do a certain kind of thing—to be a poet rather than to write poetry. That is like choosing a job for the uniform. Even loving poetry may mean only that you like to read it, not write it.

Anonymous

Write then, now that you are young, nonsense by the ream. Be silly, be sentimental, imitate Shelley, imitate Samuel Smiles; give the rein to every impulse; commit every fault of style, grammar, taste, and syntax; pour out; tumble over; loose anger, love, satire, in whatever words you can catch, coerce or create, in whatever metre, prose, poetry, or gibberish that comes to hand. But if you publish, your freedom will be checked; you will be thinking what people will say; you will write for others when you ought to be writing for yourself. And what point can there be in curbing the wild torrent of spontaneous nonsense which is now, for a few years only, your divine gift in order to publish prim little books of experimental verses? To make money? That, we both know, is out of the question. To get criticism? But your friends will pepper your manuscripts with far more serious and searching criticism than you will get from the reviewers. As for fame, look I implore you at famous people; see how the waters of dulness spread around them as they enter; observe their pomposity, the prophetic airs; reflect that the greatest poets were anonymous; think how Shakespeare cared nothing for fame; how Donne tossed his poems into the waste-paper basket; write an essay giving a single instance of any modern English writer who has survived the disciples and admirers, the autograph hunters and the interviewers, the dinners and the luncheons, the celebrations and the commemorations with which English society so effectively stops the mouths of its singers and silences their songs.

Virginia Woolf
A Letter to a Young Poet

"But it's poetry!" That was an exclamation never heard before this mechanical age, unless with pleasurable anticipation.

Henry S. Canby

Holding the Pose: At times when second-rate artists are doing their best work they can hardly be distinguished from the truly great. Yet what they always lack is the ability to keep themselves at the required height for a sufficient length of time. Precisely at those moments when the last extraordinary straining of all their energies would be necessary, they are fated to sink into the paltry, the trivial, or the absurd.

Arthur Schnitzler
"Work and Echo"

Understand that you can have in your writing no qualities which you do not honestly entertain in yourself. Understand that you cannot keep out of your writing the indication of the evil or shallowness you entertain in yourself. If you love to have a servant stand behind your chair at dinner, it will appear in your writing; if you possess a vile opinion of women, or if you begrudge anything, or doubt immortality, these will appear by what you leave unsaid more than by what you say. There is no trick or cunning by which you can have in your writing that which you do not possess in yourself.

Walt Whitman
Memoranda for *Leaves of Grass*

But the end of contemplating the eternal beauties, and doing nothing to yoke them with time, is smugness, and stagnation, and sterility.

Rebecca West
Harriet Hume

Temperament: When we speak of the artistic temperament we are usually referring to the sum quantities which hinder the artist in producing.

Arthur Schnitzler
"Work and Echo"

No matter how the poet may sweat and fast to produce his ode, the chances are that in the poem he will visualize himself as reclining somewhere on a mossy bank beside a running brook. Sir Thomas Wyatt celebrated his bed as "the body's ease" and "quieter of the mind." Few have been so frank as Wordsworth, who admits lying in vacant as well as pensive mood, but many have professed with Coleridge that they were fain to

dream away the entrusted hours
On rose-leaf beds, pampering the coward heart
With feelings all too delicate for use.

Keats, "on Skiddaw's mount lay supine, midway th' ascent." Is it any wonder, then, that the reader, remembering in addition that Coleridge composed "Kubla Khan" while asleep in a chair, considers the writing of poetry a lazy man's occupation? The public, not unreasonably, perhaps, is prone to take their words literally. The "pernicious nonsense" of the "essential laziness" of poets is, sad to say, a pleasant fiction largely of their own invention.

Raymond F. Howes

We make ourselves a place apart
Behind light words that tease and flout,
But oh, the agitated heart
Till someone find us really out.

Robert Frost, "Revelation"
A Boy's Will

The world is a perpetual caricature of itself; at every moment it is the mockery and contradiction of what it is pretending to be. But as it nevertheless intends all the time to be something different and highly dignified, at the next moment it corrects and checks and tries to cover up the absurd thing it was; so that a conventional world, a world of masks, is superimposed on the reality, and passes in every sphere of human interest for the reality itself. Humor is the perception of this illusion, whilst the convention continues to be maintained, as if we had not observed its absurdity.

George Santayana
Soliloquies in England

People who read books without writing them are likely to form a simple picture of any celebrated author. He is John X or Jonathan Y, the man who wrote such a fascinating novel about Paris, about divorce, about the Georgia crackers—the man who drinks, the man who ran off with the doctor's wife—the bald-headed man who lectured to the Wednesday Club. But to writers, especially to young writers in search of guidance, the established author presents a much more complicated image, and one that is assembled from many sources. His books are indeed a principal source, but there is also to be considered his career, the point from which it started, the direction in which it seems to be moving. There is his personality as revealed in chance interviews or caricatured in gossip; there are the values he assigns to other writers; and there is the value placed on himself by his younger colleagues in those kitchen or barroom gatherings at which they pass judgment with the harsh finality of a Supreme Court—John X has got the real stuff, they say, but Jonathan Y is terrible—and they bring forward evidence to support these verdicts. The evidence is mulled over, all the details are fitted together like the pieces of a jigsaw puzzle, until they begin to form a picture, vague and broken at first, then growing more distinct as the years pass by: the X or Y picture, the James Joyce, Paul Valéry, or T. S. Eliot picture. But it is not so much a picture when completed: it is rather a map or diagram which the apprentice will use in planning his own career.

Malcolm Cowley
Exile's Return

Bad literature justifies itself by treating more important matters than good writers have the courage to touch upon; violent sentiments, adultery, ostracism, guilt, and redemption.

Glenway Wescott, "A Guilty Woman"
Goodbye Wisconsin

The miserable man may think well and express himself with great vehemence, but he cannot make beautiful things, for Aphrodite never rises from any but a tide of joy.

William Butler Yeats

Men are free when they are in a living homeland, not when they are straying and breaking away. Men are free when they are obeying some deep, inward voice of religious belief. Men are free when they belong to a living, organic believing community, active in fulfilling some unfulfilled, perhaps unrealized purpose. Not when they are escaping to some wild west. The most unfree souls go west, and shout of freedom. Men are freest when they are most unconscious of freedom. The shout is a rattling of chains, always was.

D. H. Lawrence
Studies in Classic American Literature

It was Chrysis' theory of life that all human beings—save a few who seemed to possess some secret from the gods—merely endured the slow misery of existence, hiding as best they could their consternation that life had no wonderful surprises after all and that its most difficult burden was the incommunicability of love.

Thornton Wilder
Woman of Andros

We grow neither better nor worse as we get old, but more like ourselves.

May Lamberton Becker
"The Reader's Guide"

Thoreau's quality is very penetrating and contagious; reading him is like eating onions—one must look out or the flavor will reach his own page. But my current is as strong in my channel as Thoreau's in his.

John Burroughs
Journal

People do not ask painters to go places and paint pictures for nothing, but they are forever trying to graft entertainment off of poets.

Don Marquis

They that write of poisons, and of creatures naturally disposed to the ruin of man, do as well mention the flea as the viper, because the flea, though he kill none, he does all the harm he can.

John Donne
"Devotions"

Nothing in our age, I have observed, is more preposterous, than the running judgments upon Poetry, and Poets; when we shall hear those things commended, and cry'd up for the best writings, which a man would scarce vouchsafe to wrap any wholesome drug in; he would never light his tobacco with them. And those men almost named for Miracles, who are not yet so vile, that if a man should go about to examine and correct them, he must make all they have done but one blot. Their good is so entangled with their bad, as forcibly one must draw on the others death with it.

Ben Jonson
Timber: or Discoveries

The basis of literary friendships is mixing the poisoned bowl.

Oscar Wilde

Noise is the most impertinent of all forms of interruption. It is not only an interruption, but a disruption of thought. Of course, where there is nothing to interrupt, noise will not be so particularly painful.

Schopenhauer
Studies in Pessimism

There is nothing worse for our trade than to be in style:
He that goes naked goes farther at last than another:

Wrap the bard in a flag or a school and they'll jimmy his
Door down and be thick in his bed—for a month:

(Who recalls the address now of the Imagists?)
But the naked man has always his own nakedness:
People remember him forever his live limbs.

Archibald MacLeish, "Invocation to the Social Muse"
Poems: **1924-1933**

What American literature needs is not more poets (we could dispense with most of those already writing), but mature poets who are willing to devote their whole time to the most difficult of arts.

Malcolm Cowley,
"The Business of Being a Poet"

Nine-tenths of the best poetry in the world has been written by poets less than thirty-five years old; a great deal more than half of it has been written by poets under twenty-five. One always associates poetry with youth, for it deals chiefly with ideas that are peculiar to youth, and its terminology is quite as youthful as its contents. When one hears of a poet past thirty-five, he seems somewhat unnatural and a trifle obscene; it is as if one encountered a graying man who still played Chopin waltzes and believed in elective affinities.

H. L. Mencken, "The Poet and His Art"
Prejudices, 3d Series

He hopes to live by writing poems, and yet he has no assurance that his poems will be accepted by magazines. If they happen to be accepted, he has no assurance that they will be regarded as anything else than a free contribution to the cause of letters. Let us assume, however, that he is paid for his work at the rate of fifty cents a line, and that being exceptionally prolific he can produce the equivalent of eight or nine sonnets every month. In this case, granted that all his poems are printed, he will be earning about $14 a week—approximately as much as the striking mill-hands in North Carolina.

Malcolm Cowley,
"The Business of Being a Poet"

It is felt, pretty widely, that poetry is an effeminate business, and that poets are not "men." When a poet somehow becomes news, the papers are at pains to state that he wears his hair short, enjoys his beer, and attends boxing matches.

L. A. G. Strong
Common Sense About Poetry

I had rather hear a brazen canstick turned
Or a dry wheel grate on the axle-tree;
And that would set my teeth nothing on edge,
Nothing so much as mincing poetry.

Shakespeare
Henry IV

I have been breaking silence these twenty-three years and have hardly made a rent in it.

Henry David Thoreau
Journals

There are also the false poets, the bad poets, who rush about, reading their stuff to anyone who will listen: eager for any audience, however unskilled, and vexing even strangers in their indecent haste to expose their writings. The true poet does not behave in this fashion; and therefore, if the ordinary reader has ever been subjected to this kind of treatment, it will have been one of these preposterous asses, who thereby get a bad name for the craft they are aping.

L. A. G. Strong
Common Sense About Poetry

No matter how sagacious or how revered the teacher, at some point you will find yourself beginning to diverge from him. For sooner or later, every individual has to fall back on that residual and personal parcel of conviction which is true for himself alone.

Christopher Morley
Inward Ho!

By all means use sometimes to be alone.
Salute thyself: see what thy soul doth wear.
Dare to look in thy chest; for 'tis thine own;
And tumble up and down what thou find'st there.
Who cannot rest till he good fellows find,
He breaks up house, turns out of doors his mind.

George Herbert
"The Church Porch"

I can no longer expect to be revisited by the continuous excitement under which in the early months of 1895 I wrote the greater part of my other book.

A. E. Housman
Preface to *Last Poems*

Success is, indeed, as Trollope says somewhere, a necessary poison; but they are fortunate, he wisely adds, to whom it comes late in life and in small doses . . . the number of miscarriages of talent, the rate of infant mortality among gifts of promise, seem to be ever increasing. And indeed, with all the advertisement and premature publicity of our time, where can we hope to find that leisurely ripening of talent in the shade of obscurity, that slow development by experiment and failure, by which it can best be mellowed and matured?

Logan Pearsall Smith
"The Prospects of Literature"

I doubt if Emerson could trundle a wheelbarrow through the streets, because it would be out of character. One needs to have a comprehensive character.

Henry David Thoreau
Journals

When you meet, in the flesh, a writer whose work has seemed to you to have tragic force, you are apt to feel that, face to face and talking with him, you are, in essentials, further removed from him than you were when you only read his books. . . . Compared with that self-revealer, the man before you seems like a creature withdrawn into a shell. Between you and him there has now arisen the estranging film of defensive reticence which separates nearly all of us from our friends.

C. E. Montague, "The Delights of Tragedy"
A Writer's Notes on His Trade

The conversation of authors is not so good as might be imagined: but, such as it is (and with rare exceptions) it is better than any other. The proof of which is, that when you are used to it, you cannot put up with any other.

William Hazlitt
"On the Conversation of Authors"

Where the poet of the past was glad to share and quick to express the passions and foibles of those about him, the poet of today is proud only of his differences. It is no longer the self who desires a closer connection with and "a greater knowledge of human nature"; it is, as Virginia Woolf wrote, "a self that sits alone in a room at night with the blinds drawn . . . much less interested in what we have in common than what he has apart." In short, the poet, for all his volubility, no longer believes in his high purpose, nor in himself. He seeks to charm or pique or entertain; he cannot exalt. He no longer delights in the passionate "goings-on of the Universe" nor is he "habitually impelled to create them" for the act of creation is an act of faith, and he has no faith in them. He does not really believe—and I may as well come out with the stilted and inevitable phrase—in the destiny of man.

Louis Untermeyer, "Poets to Come!"
Play in Poetry

Have patience and indulgence toward the people, take off your hat to nothing known or unknown, or to any man or number of men, go freely with powerful uneducated persons.

Walt Whitman
Preface to *Leaves of Grass*

There's a free masonry among the dull by which they recognize and are sociable with the dull, as surely as a correspondent tact in men of genius.

Ralph Waldo Emerson
Journals

Detestable is the society of mere literary men.

Emmanuel Kant

Let us honor if we can
The vertical man

Though we value none
But the horizontal one.

W. H. Auden
Invocation to *Poems*

Somebody with whom I was talking cried: "They are all only poetical persons—not poets. Who will be reading them a century hence?" To which I answered: "There are so many of them that, a century hence, they may appear a kind of Composite Poet; there may be 500 excellent poems proceeding from 100 poets mostly not so very great, but well worth remembering a century hence."

Harold Monro
Preface to *Twentieth Century Poetry*

Rousseau's children are now forgotten
And he might be forgotten, too,
If he had not sent them to an orphan asylum
To free himself for the writing of books.
But, oh, to be remembered
For deserting your children
For the sake of learning the violin
And not learn it.

Edgar Lee Masters
The New Spoon River

Nothing in literature is so perishable as eccentricity, with regard to which each generation has its own requirements and its own standard of taste; and the critic who urges contemporary poets to make their work as individual as possible is deliberately inviting them to build their structures on sand instead of rock.

Edmond Holmes
What Is Poetry?

All one's work might have been better done; but this is the sort of reflection a worker must put aside courageously if he doesn't want every one of his compositions to remain forever a private vision, an evanescent reverie.

Joseph Conrad
Notes on My Books

'Tis not every day that I
Fitted am to prophesy:
No, but when the Spirit fills
The fantastick Pannicles:
Full of fier; then I write
As the Godhead doth indite.
Thus inraged, my lines are hurl'd,
Like the Sybells, through the world.
Look how next the holy fier
Either slakes, or doth retire;
So the Fancie cools, till when
That brave Spirit comes again.

Robert Herrick, "Not Every Day Fit for Verse"
Hesperides

A long poem was a new departure for him. He felt that it was time for him to make an attempt, but he dreaded it as well. I do not suppose that anyone not a poet can realize the agony of creating a poem. Every nerve, even every muscle, seems strained to the breaking point. The poem will not be denied, to refuse to write it would be a greater torture. It tears its way out of the brain, splintering and breaking its passage, and leaves that organ in the state of a jellyfish when the task is done. And yet to have no poem to write is the worst state of all.

Amy Lowell
John Keats

To be so lighthearted
What pain was left behind;
What fetters fallen gave them
Unto this airy mind.

Æ (George Russell), "The Gay"
Vale

During periods of trouble the artist has only three things which may vouch for him: his sincerity, his spiritual richness, or his imagination.

Benjamin Crémieux
"Inquiétude et Réconstruction"

The crowd was always near; he ran to it
Glad to forget a moment how this wrong
Done to himself was eating bit by bit
The delicate food he should have saved for song.
Stuffing his ears, he talked to everybody:
The smart, the lazy, the polite, the shoddy.

Harrison Dowd

Like all artists, Byron and Shelley wrote in order to console themselves for not living, and a man of action appeared to them as an enviable phenomenon.

André Maurois
Ariel

I was in one of those disillusioned moods which come to writers bankrupt of ideas, bankrupt of confidence, a prey to that recurrent despair, the struggle which makes the profession of the pen "a manly one." My eyes wandering over that fine countryside took in the loveliness thereof with the profound discontent of one who, seeing beauty, feels that he cannot render it.

John Galsworthy, "A Strange Thing"
Tatterdemalion

A second chance—that's the delusion. There never was to be one. We work in the dark—we do what we can—we give what we have. Our doubt is our passion, and our passion is our task. The rest is the madness of art.

Henry James
The Middle Years

The poet must always prefer the community where the perfected minds express the people, to a community that is vainly seeking to copy perfected minds.

William Butler Yeats, "The Galway Plains"
Ideas of Good and Evil

The truth to be driven home is not that the poet is important. The truth to be driven home is that the poet is important only so long as he acts as poet. The intuitions of the poet are valid and may be accepted only because his loyalty is to his art, because his sole test of the acceptability of a word or a phrase or a poem is the test of his art and not the test of his politics or his social indignation.

Archibald MacLeish
"The Poetry of Karl Marx"

It is a happy thing that there is no royal road to poetry. The world should know by this time that one cannot reach Parnassus except by flying thither. Yet from time to time more men go up and either perish in its gullies fluttering excelsior flags or else come down again with full folios and blank countenances. Yet the old fallacy keeps its ground. Every age has its false alarms.

Gerard Manley Hopkins, "Early Diaries"
Notebooks and Papers

Anyone can run to excesses,
It is easy to shoot past the mark,
It is hard to stand firm in the middle.

Ezra Pound, XIII
A Draft of Thirty Cantos

It may happen that poets will be made more often by their sins than by their virtues, for general praise is unlucky, as the villages know, and not merely as I imagine—for I am superstitious about these things—because the praise of all but an equal enslaves and adds a pound to the ball at the ankle with every compliment.

William Butler Yeats, "Discoveries"
The Cutting of an Agate

And here is the natural place to confess that any poet, dramatist, or novelist, who declares that he is indifferent whether or not people give him attention, is either an ass or a liar; anyhow, he is not natural.

H. M. Tomlinson
"The Problems of a Novelist"

What are the great poetical names of the last hundred years or so? Coleridge, Wordsworth, Byron, Shelley, Landor, Keats, Tennyson, Browning, Arnold, Morris, Rossetti, Swinburne—we may stop there. Of these, all but Keats, Browning, and Rossetti were University men; and of these three, Keats, who died young, cut off in his prime, was the only one not fairly well-to-do. It may seem a brutal thing to say, and it is a sad thing to say: but as a matter of hard fact the theory that poetical genius bloweth where it listeth, and equally in poor and rich, holds little truth. As a matter of hard fact, nine out of ten of these twelve were University men: which means that somehow or other they procured the means to get the best education England can give. As a matter of hard fact, you know that of the remaining three Browning was well-to-do, and I challenge you that, if he had not been well-to-do, he would no more have attained to writing *Saul,* or *The Ring and the Book,* than Ruskin would have attained to writing *Modern Painters* if his father had not dealt prosperously in business. Rossetti had a small private income; and moreover he painted. There remains but Keats; whom Atropos slew young, as she slew John Clare in a madhouse, and James Thomson by the laudanum he took to drug disappointment.

These are dreadful facts, but let us face them. It is—however dishonouring to us as a nation—certain that by some fault in our commonwealth, the poor poet has not in these days, nor has he had for two hundred years, a dog's chance. Believe me—and I have spent a great part of the last ten years in watching some 320 Elementary Schools—we prate of democracy, but actually a poor child in England has little more hope than had the son of an Athenian slave to be emancipated into that intellectual freedom of which great writings are born.

A. Quiller-Couch, "The Practice of Writing"
The Art of Writing

It does not speak favorably for the taste and humor of Detroit that its intelligentsia sniffed dire propaganda in Rivera's witchery; that it suspected anti-religious parody in the scene of a child being vaccinated. Nothing is to be thought of this except that a society dominated by captains of industry and their women folk will crave either the softest or the most exotic art.

Frank Jewett Mather, Jr.
"Rivera's American Murals"

The public really love in art that which is banal and long familiar, that to which they have grown accustomed.

Anton Chekhov
Notebooks

I scarcely need to tell you that all the pioneer poets—even such poets as Wordsworth and Keats—have been disagreed with during their lifetime. The name of Wordsworth could not be mentioned until he was past fifty and sixty without an outburst of a vulgar nature from the press. It is not the slightest use for reviewers to fly into a temper and say that it is only the mad artists who are roughly treated by the crowd. For it can be proved that such treatment, varied by heart-breaking neglect, has been meted out to every artist since the time of Shakespeare.

Edith Sitwell, "Experiment in Poetry"
Tradition and Experiment

And in spite of the immense amount of poetry published and read today, the personality truly and naturally poetic seems to be becoming rarer and rarer. It may be true that the kind of dignity and distinction which have been characteristic of the poet in the past are becoming more and more impossible in our modern democratic society and during a period when the ascendancy of scientific ideas has made man conscious of his kinship with the other animals and of his subjection to biological and physical laws rather than of his relation to the gods. It was easy for the lyric poet, from Wyatt's age to Waller's, to express himself both directly and elegantly, because he was a courtier, or, in any case, a member of a comparatively small educated class, whose speech combined the candor and naturalness of conversation among equals with the grace of courtly society. It was possible for him honestly to take up a residence in an intellectual world where poetic images stood for actualities because the scientific language and technique for dealing with these actualities had not yet come to permeate thought. But the modern poet who would follow this tradition, and who would yet deal with life in any large way, must create for himself a special personality, must maintain a state of mind, which shall shut out or remain indifferent to many aspects of the contemporary world.

Edmund Wilson
Axel's Castle

Hypocrisy and suave intrigue,
Successful impudence and lying,
Lawlessness with law in league,
Talent in the gutter dying—
Cant,
Rant,
And superstition
Are the favourites of Tradition—

Old French song

The man or boy of genius is very generally hated or scorned by the average man or boy until the day come for him to charm them into unwilling homage. Until that day he has often to cry with Blake, "Why was I not born with a different face?" for his abstracted ways and strange interests arouse that hatred of the uncommon which lies deep in the common heart. It is said that if you tie a piece of red cloth to a sea-gull's leg its fellow-gulls will peck it to death. Shelley, tormented by the gull-like animosity of his school-fellows, plunged a pen through the hand of a tormentor. Blake leant out from a scaffolding where he sat at work and flung a Westminster student from a cornice, whither he had climbed the better to tease him.

William Butler Yeats
Introduction to *Blake's Poems*

Those who are able to produce poor poetry, and whose friends know it, who yet refrain from exercising their acknowledged powers, enjoy the unqualified approval of the nine Muses.

Ik Mitchell
Memoirs of an Editor

Happy is it, that the mass of mankind eat and drink, and sleep, and perform their several tasks, and do as they like without us—caring nothing for our scribblings, our carpings, and our quibbles: and moving on the same, in spite of our fine-spun distinctions, fantastic theories, and lines of demarcation, which are like chalk-figures to be danced out before morning.

William Hazlitt
"On the Conversation of Authors"

A man of talents, who shrinks from a collision with his equals or superiors, will soon sink below himself. We improve by trying our strength with others, not by showing it off. A person who shuts himself up in a little circle of dependents and admirers for fear of losing ground in his own opinion by jostling with the world at large, may continue to be gaped at by fools, but will forfeit the respect of sober and sensible men.

William Hazlitt
"Characteristics"

The occasional poet is circumscribed by the narrowness of his subject. Whatever can happen to man has happened so often, that little remains for fancy or intervention. We have all been born; we have most of us been married; and so many have died before us, that our deaths can supply but few materials for a poet.

Samuel Johnson, "John Dryden"
Lives of the Poets

Rhymes and rhymers pass away, poems distilled from
 poems pass away,
The swarms of reflectors and the polite pass, and leave
 ashes,
Admirers, importers, obedient persons, make but the soil
 of literature.
America justifies herself, give it time, no disguise can de-
 ceive it or conceal from it, it is impassive enough,
Only toward the likes of itself will it advance to meet
 them,
If its poets appear it will in due time advance to meet
 them, there is no fear of a mistake,
The proof of a poet shall be sternly deferred till his country absorbs him as affectionately as he has absorbed it.

Walt Whitman, "By Blue Ontario's Shore"
Leaves of Grass

There are as many arts as there are artists—the number is not seven, but countless as the stars. We group them in constellation for our convenience, not theirs; seven units are more easily handled than a trillion. The confusions in regard to them are countless, too; the actual number is far greater; but they may also be gathered for our convenience into seven groups—"seven" has the perfume of a mystic tradition kept fragrant by the superstition of generations of men. So I begin with a roll-call of them: Poets write for money; poets are influenced by their environment; poets write in metres; poets write tragedies and comedies; poets are moral or immoral; poets are democratic or aristocratic; poets use figures of speech.

J. E. Spingarn
"The Seven Arts and the Seven Confusions"
Creative Criticism

A poet is no rattle-brain, saying what comes upper-most, and, because he says everything, saying, at last, something good; but a heart in unison with his time and country. The Genius of our life is jealous of individuals, and will not have any individual great, except through the general. There is no choice to genius. A great man does not wake up on some fine morning and say, "I am full of life, I will go to sea, and find an Antarctic continent: today I will square the circle: I will ransack botany, and find a new food for man: I have a new architecture in my mind: I foresee a new mechanic power": no, but he finds himself in the river of thoughts and events, forced onward by the ideas and necessities of his contemporaries. He stands where all the eyes of men look one way, and their hands all point in the direction in which he should go.

Ralph Waldo Emerson, "Shakespeare"
Representative Men

And, talking of imagination, do you know the Black Thought, Gentlemen? I am loath to remind you of it in this fenced and pleasant place, but it is the one emotion that all men of imagination have in common. It is a horror of great darkness that drops upon a man unbidden, and drives him to think lucidly, connectedly, and with Cruikshank detail, of all the accidents whereby, through no fault of his own, he may be cut off from his work, and forced to leave those he loves defenceless to the world. You know the Black Thought, Gentlemen? It possesses some men in the dead of night; some in the sunshine; some when they are setting their palettes; some when they are stropping their razors; but only the very young, the very sound, the very single, are exempt.

Rudyard Kipling
A Book of Words

XVIII

The Poet's World

Wherever a man opens his eyes on the world as a poet, he is stricken into expression of its wonder, its abundance and beauty, its lawful variety, or its vigorous astonishments. This feeling makes the poet. It may be cruelty or waste that astonishes him, but he knows these things for their equalizing weight in the scales of life. Or it may be patterns in the snowflake or the whirlwind he sees; or the recurrence of human hope alternating with human chaos; a river of time bringing wreckage past his look-out, then ships steering under their own power. But it is always as if he comes to his native land a stranger. Everything cries for his attention, and he sees what is perfect of its kind—perfectly good or perfectly bad. Because he has never seen it before, it has never been seen.

Chaucer had that fresh pleasure in life, and we may believe he spoke for himself when he made the Wife of Bath say, "It tikleth me unto my herte rote that I have had my world as in my tyme." Shakespeare had it; Hamlet was one of many who said for him, "This brave o'erhanging firmament." George Herbert felt it when he wrote

The starres have us to bed,
Night draws the curtain, which the sunne withdraws;
Musick and light attend our head,
All things unto our flesh are kinde
In their descent and being; to our minde
In their ascent and cause.

Keats, Donne, Pepys (he had the poet's eagerness) and Browning, and Hopkins, all relished life and the world, in its wholeness and in its infinite parts, writing with a capacity for excitement beyond that of most men.

When the poet tries to set down his vivid sense of his world, he may either chant the catalogue of its glories, or cry out its pains, or soar in a brief lyric concentration of the one loveliest moment of time. If he chants, then he piles up, like Chaucer, or Whitman, or Brooke, the bounty he has inherited. At the highest pitch is the "Song to David" by Christopher Smart. If he turns his wonder to pure song, he cries like Gerard Manley Hopkins, "Look, look up at the skies!" or like Emily Dickinson he catches up the little things of earth in a breathless run of words with a fierce light on them. Robinson Jeffers, standing a long way off from mankind, in his compassion says, "You making haste haste on decay: not blame-worthy; life is good, be it stubbornly long or suddenly a mortal splendor: meteors are not needed less than mountains: shine, perishing republic." And the spirit of exaltation always smoulders, always ready to break into fire. When a well-meaning friend asked Blake, "When the sun rises, do you not see a round disk of fire something like a guinea?" he said, "Oh no, I see an immeasurable company of the heavenly host crying Holy Holy Holy is the Lord God Almighty."

The poet sees in all things the extra dimension of time. Whatever his eye falls on is passing by, and he knows it; he snatches at it with words, never reconciled to its passing, yet delighting in its onward show. English poetry is full of this haste, of Housman's "Take my hand quick and tell me." It has been so ever since the unknown Anglo-Saxon wrote of life, the bird, flying from the night and storm into the bright banquet-hall, where song and fire glow, and flying out again into the night. But the poet feels the excitement more than the sadness of such a swift passing. He stares, he touches, he runs to meet, and in imagination throws himself into other lives, and can never get enough. There crowds into his mind an awareness of all that goes on in any moment of time, with him or away from him, so that in poetry he takes a long look forward and back into time and across the world.

There also brims in him the love of things for their own sake: the taste of food, the feeling of air on the skin, the sound of voices, the look of trees in their straightness, and the changes of light and weather on roads, houses, hills, and the faces of men and women. The weight of tools and weapons, the crash of surf, man's brave architecture lifting roofs under heaven, the smell of rain, and the ring of bells—he loves these, and a thousand other reasons for not dying.

But the poet is not always in the mood to see or exult over light and abundance. Whatever it is that poets are made of, it is partly salt. Living is sometimes despair and loss, and the black hour comes when one cannot rejoice. At another hour corrective satire breaks from poets harried and angered by the difference between man's behavior and man's ideals. They strike to protect the life they cherish. Yet the anger comes from the same man, and the same source in the man, which is his intensity of consciousness. Either way the poet sees his world, his work is to write down what he sees, and it is this way, says Vernon

Lee, "being the response to man's organized and unceasing cravings for strength, clearness, order, dignity and sweetness, for a life intenser and more harmonious, that what man writes comes to be greater than what man is."

But there is always at bottom that earthy pleasure in anything good of its kind; it makes any experience vivid. The poet's range seems to be several octaves more in either direction than the ordinary instrument, and, like a concert piano, he is tuned a half-note higher for brilliant performance. He may have a vision as vast as Milton's of lost paradise, or he may see with Blake the world in a grain of sand. He may, like Ralph Hodgson, "hear the whole harmonious hymn of being roll," or like Chaucer he may simply be enormously amused by the perfection of charlatanism in the wily Pardoner—the perfect rascal. The poet needs only these representative bits of life to make him remember all they stand for. At once he sees the clean thrust of the blow struck, and feels the pain of the one who falls under the blow. He gets the satisfaction the striker gets, physically, and at the same time he rouses to indignation for the defeated, beaten without cause and hopeless of striking back. The poet may not take sides, one or the other; the poet takes both sides, all sides. That is the work he knows he has to do.

When in the world one side or the other would conscript the poet in its service, arguing that it is his duty, saying

> And now we hear
> All day in the dark stairway of the blood
> Rebellion climbing to that little room,
> The heart, there to demand great reckoning.
> We wait. We welcome one event so taut
> That action beats upon it like a drum,

then the poet, whose work it is to watch the world's oppositions and victories and surrenders, will reply,

Poetry runs to help that sharp tattoo,
But all for its relish in the ultimate,
To stretch itself in storm; as poetry would
To be there first where time with streaming flags
Declares new boundaries; as poetry would
To marvel at a green tree wound with sun,
To see a young man live almost unscarred,
Mature in danger, passionate for peace,
Who wears flesh tight about his bones and bright,
His breath too quick for strangling, and his will,
With caring for his generation, harsh.
Poetry serves the living; rounds one hope
Or all; gives grace, and sweeps that grace with light;
Reminds all men that Time with sliding step,
And Death with sudden stride, walk at their heels.
But gives, warns, glorifies, in freedom best.
Poetry flashes, cries, contends, rides hard.
Poetry rings right, marvels, summons to life
The soldier thoughts in arms lain down to sleep.
But these: the bonfire burning in the rain,
The moment made of light, the harvesters,
The longed-for dead; all these are poetry.
And these: blind skull, blue wind, persistent love,
And change, and memory, and grief: all these.
The world is one to poetry: the hawk
That hovers marking down its prey, plunges,
And strikes, is ignorant of county names.

Someone has said that the sixth sense is an awareness of the gods, and the seventh a skill in nonsense. An eighth may be memory. To a highly sensitive set of the more usual five, the poet adds these, and some others. One of the others is a sense for words. Another is the sense of significance, which is the sense that makes representative bits of life enough to work with. The poet works also with the sense of space, an airman's sight of the particular piece of cosmos or geography where the poet stands. The sight may be double and simultaneous. The sense of time, the sense of structure, the sense of truth, also reveal the world to the poet, and bring the world straighter into his poem. But the sense of delight, or wonder, or strangeness, whatever it may be named, somehow quickens all these. It is not necessarily pleasure, but it is always aliveness. The sense of wonder is the eye, so to speak, that lets life into the mind, the heart, the bone. The sense of wonder emphasizes with Blake's "bounding line and its infinite inflections and movements" all his sensual and intellectual experience. The sense of wonder is the beginning of poetry.

It is first necessary to see the world through the poet's eyes and get some understanding of this sense, if we are to know what makes his work definite and different. The secret lies in a special consciousness of existence. The poet knows that he is. The poet knows who he is. The poet knows where he is. He is alive in time and space, the newest member of earth's miraculous voyage. He is acutely aware of the precarious exact crossing of his native latitude and longitude, and of where to lay his hand upon the subtle knot that makes him man. He stands there open to the four seasons and the twelve winds; his eyes are wide, his ears are keen, he feels earth hard under the heel, and the blood rich in his body, and he writes his poetry.

My Heart in Hiding Stirred

It is now five of the clock, and the sun is going apace on his journey: and fie sluggards, who would be asleep: the bells ring to prayer, and the streets are full of people, and the highways stored with travelers: the scholars are up and going to school, and the rods ready for the truants' correction: the maids are at milking, and the servants at plough, and the wheel goes merrily while the mistress is by: the capons and the chickens must be served without door, and the hogs cry till they have their swill: the shepherd is almost gotten to his fold, and the herd begins to blow his horn through the town. The blind fiddler is up with his dance and song, and the alehouse door is unlocked for good fellows: the hounds begin to cry after the hare, and horse and foot follow after the cry: the traveler is now well on his way, and if the weather be fair, he walks with the better cheer: the carter merrily whistles to his horse, and the boy with his sling casts stones at the crows: the lawyer now begins to look at his case, and if he give good counsel, he is worthy of his fee. . . .

Nicholas Breton
The Fantasticks

Strange the world about me lies,
Never yet familiar grown;
Still disturbs me with surprise,
Haunts me with a face half-known.

William Watson
"World-Strangeness"

The world of girls' beautiful faces, bodies, and clothes, quiet afternoons, graceful birds, great words, tearful music, mind-joying poetry, beautiful livings, loved things, known things: a to-be-used and known and pleasure-to-be-giving world.

Eli Siegel, "Hot Afternoons Have Been In Montana"
***Prize Poems* 1913-1929**

The world is a dream, O Finn. The world is a dream of our hearts. We can make it and mould it, O captain, according to the shape of our will. With truth, with courage and love, hard it would be not to triumph. And if we are broken at last, the world is a dream, O Finn.

Where we loved we are one. We are only what we have remembered. The wave of Rughraidhe lashing the shore, the lowing of oxen in Maghmaoin, the seagull's scream in distant Iorrus. The murmur of the streams in Sliabh Mis, the yell of the hounds at Drumlis, the noise of the fawns round Sliabh gCua. The hound's deep bay at twilight's fall and the barque's sharp grating on the shore. For where we have loved we are one.

Darrell Figgis
The Return of the Hero

One star fell, and another, as we walked.
Lifting his hand toward the west, he said—
How prodigal that sky is of its stars.
They fall and fall, and still the sky is sky.
Two more have gone, but heaven is heaven still.

Let us be reckless of our words and worlds,
And spend them freely as the tree his leaves;
And give them where the giving is most blest.
What should we save them for—a night of frost?
All lost for nothing, and ourselves a ghost.

Conrad Aiken, LVII
Preludes for Memnon

The spell of arms and voices: the white arms of roads, their promise of close embraces, and the black arms of ships that stand against the moon, their tale of distant nations. They are held out to say: we are alone—come.

James Joyce
Portrait of the Artist as a Young Man

It was but some days ago
When for my love and me, earth as of old
Made a green bed and drenched the air with gold,
And to our leaping pulse opposed her slow
Antiphony.

Shaemas O'Sheel
"Landscape With Figures 1850"

You never enjoy the world aright, till the Sea itself floweth in your veins, till you are clothed with the heavens, and crowned with the stars: and perceive yourself to be sole heir of the world, and more than so, because men are in it who are every one sole heirs as well as you.

Thomas Traherne
"Centuries of Meditation"

When all we are is cut and set
Two crystals in Death's bracelet;
When all we have lies curved together
On God's long wing, like feather and feather,
It's probable that we'll forget
Climate and cloud and earth and weather.

Before we are dissolved in Light,
Or moulded motionless, on Flight,
Let us minutely move together,
Piteously promising one another,
Ecstatic midge and passionate mite—
To worship earth and relish weather.

Winifred Welles
"Song Before Entering Paradise Forever"
Blossoming Antlers

Till your spirit filleth the whole world, and the stars are your jewels; till you are as familiar with the ways of God in all Ages as with your walk and table: till you are intimately acquainted with that shady nothing out of which the world was made: till you love men so as to desire their happiness, with a thirst equal to the zeal of your own: till you delight in God for being so good to all: you never enjoy the world. Till you more feel it than your private estate, and are more present in the hemisphere, considering the beauties and the glories there, than in your own house: Till you remember how lately you were made, and how wonderful it was when you came into it: and more rejoice in the palace of your glory, than if it had been made today morning.

Thomas Traherne
"Centuries of Meditation"

I saw Eternity the other night
Like a great ring of pure and endless light,
All calm it was and bright;
And round it, Time, in hours, days, years,
Driven by the spheres,
Like a vast shadow moved, in which the world
And all her train were hurled.

Henry Vaughan
"The World"

From the beginning, it has been native to all poets and prophets. It is a condition dependent upon one thing alone—a mood of wonder, childlike in its freshness. What is man's great privilege, his exceptional experience? Consciousness and again consciousness, and it is in a passionate imaginative consciousness our true rewards are to be won.

Llewelyn Powys
Now That the Gods are Dead

Rightly to perceive a thing, in all the fulness of its qualities, is really to create it. So, on perfect holidays, you recreate the world and sign on again as a pleased and enthusiastic member of the great airship's company.

C. E. Montague
The Right Place

I hold him happiest
Who, before going quickly whence he came,
Hath looked ungrieving on these majesties,
The world-wide sun, the stars, waters, and clouds
And fire. Live, Parmeno, a hundred years
Or a few weeks, these thou wilt always see,
And never, never, any greater thing.

Menander

Shakespeare, too, does not look at a thing, but into it, through it; so that he constructively comprehends it, can take it asunder and put it together again; the thing melts, as it were, into light under his eye, and anew creates itself before him. That is to say, he is a Poet. For Goethe, as for Shakespeare, the world lies all translucent, all fusible we might call it, encircled with wonder; the Natural in reality the Supernatural, for to the seer's eyes both become one.

Thomas Carlyle
"Goethe"

Look thy last on all things lovely
Every hour. Let no night
Seal thy sense in deathly slumber
  Till to delight
Thou have paid thy utmost blessing;
Since that all things thou wouldst praise

Beauty took from those who loved them
In other days.

Walter de la Mare, "Farewell"
Motley and Other Poems

I am always struck by the centrality of the observer's position. He always stands fronting the middle of the arch and does not suspect at first that a thousand hills behold the sunset sky from equally favorable positions.

Henry David Thoreau
Journals

Lord! What a stir Stankes makes, with his being crowded in the streets, and wearied walking in London, and would not be wooed to go to a play, nor to Whitehall, or to see the Lions, though he were carried in a coach. I never could have thought there had been on earth a man so little curious in the world as he is.

Samuel Pepys
Diary

The coolness of sheets, the warmth of blankets, the look of the little blue flames dancing on the top of a fire of hard coal, the taste of bread, or milk, or honey, or wine or of oil, of well-baked potatoes, or earth-tasting turnips! —the taste of the airs, dry or moist, that blow in through our opened windows, the look of the night-sky, the sounds of twilight or of dawn, the hoarse monotone of a distant pine-wood or of pebble-fretted waves—all these things as one feels them are materials, eternal and yet fleeting, of the art of being alive upon the earth.

John Cowper Powys
The Meaning of Culture

This day and May 11 (1871) the bluebells in the little wood between the College and the highroad and in one of the Hurst Green cloughs. In the little wood, opposite the light, they stood in blackish spreads or sheddings like the spots on a snake. The heads are then like thongs and solemn in grain and grape-color. But in the clough, through the light, they came in falls of sky-colour washing the brows and slacks of the ground with vein-blue, thickening at the double, vertical themselves and the young grass and brake fern combed vertical, but the brake struck the upright of all this with light winged transomes. It was a lovely sight. The bluebells in your hand baffle you with their inscape, made to every sense: if you draw your fingers through them they are lodged and struggle with a shock of wet heads; the long stalks rub and click and flatten to a fan on one another like your fingers across themselves would when you passed the palms hard across one another, making a brittle rub and jostle like the noise of a hurdle strained by leaning against; then there is the faint honey smell and in the mouth the sweet gum when you bite them. But this is easy, it is the eye they baffle. They give one a fancy of panpipes and of some wind instrument with stops—a trombone perhaps. The overhung necks—for growing they are little more than a staff with a simple crook but in water, where they stiffen, they take stronger turns, in the head like sheephooks or, when more waved throughout, like the waves riding through a ship that is being smacked—what with these overhung necks and what with the crisped ruffled bells dropping mostly on one side and the gloss these have at their footstalks they have an air of the knights at chess.

Gerard Manley Hopkins, "Journal"
Notebooks and Papers

I am living this 27th day of June, 1847—a dull cloudy day and no sun shining. The clink of the smith's hammer sounds feebly over the roofs, and the wind is sighing gently as if dreaming of cheerfuller days. The farmer is ploughing in yonder fields, craftsmen are busy in the shops, the trader stands up in the counter, and all works go steadily forward.

Henry David Thoreau
Journals

Aug. 27—A day when all things are ours and possible, when things to write about, characters to interpret, stand out as clear as the dark still spruces against the bluest of blue skies.

Ruth Blodgett
Unpublished Notebooks

Life falls away from people who neglect
To seek its marvels; early are destroyed
The wilful stupid and the wilful blind.

Helene Mullins, "Now Learn, O Cynic"
Streams from the Source

It is candle light. The fishes leap, the meadows sparkle with the coppery light of fire-flies. The evening star, multiplied by undulating water, is like bright sparks of fire continually ascending.

Henry David Thoreau
Journals

From my western balcony-window, I watched the light
Deepen under solid leaves along the hill
And under ledges I had never seen
On the mountain-range and sharpen the sides of boats . . .

And so it had been under my ribs with music
And with wine, a lovely deepening of the light
A body carries on its own small hill:
I laughed aloud, joining bright earth with earth.

Witter Bynner, "Dawn"
Indian Earth

I caught this morning morning's minion, Kingdom of daylight's dauphin, dapple-dawn-drawn Falcon, in his riding
Of the rolling level underneath him steady air, and striding
High there, how he rung upon the rein of a wimpling wing
In his ecstasy! Then off, off forth on swing,
As a skate's heel sweeps smooth on a bow-bend: the hurl and gliding
Rebuffed the big wind. My heart in hiding
Stirred for a bird,—the achieve of, the mastery of the thing!

Gerard Manley Hopkins, "The Windhover"
Poems

The true spirit of delight, the exaltation, the sense of being more than man, which is the touchstone of the highest excellence, is to be found in mathematics as surely as in poetry. Real life is to most men a long second-best, a perpetual compromise between the ideal and the possible; but the world of pure reason knows no compromise, no practical limitations, no barrier to creative activity.

Bertrand Russell, "The Study of Mathematics"
Philosophical Essays

Sing now the birds: on every bough a bird sings;
Slowly at first, then fast and faster,

Till the walled garden thrills and shrills with music:
The cricket beneath the violet aster

Cries his joy to heaven as the first beam strikes him—
The foxgloves bend beneath a weight of bees;
Praise! Praise! Praise! the chorus rises;
Drowsily, happily, dumbly sway the trees.

Conrad Aiken
The Pilgrimage of Festus

Eternity was manifest in the Light of the Day, and sometimes infinite behind everything appeared: which talked with my expectation, and moved my desire. The city seemed to stand in Eden, or to be built in Heaven. The streets were mine, the temple was mine, the people were mine, their clothes and gold and silver were mine, as much as their sparkling eyes, fair skins and ruddy faces. The skies were mine, and so were the sun and moon and stars, and all the world was mine; and I the only spectator and enjoyer of it.

Thomas Traherne
"Centuries of Meditation"

I put my ear to one of the posts, and it seemed as if every pore of the wood was filled with music, labored with the strain—as if every fibre was affected and being seasoned or timed, rearranged according to a new and more harmonious law. Every swell and change or inflection of tone pervaded and seemed to proceed from the wood, the divine tree or wood, perchance—to keep it from rotting—to fill its pores with music!

Henry David Thoreau
Journals

Within, by a wildfire cedar-lit,
my fine green villains clasp their violins.

there was no lack of brilliant light. Our music
rose. There was the winding of the forest-horn,
and troubles, all that troop with music, raught us.

Eric Schroeder
"The Winter Palace"

The heavens opened for the sunset tonight. When I had thought the day folded and sealed, came a burst of heavenly bright petals. I sat behind the window, pricked with rain, and looked until that hard thing in my breast melted and broke into the smallest fountain, murmuring as aforetime, and I drank the sky and the whisper.

Katherine Mansfield
Journals

Look at the stars! Look, look up at the skies!
O look at all the fire-folk sitting in the air!
The bright boroughs, the circle-citadels there!
Down in dim woods the diamond delves! the elves'-eyes!
The grey lawns cold where gold, where quick-gold lies!
Wind-beat white beam; airy abeles set on a flare!
Flake-doves sent floating forth at a farmyard scare!

Gerard Manley Hopkins, "The Starlight Night"
Poems

In his loneliness and fixedness he yearneth toward the journeying Moon, and the stars that still sojourn, yet still move onward; and everywhere the blue sky belongs to them, and is their appointed rest and their native country and their own natural home, which they enter unannounced, as lords that are certainly expected, and yet there is a silent joy at their arrival.

Samuel Taylor Coleridge
Prose Argument to *The Ancient Mariner*

The Horned Violet is a pretty thing, gracefully lashed. Even in withering the flower ran through beautiful inscapes by the screwing up of the petals into straight little barrels or tubes. It is not that inscape does not govern the behaviour of things in slack and decay as one can see even in the pining of the skin in the old and even in a skeleton but that horror prepossesses the mind, but in this case there was nothing in itself to shew even whether the flower were shutting or opening.

Gerard Manley Hopkins, "Journal 1871"
Notebooks and Papers

To mount a hill is to lift with you something lighter and brighter than yourself or than any meaner burden. You lift the world, you raise the horizon; you give a signal for the distance to stand up. It is like the scene in the Vatican when a Cardinal, with his dramatic Italian hands, bids the kneeling groups arise. He does more than bid them. He lifts them, he gathers them up, far and near, with the upward gesture of his expressive force. Or it is as when a conductor takes his players to successive heights of music. You summon the sea, you bring the mountains, the distances unfold unlooked-for wings and take an even flight. You are but a man lifting his weight on the upward road, but as you climb the circle of the world goes up to face you.

Alice Meynell
The Spirit of Place

I got up the mountain edge, and from the top saw the world stretcht out—cornlands and forest, the river winding among meadow-flats, and right off, like a hem of the sky, the moving sea, with snatches of foam, and large ships reaching forward, out-bound. And then I thought no more, but my heart leapt to meet the wind, and I ran, and ran. I felt my legs under me, I felt the wind buffet me, hit me on the cheek; the sun shone, the bees swept past me singing; and I too sang, shouted, World, World, I am coming!

Maurice Hewlett
Pan and the Young Shepherd

This light is the very flush of spring; it is innocent and
 warm;
It is gentle as celestial rain; it is mellow as gold;
Its pure effulgence may unbind the form
Of a blossoming tree; it may quicken fallow mould.

This light is various and strange; its luminous hue
May transmute the bleakest dust to silver snow;
Its radiance may be caught within a pool, a bead of dew;
It may contract to the sheerest point; it may arch to a bow.

This light is heaven's transcendent boon, a beam
Of infinite calm; it will never cease;
It will illuminate forever the aether-stream;
This light alone can lead me to peace.

Theodore Roethke
"This Light"

What is marvellous? what is impossible or vague? after you have just once opened the space of a peach-pit and given audience to the far and near and to the sunset and had all things enter with electric swiftness softly and duly without confusion or jostling or jam.

Walt Whitman
Preface to *Leaves of Grass,* 1855

First saw the Northern Lights. My eye was caught by beams of light and dark very like the crown of horny rays the sun makes behind a cloud. At first I thought of silvery cloud until I saw that these were more luminous and did not dim the clearness of the stars in the Bear. They rose slightly radiating thrown out from the earthline. Then I saw soft pulses of light one after another rise and pass upwards arched in shape but waveringly and with the arch broken. They seemed to float, not following the warp of the sphere as falling stars look to do but free though concentrical with it. This busy working of nature wholly independent of the earth and seeming to go on in a strain of time not reckoned by our reckoning of days and years but simpler and as if correcting the preoccupation of the world by being preoccupied with and appealing to and dated to the day of judgement was like a new witness to God and filled me with delightful fear.

Gerard Manley Hopkins, "Journal 1870"
Notebooks and Papers

How silent, how spacious, with room for all, yet without place to insert an atom—in graceful succession, in equal fulness, in balanced beauty, the dance of the hours goes forward still. Like an odor of incense, like a strain of music, like a sleep, it is inexact and boundless. It will not be dissected, nor unravelled, nor shown.

Ralph Waldo Emerson, "Nature"
Conduct of Life

Nevertheless it is the eve. Let us accept all inflows of vigor and real tenderness. And at dawn, armed with an eager patience, we shall enter splendid towns.

Rimbaud
Une Saison en Enfer

The light in her beautiful, formal room was dim, though it would do, as everything would always do; the hot wind had kept out lamps, but there was a pair of clusters of candles that glimmered over the chimney-piece like the tall tapers of an altar. The windows were all open, their redundant hangings swaying a little, and he heard once more, from the empty court, the small plash of the fountain. From beyond this, and as from a great distance—beyond the court, beyond the *corps de logis* forming the front—came, as if excited and exciting, the vague voice of Paris. Strether had all along been subject to sudden gusts of fancy in connection with such matters as these—odd starts of the historical sense, suppositions and divinations with no warrant but their intensity. Thus and so, on the eve of great recorded dates, the days and nights of revolution, the sounds had come in, the omens, the beginnings broken out.

Henry James
The Ambassadors

We do not commonly live our life out to the full; we do not fill all our pores with our blood; we do not inspire and expire fully and entirely enough, so that the wave, the comber of each inspiration shall break upon our extremest shores, rolling till it meets the sea which bounds us, and the sound of the surf comes back to us. Might not a bellows assist us to breathe? That our breathing should create a wind on a calm day! We live but a fraction of our life. Why do we not let on the flood, raise the gates, and set all our wheels in motion? He that hath ears to hear, let him hear.

Henry David Thoreau
Journals

XIX

The Poet's Nature

Any description of the poet as human being, or as poet, for that matter, must indicate his inclusiveness. Though his range is widely extensive and deeply intensive, he springs to attention at any border, at any level. He can be Hamlet, or Falstaff. He can be Macduff, as Whitman meant when he said that he, too, "knitted the old knot of contrariety, had guile, lust, hot wishes I dared not speak, was wayward, vain, greedy, shallow." But there is also John Keats, "happy as a man can be . . . with the yearning passion I have for the beautiful, connected and made one with the ambition of my intellect," and there is William Butler Yeats, "blest by everything, everything I look upon is blest," in one mood, or in another "timid, entangled, empty and abashed." Crosland thrusts forward his "furious wise will and heart of stone," and D. H. Lawrence cries out his passionate conviction that, "My great religion is a belief in the blood!" Sir Thomas Browne had "all Africa and her prodigies" in him. Conrad Aiken bids his readers with him "laugh with fool's delight that heavenly folly made the world so bright."

The poet, Bliss Perry once said, has always been *"genus irritable"*—the irritable kind. But not, of course, in the ordinary sense. He is easily irritated—that is, easily stirred, awaked, roused into words; quickly made glad; often driven to excesses of impatience, anger, exaltation, love, terror. John Donne must have the soul descend to affections, "else a great Prince in prison lies"; and Shakespeare marks "the expense of spirit in a waste of shame"; Masefield remembers as most poets do that "man with his burning soul has but an hour of breath"; Emerson walks across Cambridge Common, "glad almost to the brink of fear"; and Katherine Mansfield in the grimness of grief writes in her journal, "Today I am hardening my heart. I am walking all around my heart and building up the defences"; Keats feels "an awful warmth about my heart like a load of immortality." All these, poured out though they are extravagantly on the page, are not a fraction of the poet's capacity and variety. There was Milton, who knew the courts of heaven, and Villon, who knew the alleys of Paris. Chaucer rode down to Canterbury with priests, shipmen, millers, knights, and nuns; George Herbert lived in the retirement of a country parish and his mother's house. Blake was mad. Or was he sane? And Alexander Pope was very sane.

"Not only poems, but songs, snatches, and raptures of a flaming spirit," said a seventeenth-century writer, of the psalms of David. It is the heat of the blood that differentiates the poet. It was clever of Oscar Wilde to say that several drinks of whiskey can produce an effect very similar to intoxication. But in one of the finest of short poems in English, James Thomson says, "He reeleth with his own heart, that great rich vine."

And it is not an accident that the poet is articulate; sometimes one feels that writers of all kinds have an unfair advantage over the rest of the world, because they can get a hearing for their pains and joys; as if no one else felt pain and joy at all. Sometimes this deludes the poet into the smugness of naming himself the voice of the silent, self-elected. But the special quality of the poet begins with the involuntary voice. With such a necessity laid on him, seeing as he does a golden outline that defines everything between himself and the sun, he may not silence the sense of vivid life in himself. It beats and surges into a declaration of being, an emphatic I Am: the world was thus when I was in it—active, growing, decaying, complex, passionate, pitiful, miraculous. It is simply that a current passes through his body; sometimes it convulses him with its enormous voltage, but more often he is a good conductor, pure metal, and passes on the flow of life to later times and other men. Poetry for this (figurative) reason is dangerous to read, like touching a bare wire, for people who are afraid of the life in the wires.

Because the drift of days seldom makes the average man shiver and glow with the sudden shock of the whole meaning of life, he feels in the unusual behavior of the poet something deplorable, because it is unusual. The average man has also had unpleasant experience of the poet of mixed baser metal, the imperfect conductor of the current. But the real poet is a norm for mankind: In the quality of his living the man all would wish to be. T. W. H. Crosland reminds us of the old falsehood that a writer of poems, especially of sonnets, is a person in precarious health, or of abnormal behavior. But, he says, as a matter of fact, the great poets "are not only the sanest people in the world, but physically and temperamentally the toughest." Men and women weak in body and nerves burn out after a little of the current has passed through them; they cannot stand it. But in the great spirits, such as Shakespeare, Goethe, Dante, Chaucer, or Yeats, there is a calmness and a confident strength. They are in accord with the force flowing through them; there is room enough in them, and there are no obstructions.

But metaphors are a view from one side. To speak of poets as good conductors is to imply passive reception and release; the figure is not the whole truth. This is because the poet also imparts a special quality to the life flowing through him, so that it is changed by the passage. One element of this change is the new rhythm that he gives to the stream of life. It has been his study to discover his special inner rhythm; all life that enters his perception beats thereafter to that unmistakable vibration. He also colors the life he feels with his powerful affection for it, which is another sort of change. Proust, though not a versifier, transmitted his sense of life colored by caring over the detail of every scene and hour, reluctant to be called away even to the next hour and the following episode. It may be that a sharp sense of the appalling limits of time is what makes the poets wish to linger and intensify. But after all, the poet is one who, because he feels in the air time rushing by, knows more than most about it, and has power over it. He can stop time. By his passionately scrupulous examination of one moment, he can recreate it as it is and let it go, knowing as Wycliffe knew that "word, wynde, and mannes mind is full short, but letter written dwelleth." The poet, who can free all men as well as himself from time, loves what he writes of, and writes of what he loves. If he protests, if he mourns, if he hates, and writes about that, his love is not far; it is that powerful affection thwarted of which he speaks. And to a certain extent he loves the hateful thing, if only it has life in it. "As to the poetic character itself," wrote Keats in a letter, "it lives in gusto, be it foul or fair, high or low, rich or poor, mean or elevated—it has as much delight in conceiving an Iago as an Imogen."

Wherever the poet stands, the hills and houses and the thinking of mankind center on him like the spokes of a wheel or the threads of a spider's web. He looks out in every direction with as fresh an excitement as if the world had never been thrust upon the eyes of men till then. This is a mad conviction, but it is the key to the mystery, what Goethe calls "the open secret," open to all, seen by almost none. It never occurs to him not to dare say what he sees; to him it is an overwhelming wonder that he is there at all, and it seems only natural that so placed he should communicate his astonishment and delight. This confidence is an element of genius, but every poet shares it. He feels a kind of godhead; not egotistic assumption, but the fulness of life and his nearness to the source. In vision he has space and time for latitude, as well as such intense apprehension that the commonplace is miraculous and the near-at-hand a wonder fetched home for his pleasure. Wherever the scale of things seems meager to him, because the gods were tired, or daylight not illumination enough, he heightens through his own creativeness the proportions, and he focuses a single beam of light which the sun shall not dim by going down. When natural music is faint to the ears of mankind, the poet magnifies it. Gaps in the created order are his to fill, or at the least to foresee; and the future, however impenetrable a curtain it seems to drop between it and ourselves, is his to prophesy. To do these things: to sharpen, to re-enforce, to heighten, to prophesy, is to exercise his highest power, that of creator.

The Man Aware of Himself

Here was a task as great as the world. And he who stood before it and beheld it was unknown and struggling under the necessity of earning his bread. He was quite alone, and if he had been a real dreamer, he would have dreamed a deep and beautiful dream—one of those long, long dreams in which a life would pass like a day. But this young man who worked in the factory at Sèvres was a dreamer whose dream rose in his hands, and he began immediately its realization. He sensed where he had to begin. A quietude which was in him showed him the wise road. Here already Rodin's deep harmony with nature revealed itself; that harmony which the poet George Rodenbach calls an elemental power. And, indeed, it is an underlying patience in Rodin which renders him so great; a silent, superior forbearance resembling the wonderful patience and kindness of Nature that begins creation with a trifle in order to proceed silently and steadily toward abundant consummation. Rodin did not presume to create the tree in its full growth. He began with the seed beneath the earth as it were. And this seed grew downward, sunk deep its roots and anchored them before it began to shoot upward in the form of a young sprout. This required time, time that lengthened into years. "One must not hurry," said Rodin to the few friends who gathered about him, in answer to their urgence.

Rainer Maria Rilke
Auguste Rodin

I am not a liberal, not a conservative, not a believer in gradual progress, not a monk, not an indifferentist. I should like to be a free artist and nothing more. I regard trade-marks and labels as a superstition. My holy of holies is the human body, health, intelligence, talent, inspiration, love, and the most absolute freedom—freedom from violence and lying, whatever forms they may take. This is the program I would follow if I were an artist.

Anton Chekhov
Letters

Now it appears to me that almost any man may, like the spider, spin from his own inwards his own airy citadel—the points of leaves and twigs on which the spider begins her work are few, and she fills the air with a beautiful circuiting.

John Keats
Letters

The feast of love is music,
And the wine of love is song.
When love sits down to the banquet,
Love sits long,

Sits long, and arises drunken,
But not with the feast and the wine.
He reeleth with his own heart,
That great, rich Vine.

James Thomson
"The Vine"

The great angels of annunciation create the beauty of their own real names. Who now finds Shakespeare ridiculous? And how lovely a name is Keats?

Havelock Ellis, "The Art of Writing"
The Dance of Life

The Genius of Poetry must work out its own salvation in a man: It can not be matured by law and precept, but by sensation and watchfulness in itself—that which is creative and must create itself. In Endymion, I leaped headlong into the sea, and thereby have become better acquainted with the Soundings, the quicksands, and the rocks, than if I had stayed upon the green shore, and piped a silly pipe, and took tea and comfortable advice. I was never afraid of failure; for I would sooner fail than not be among the greatest.

John Keats
Letters

Often we must entertain,
Tolerantly if we can,
Ancestors returned again
Trying to be modern man.
Gates of memory are wide;
All of them can shuffle in,
Join the family, and, once inside,
Alas, what a disturbance they begin!
Creatures of another time and mood,
They wrangle, they dictate;
Bawl their experience into brain and blood,
Call themselves Fate.

Harold Monro
Strange Meetings

A man of adequate vitality and zest will surmount all misfortunes by the emergence after each blow of an interest in life and the world which cannot be narrowed down so much as to make one loss fatal. To be defeated by one loss or even by several is not something to be admired as a proof of sensibility, but something to be deplored as a failure in vitality. All our affections are at the mercy of death, which may strike down those whom we love at any moment. It is therefore necessary that our lives should not have that narrow intensity which puts the whole meaning and purpose of our life at the mercy of an accident.

Bertrand Russell
The Conquest of Happiness

Joy is man's passage from a lesser to a greater perfection.

Spinoza, "The Origin and Nature of the Emotions"
Ethics

Look thou within: within thee is the fountain of good, and it will ever spring, if thou wilt ever delve.

Marcus Aurelius

My great religion is a belief in the blood, the flesh, as being wiser than the intellect. We can go wrong in our minds. But what our blood feels and believes and says, is always true. The intellect is only a bit and a bridle. What do I care about knowledge? All I want is the answer to my blood, direct, without fribbling intervention of mind, or moral, or whatnot. I conceive a man's body as a kind of flame, like a candle-flame, forever upright and yet flowing: and the intellect is just the light that is shed on to the things around. And I am not so much concerned with the things around—which is really mind—but with the mystery of the flame forever flowing, coming God knows how from out of practically nowhere, and being itself, whatever there is around it, that lights it up. We have got so ridiculously mindful, that we never know that we ourselves are anything—we think there are only the objects we shine upon. And there the poor flame goes on burning ignored, to produce this light. And instead of chasing the mystery in the fugitive, half-lighted things outside us, we ought to look at ourselves, and say, "My God, I am Myself!"

D. H. Lawrence
Letters

Come, said my soul,
Such verses for my body let us write, (for we are one)

That should I after death invisibly return,
Or, long, long hence, in other spheres,
There to some group of mates the chants resuming,
(Tallying earth's soil, trees, winds, tumultuous waves,)
Ever with pleased smile I may keep on,
Ever and ever yet the verses owning—as, first, I here and
now,
Signing for soul and body, set to them my name.

Walt Whitman
Invocation to *Leaves of Grass*

I believe I can tell the particular little chances that filled my head first with such chimes of verse, as have never since left ringing there; for I remember, when I began to read, and to take some pleasure in it, there was wont to lie in my mother's parlor (I know not by what accident, for she herself never in her life read any book but of devotion) but there was wont to lie Spenser's works. This I happened to fall upon, and was infinitely delighted with the stories of the knights, and giants, and monsters, and brave houses, which I found everywhere there (though my understanding had little to do with all this) and by degrees, with the tinkling of the rhyme and dance of the numbers; so that, I think, I had read him all over before I was twelve years old, and was thus made a poet.

Abraham Cowley
"Of Myself"

Ah! but verses amount to so little when one begins to write them young. One ought to wait and gather sense and sweetness a whole life long, and a long life is possible, and then, quite at the end, one might perhaps be able to write ten good lines. For verses are not, as people imagine, simple feelings (we have these soon enough); they are experiences. In order to write a single verse, one must see many cities, and men and things; one must know animals and the flight of birds, and the gestures that the little flowers make when they open out in the morning. One must be able to return in thought to roads in unknown regions, to unexpected encounters, and to partings that had been long foreseen; to days of childhood that are still indistinct, and to parents whom one had to hurt when they sought to give some pleasure which one did not understand (it would have been a pleasure to someone else); to childhood's illnesses that so strangely begin with such a number of profound and grave transformations, to days spent in rooms withdrawn and quiet, and to mornings by the sea, to the sea itself, to oceans, to nights of travel that rushed along loftily and flew with all the stars—and still it is not enough to be able to think of all this. There must be memories of many nights of love, each one unlike the others, of the screams of women in labor, and of women in childbed, light and blanched and sleeping, shutting themselves in. But one must also have been beside the dying, must have sat beside the dead in a room with open windows and with fitful noises. One must be able to forget them when they are many and one must have the immense patience to wait until they come again. For it is the memories themselves that matter. Only when they have turned to blood within us, to glance and gesture, nameless and no longer to be distinguished from ourselves—only then can it happen that in a most rare hour the first word of a poem arises in their midst and goes forth from them.

Rainer Maria Rilke
The Notebook of Malta Laurids Brigge

The man who is aware of himself is henceforward independent; and he is never bored, and life is only too short, and he is steeped through and through with a profound yet temperate happiness. He alone lives, while other people, slaves of ceremony, let life slip past them in a kind of dream. Once conform, once do what other people do because they do it, and a lethargy steals over all the finer nerves and faculties of the soul. She becomes all outer show and inward emptiness; dull, callous, and indifferent.

Virginia Woolf, "Montaigne"
The Common Reader

I have written this that you might see I have my share of the highest pleasure, and that though I may choose to pass my days alone, I shall be no solitary. The only thing that can ever affect me personally for more than one short passing day is any doubt about my powers for poetry: I seldom have any, and I look with hope to the nighing time when I shall have none. I am as happy as a man can be, with a yearning passion I have for the beautiful, connected and made one with the ambition of my intellect.

John Keats
Letters

The poet mused upon the dusky height,
  Between two stars towards night,
His purpose in his heart. I watched, a space,
  The meaning of his face:
There was the secret, fled from earth and skies,
  Hid in his grey young eyes.
My heart and all the Summer wait his choice,
  And wonder for his voice.
Who shall foretell his songs, and who aspire
  But to divine his lyre?
Sweet earth, we know thy dimmest mysteries,
  But he is lord of his.

Alice Meynell, "In Early Spring"
Poems

"Why are thy songs so short?" a bird was once asked. "Is it because thou art short of breath?"

"I have very many songs, and I should like to sing them all."

Daudet
Copied in Chekhov's *Notebook*

I do not ask of God that He should change anything in events, but that He should change me in regard to things, so that I might have the power to create my own universe about me, to govern my dreams, instead of enduring them.

Gérard de Nerval

It is essential in this world to be indifferent. Only those who are indifferent are able to see things clearly, to be just, and to work. Of course, I am only speaking of intelligent people of fine natures; the empty and selfish are indifferent anyway.

Anton Chekhov
Letters

Ah, when to the heart of man
Was it ever less than a treason
To go with the drift of things,
To yield with a grace to reason,
And bow and accept the end
Of a love or a season?

Robert Frost, "Reluctance"
A Boy's Will

It is said that a poet has died young in the breast of the most stolid. It may be contended, rather, that this (somewhat minor) bard in almost every case survives, and is the spice of life to his possessor. Justice is not done to the versatility and unplumbed childishness of man's imagination. His life from without may seem but a rude mound of mud; there will be some golden chamber at the heart of it, in which he dwells delighted; and for as dark as his pathway seems to the observer, he will have some kind of bull's eye at his belt.

R. L. Stevenson, "The Lantern-Bearers"
Across the Plains

Rave how thou wilt; unmoved, remote,
That inward presence slumbers not,
Frets out each secret from thy breast,
Gives thee no rally, pause, or rest,
Scans close thy very thoughts, lest they
Should sap his patient power away,
Answers thy wrath with peace, thy cry
With tenderest taciturnity.

Walter de la Mare, "Haunted"
The Listeners

I felt my own smile with my fingers—and lost it at once. No matter; it was certainly I who had inspired this concerted impulse of the fingers; something more than the bone was demonstrably mine, then—something called inspiration. Their impulse had depended on my inspiration, expressed by my bones, plus a reflecting machine called a mirror. I was therefore free among all these prisoners; I could disentangle myself from this snare of mirrors—they, never. I was the original, they the substitutes; I was the music, they the gramophone records.

Stella Benson
"Reflections in a Mirror"

When such as I cast out remorse
So great a sweetness flows into the breast

We must laugh and we must sing,
We are blest by everything,
Everything we look upon is blest.

William Butler Yeats
"Dialogue of Self and Soul"
The Winding Stair

The poets who describe Nature most minutely and most faithfully are not usually the great poets. That is intelligible because the poet—even the poet in the wide sense who also uses prose—is primarily the instrument of human emotion and not of scientific observation. Yet that poet possesses immense resources of strength who early in life has stored within him the minute knowledge of some field of the actual external world.

Havelock Ellis, "The Art of Writing"
The Dance of Life

Emphatically may it be said of the poet, as Shakespeare hath said of man, that "he looks before and after." He is the rock of defence for human nature; an upholder and preserver, carrying everywhere with him relationship and love. In spite of differences of soil and climate, of language and manners, of laws and customs: in spite of things silently gone out of mind, and things violently destroyed; the poet binds together by passion and knowledge the vast empire of human society, as it is spread over the whole earth, and over all time.

William Wordsworth
Preface to *Lyrical Ballads*

Earth's wheels run oiled with blood. Forget we that.
Let us lie down and dig ourselves in thought.
Beauty is yours and you have mastery.
Wisdom is mine and I have mystery.

We two will stay behind and keep our troth.
Let us forego men's minds that are brutes' natures,
Let us not sup the blood which some say nurtures,
Be we not swift with swiftness of the tigress.
Let us break ranks from those who trek from progress.
Miss we the march of this retreating world
Into old citadels that are not walled.
Let us lie out and hold the open truth.

Wilfred Owen
An early version of "Strange Meetings"
Poems

But poets, or those who imagine and express this indestructible order, are not only the authors of language and of music, of the dance and architecture and painting: they are the institutors of laws, and the founders of civil society and the inventors of the arts of life, and the teachers, who draw into a certain propinquity with the beautiful and the true that partial apprehension of the agencies of the invisible world which is called religion. Hence all original relations are allegorical, or susceptible of allegory, and like Janus have a double face of false and true. Poets, according to the circumstances of the age and nation in which they appeared were called in the earlier epochs of the world legislators or prophets: a poet essentially comprises and unites both these characters. For he not only beholds intensely the present as it is, but he beholds the future in the present, and his thoughts are the germs of the flower and the fruit of the latest time.

Percy Bysshe Shelley
Defence of Poetry

No live man is without an arbitrary passion for some experience. Indeed, the defect of many of those most scornful of poetry is not that they are strong in the practical life, but that the attachment to some single state has got the better of them. The greatly poetic differ from them only in the healthy variety of their loves, prevailing everywhere and always.

Max Eastman, "Poetic People"
The Enjoyment of Poetry

Love at the lips was touch
As sweet as I could bear;
And once that seemed too much;
I lived on air

That crossed me from sweet things,
The flow of—was it musk
From hidden grapevine springs
Down hill at dusk?

I had the swirl and ache
From sprays of honeysuckle
That when they're gathered shake
Dew on the knuckle.

I craved strong sweets, but those
Seemed strong when I was young;
The petal of the rose
It was that stung.

Now no joy but lacks salt
That is not dashed with pain
And weariness and fault;
I crave the stain

Of tears, the aftermark
Of almost too much love,
The sweet of bitter bark
And burning clove.

When stiff and sore and scarred
I take away my hand
From leaning on it hard
In grass and sand,

The hurt is not enough:
I long for weight and strength
To feel the earth as rough
To all my length.

Robert Frost, "To Earthward"
New Hampshire

It is not in his personal emotions, the emotions provoked by particular events in his life, that the poet is in any way remarkable or interesting. His particular emotions may be simple or crude or flat. The emotion in his poetry will be a very complex thing, but not with the complexity of the emotions of people who have very complex or unusual emotions in life. One error, in fact, of eccentricity in poetry is to seek for new human emotions to express; and in this search for novelty in the wrong place it discovers the perverse. The business of the poet is not to find new emotions but to use the ordinary ones and, in working them up into poetry, to express feelings which are not in actual emotions at all. And emotions which he has never experienced will serve his turn as well as those familiar to him. Consequently, we must believe that "emotion recollected in tranquillity" is an inexact formula. For it is neither emotion nor recollection nor, without distortion of meaning, tranquillity. It is a concentration, and a new thing resulting from the concentration, of a very great number of experiences which to the practical and active person would not seem to be experiences at all; it is a concentration which does not happen consciously or of deliberation. These experiences are not "recollected" and they finally unite in an atmosphere which is "tranquil" only in that it is a passive attending upon the event. Of course this is not quite the whole story. There is a great deal, in the writing of poetry, which must be conscious and deliberate. In fact, the bad poet is usually unconscious where he ought to be conscious, and conscious where he ought to be unconscious.

T. S. Eliot, "Tradition and the Individual Talent"
Selected Essays 1917-1932

The mass of men are very unpoetic, yet that Adam that names things is always a poet.

Henry David Thoreau
Journals

So long as a man likes the splashing of a fish, he is a poet; but when he knows that the splashing is nothing but the chase of the weak by the strong, he is a thinker; but when he does not understand what sense there is in the chase, or what use the equilibrium which results from destruction, he is becoming silly and dull, as he was when he was a child.

Anton Chekhov
Notebooks

Poets—the best of them, are a very chameleonic race; they take the color not only of what they feed on, but of the very leaves under which they pass.

Percy Bysshe Shelly
Letters

As to the poetic character itself (I mean that sort, of which, if I am anything, I am a member; that sort distinguished from the Wordsworthian or egotistical sublime), it is not itself—it has no self—it is everything and nothing—it has no character—it enjoys light and shade—it lives in gusto, be it foul or fair, high or low, rich or poor, mean or elevated—it has as much delight in conceiving an Iago as an Imogen. A poet is the most unpoetical of anything in existence, because he has no identity; he is constantly in for, and filling, some other body.

John Keats
Letters

What is the poet's ecstasy? A flying.
The soul, unjessed, darts upward, crying, crying,
The spirit flowing and the body drying.

There in a country where no self can blind it,
The soul goes flying with no past behind it
And neither friend nor enemy can find it.

Eileen Duggan, "Ecstasy"
Poems

David's Psalms are not only poems but songs, snatches and raptures of a flaming spirit. And this indeed I observe to the honour of poets; I never found them covetous or scrapingly base. The Jews had not two such kings in all their catalogue, as Salomon and his father, poets both. There is a largeness in their souls beyond the narrowness of other men; and why may we not then think, this may embrace more both of heaven and of God? I cannot but conjecture this to be the reason that they, most of them, are poor; they find their minds so solaced with their own flights that they neglect the study of growing rich. Besides, they are for the most part mighty lovers of their palates, and this is a known impoverisher. And they are all friends to the grape and liquor, though I think many, more out of a ductile nature and their love to pleasant company, than their affection to the juice alone. They are all of free natures, and are the truest definition of that philosopher's man, which gives him animal risible. Their grossest fault is that you may conclude them sensual, yet this does not touch them at all. Ingenious for the most part they are. I know there be some rhyming fools; but what have they to do with poetry?

Owen Feltham
"Of Poets and Poetry"

Poet and Prophet differ greatly in our loose modern notions of them. In some old languages, again, the titles are synonymous; Vates means both Prophet and Poet: and indeed at all times, Prophet and Poet, well understood, have much kindred of meaning. Fundamentally indeed they are still the same; in this most important respect especially, that they have penetrated both of them into the sacred mystery of the Universe; what Goethe calls "the open secret." "Which is the great secret?" asks one— "The open secret,"—open to all, seen by almost none.

Thomas Carlyle, "The Hero as Poet"
On Heroes, Hero-Worship, and the Heroic in History

Among primitive men the poet is merely one of many whom a group experience has wrought up emotionally to such a pitch that a liberation from excitement is as strongly desired as the satisfaction of a physical need. From the group of the mourners, the rejoicing, the enraged, the terror-stricken, there leaps forth one in whom the passion common to all has crystallized into intelligible speech; another leaps forth, perhaps a third. And each time the group of bystanders expresses its assent and inner liberation by cries and ululations. Here we observe that the poet has no existence separate from the tribe. The excitement once passed, he is a mere tribal unit like any other. He makes no demand of his tribe; the tribe makes no demand of him.

Nevertheless we shall have to assume even in this "precentor" of primitive times a specific gift: in some small measure, at least, a god gave him, above his brethren, the power to utter what he suffered. If and whenever this individual gift was heightened, the man in question became capable of reacting to stimuli not powerful enough to excite the tribal group. He no longer uttered his cry only under the immediate stimulus of death, war, hunger. The vivid recollection of these things sufficed him. And thus took place the first liberation of poetry from the immediate occasion, the first poetic projection of the past and distant. Our man with his individual emotion is now seen to stand among his calmer tribesmen, whom he draws into the circle of his own mood. Thus he becomes to them the seer, the inspired one, the vessel of a divine revelation. And this conception, which has never been wholly separated from the image of the poet, has been emphasized in very varying degrees at different times.

Richard Moritz Meyer
"The Modern Poet"

Planners, builders, laborers, schemers, executives, make a city, a country, a university, habitable, give them their bones and their blood. Poets and novelists make us appreciate the life we live in them, give them their souls.

Henry S. Canby
"Thanks to the Artists"

Come with rain, O loud Southwester!
Bring the singer, bring the nester;
Give the buried flower a dream;
Make the settled snow-bank steam;

Find the brown beneath the white;
But whate'er you do to-night,
Bathe my window, make it flow,
Melt it as the ice will go;
Melt the glass and leave the sticks
Like a hermit's crucifix;
Burst into my narrow stall;
Swing the picture on the wall;
Run the rattling pages o'er;
Scatter poems on the floor;
Turn the poet out of door.

Robert Frost, "To the Thawing Wind"
A Boy's Will

. . . what is meant by the word Poet? He is a man speaking to men: a man, it is true, endowed with a more lively sensibility, more enthusiasm and tenderness, who has a greater knowledge of human nature, and a more comprehensive soul, than are supposed to be common among mankind; a man pleased with his own passions and volitions, and who rejoices more than other men in the spirit of life that is in him; delighting to contemplate similar volitions and passions as manifested in the goings-on of the universe, and habitually impelled to create them where he does not find them.

William Wordsworth
Preface to *Lyrical Ballads*

So too I cannot understand how a Mirabeau, with that great glowing heart, with the fire that was in it, with the bursting tears that were in it, could not have written verses, tragedies, poems, and touched all hearts in that way had his course of life and education led thitherward. The grand fundamental character is that of Great Man:

that the man be great. Napoleon has words in him which are like Austerlitz battles. Louis Fourteenth's Marshals are a kind of poetical men withal; the things Turenne says are full of sagacity and geniality, like the sayings of Samuel Johnson. The great heart, the clear deep-seeing eyes: there it lies; no man whatever, in what province soever, can prosper at all without these.

Thomas Carlyle, "The Hero as Poet"
On Heroes, Hero-Worship, and the Heroic in History

And thus, in full, there are four classes: the men who feel nothing, and therefore see truly; the men who feel strongly, think weakly, and see untruly (second order of poets); the men who feel strongly, think strongly, and see truly (first order of poets); and the men who, strong as human creatures can be, are yet submitted to influences stronger than they, and see in a sort untruly, because what they see is inconceivably above them. This last is the usual condition of prophetic inspiration.

John Ruskin, "Of the Pathetic Fallacy"
Modern Painters

One more royal trait properly belongs to the poet. I mean his cheerfulness, without which no man can be a poet—for beauty is his aim. He loves virtue, not for its obligations, but for its grace: he delights in the world, in man, in woman, for the lovely light that sparkles from them. Beauty, the spirit of joy and hilarity, he sheds over the universe. And the true bards have been noted for their firm and cheerful temper. Homer lies in sunshine; Chaucer is glad and erect . . . not less sovereign and cheerful —much more sovereign and cheerful, is the tone of Shakespeare. His name suggests joy and emancipation to the heart of men. If he should appear in any company of human souls, who would not march in his troop?

Ralph Waldo Emerson, "Shakespeare"
Representative Men

Into the middle of my thought I crept
And on the bosom of the angel lay,
Lived all my life at once; and oh I wept
My own future to be.

Stanley Kunitz, "The Words of the Preacher"
Intellectual Things

Perhaps only the poet knows how close he comes sometimes to the boundaries of that other country where self is lost in the stored memories of the race, intelligence in instinct, and humanity in a great animal kinship. He is often amazed by his own intuitive flashes, but not too much amazed, if he is a true artist, to get them down on paper in some sort of intelligible order. If he can convey to his readers the sense of mysterious origin with which the suggestion endowed his mind, then he has succeeded. Someone has whispered in his ear, perhaps not in words, but rather in a series of bright visions like an unfolding dream. He must make these visions materialize in words, and he must get them down with the dew of his astonishment still on them. We recognize the results of such moments wherever we find them, whether Blake is telling us of the lion's ruddy eyes that flowed with tears of gold, or staid New England Emerson suddenly intones: "Daughters of Time, the hypocritic Days, muffled and drab like solemn dervishes. . . ."

Jessica Nelson North
"Quality in Madness"

I had not taken the first step in knowledge;
I had not learned to let go with the hands,
As still I have not learned to with the heart,
And have no wish to with the heart—nor need,
That I can see. The mind—is not the heart.
I may yet live, as I know others live,
To wish in vain to let go with the mind—
Of cares, at night, to sleep; but nothing tells me
That I need learn to let go with the heart.

Robert Frost, "Wild Grapes"
New Hampshire

Nothing worth speaking of happened . . . I took down some thin paper and wrote on it a little poem called St. Agnes' Eve.

John Keats
Letters

Cries the poet every day:
Ego, mei, mihi, me!

Christopher Morley
Inward Ho!

Alfred (Tennyson) is always carrying a bit of chaos around with him, and turning it into cosmos.

Thomas Carlyle

Great things happen: sometimes in a burst of instantaneous completion; oftenertimes by slow indignations, through every grade of postponement, doubtful addition, and nail-paring disgust. But they do happen, and sooner or later the man with a blessing hears about them.

Christopher Morley, "Jamie Comes to Hy-Brasil"
Romany Stain

But the sentient, the living, the laughing, the grieving—
The wild snorting poets that scour the plains
And lave in the ocean of boundless emotion
Think life is a dungeon, and howl in their chains.

John Jay Chapman
"Souls in Prison"

At length, starting to his feet (it was now winter and very cold) Orlando swore one of the most remarkable oaths of his lifetime, for it bound him to a servitude than which none is stricter. "I'll be blasted," he said, "if I ever write another word, or try to write another word, to please Nick Greene or the Muse. Bad, good, or indifferent, I'll write, from this day forward, to please myself," and here he made as if he were tearing a whole budget of papers across and tossing them in the face of that sneering loose-lipped man.

Virginia Woolf
Orlando

Imagination changes the scale of everything, and makes a thousand patterns of the woof of nature, without disturbing a single thread. Or rather—since it is nature itself that imagines—it turns to music what was only a strain; as if the universal vibration, suddenly ashamed of having been so long silent and useless, had burst into tears and laughter at its own folly, and in so doing had become wise.

George Santayana
Soliloquies in England

People made of skin and bone are just as incredible as people made of ink and paper; the Almighty allows Himself a much more frantic latitude in inventing people than we writers do. . . . Really to write about people, one must contrive to be present at a scene that—in flesh and blood—one never succeeds in witnessing; one must contrive to know people when they are alone. And I am sure that when people are alone they are entirely incredible.

Stella Benson
Pull Devil, Pull Baker

The faint conceptions I have of poems to come bring the blood frequently into my forehead.

John Keats
Letters

At times, I have got drunk on brimming eyes;
Wrestled alone with him who comes by night,
And with a drop of scalding oil have lost him:
At times, fused night with day in fervent thinking
Till the skull sweated . . .

Richard Hughes, "Travel-Piece"
Confessio Juvenis

If there is a famine of invention in the land, like Joseph's brethren we must travel far for food; we must visit the remote and rich ancients; but an inventive genius may safely stay at home; that like the widow's cruse, is divinely replenished from within; and affords us a miraculous delight.

Edward Young
"Conjectures on Original Composition"

Milton's purity is more eager. In the most exciting parts of Wordsworth you always feel, you never forget, that what you have before you is the excitement of a recluse. There is nothing of the stir of life; nothing of the brawl of the world. But Milton, though always a scholar by trade, though solitary in old age, was through life intent on great affairs, lived close to great scenes, watched a revolution, and if not an actor in it, was at least secretary to the actors.

Walter Bagehot
"Wordsworth, Tennyson and Browning, or Pure, Ornate and Grotesque Art in English Poetry"

Nobody else I ever knew has given me such a sense of having freedom, a margin of actual self-determination. . . . Firmness in refusal to comply with external forces except when his internal force is in accord, is the trait that I am most frequently astonished by in him. . . . He left Dartmouth, not because he didn't like hard work, nor because he was restless, but because he found college a mill for being made into "decent boards," and he was going to stay a growing tree. . . . No real experience comes, he thinks, when you can take the sting out of it by telling yourself you can use it in a book or otherwise. The experiences that toughen your character or furnish your mind are experiences you are submerged in. . . . He is not "a decent product of life's ironing-out." He is an original man whose extraordinariness is partly due to his never having bargained away any of the endowments of the genus man.

Sidney Cox
Robert Frost

He had been, in fact, one of those rare critical intelligences, possessed of a natural aptitude for what is best and most hopeful among their contemporaries' work—such men as, amid the hurly-burly of contemporary enthusiasm and disdain, have an instinctive leaning toward the few, usually depressed and neglected, figures who will afterwards seem to be the giants of the age in which they lived.

He had enjoyed *a sense of his own age,* had recognized its pattern while the pattern was yet incomplete, and—because it is only our misapprehension of the present which prevents our looking into the immediate future, our ignorance of today and of its real import as apart from its spurious tendencies and requirements—had anticipated many problems, both on the esthetic and on the moral plane, in which the fate of modern poetry is still concerned.

Peter Quennell
Baudelaire and the Symbolists

I may say of him here, that he is the only person I ever knew who answered to the idea of the man of genius. He is the only person from whom I ever learnt anything. He was the first poet I ever knew. His genius at that time had angelic wings and fed on manna. He talked on forever; his thoughts did not seem to come with labor and effort; but as if borne on the gusts of genius and as if the wings of his imagination lifted him from off his feet. His voice rolled on the ear like the pealing organ, and its sound alone was the music of thought. His mind was clothed with wings; and raised on them, he lifted philosophy to heaven. In his descriptions, you then saw the progress of human happiness and liberty in bright and never-ending succession, like the steps of Jacob's ladder, with airy shapes ascending and descending, and with the voice of God at the top of the ladder.

William Hazlitt
"Coleridge"

I think continually of those who were truly great.
Who, from the womb, remembered the soul's history
Through corridors of light where the hours are suns

Endless and singing. Whose lovely ambition
Was that their lips, still touched with fire,
Should tell of the Spirit clothed from head to foot in song.
And who hoarded from the Spring branches
The desires falling across their bodies like blossoms.

What is precious is never to forget
The essential delight of the blood drawn from ageless
springs
Breaking through rocks in worlds before our earth.
Never to deny its pleasure in the morning simple light
Nor its grave evening demand for love.
Never to allow gradually the traffic to smother
With noise and fog the flowering of the spirit.

Near the snow, near the sun, in the highest fields
See how these names are fêted by the waving grass
And by the streamers of white cloud
And whispers of wind in the listening sky.

The names of those who in their lives fought for life
Who wore at their hearts the fire's centre.
Born of the sun they travelled a short while towards the
sun,
And left the vivid air signed with their honour.

Stephen Spender, xxx
Poems

Most things are strong in one direction—a straw longitudinally, a board in the direction of its edge, a knee transversely to the grain—but the brave man is a perfect sphere, which cannot fall on its flat side, and is equally strong every day.

Henry David Thoreau
Journals

Man is perishable. That may be; but let us perish resisting, and if it is only nothingness that awaits us, let us act so that it will be an injustice.

Etienne de Senancour
Obermann

Whatever the poets pretend, it is plain they give immortality to none but themselves; 'tis Homer and Vergil we reverence and admire, not Achilles or Aeneas.

Jonathan Swift
"Thoughts"

. . . and grant
That I myself for portions of the year
May handle nothing and set eyes on nothing
But what the great and passionate have used
Throughout so many varying centuries
We take it for the norm.

William Butler Yeats,
"A Prayer on Going Into My House"
The Wild Swans at Coole

Our house must be honest and solid like our work. Everything we buy must be the same. Everything we wear, even. I can't stand anything false. Everything must ring like Elizabethan English and like those gentlemen I always seem to be mentioning, "the Poets." There is a light upon them, especially upon the Elizabethans and our "special" set—Keats, Wordsworth, Coleridge, Shelley, De Quincey, and Co., which I feel is like the bright star shining which must hang in the sky above Heron as we drive home. Those are the people with whom I want to live, those are the men I feel are our brothers, and the queer thing is that I feel there is a great golden loop linking them to Shakespeare's time.

Katherine Mansfield
Letters

I know what wages beauty gives,
How hard a life her servant lives,
Yet praise the winters gone:
There is not a fool can call me friend,
And I may dine at journey's end
With Landor and with Donne.

William Butler Yeats, "To a Young Beauty"
The Wild Swans at Coole

We carry with us all the wonders we seek without us: there is all Africa and her prodigies in us; we are that bold and adventurous piece of Nature, which he that studies wisely learns in a compendium what others labor at in a divided piece and endless volume.

Sir Thomas Browne
Religio Medici

With a heart of furious fancies
Whereof I am commander,
With a burning spear,
And a horse of air,
To the wilderness I wander;

With a knight of ghosts and shadows,
I summoned am to tourney:
Ten leagues beyond
The wide world's end;
Methinks it is no journey.

"Tom o' Bedlam"
Giles Earle, His Book, 1615

I see Everything I paint in this World, but Everybody does not see alike. To the Eyes of a Miser a Guinea is far more beautiful than the Sun, & a bag worn with the use of Money has more beautiful proportions than a Vine filled with Grapes. The tree which moves some to tears of Joy is in the Eyes of others only a Green thing which stands in the way. Some see Nature all Ridicule and Deformity, & by these I shall not regulate my proportions; & some scarce see Nature at all. But to the eyes of the Man of Imagination, Nature is Imagination itself. As a man is, so he sees.

William Blake
Letters

They would not find me changed from him they knew—
Only more sure of all I thought was true.

Robert Frost, "Into My Own"
A Boy's Will

The only strength for me is to be found in the sense of a personal presence everywhere, it scarcely matters whether it be called human or divine; a presence which only makes itself felt at first in this and that particular form and feature. Into this presence we come, not by leaving behind what are usually called earthly things, or by loving them less, but by living more intensely in them; for it is literally true that this world *is* everything to us, if only we choose to make it so, if only we "live in the present" *because* it is eternity.

R. L. Nettleship
Letters

I thank God, and with joy I mention it, I was never afraid of Hell, nor never grew pale at the description of that place.

Sir Thomas Browne
Religio Medici

If a person liked anything, if he took snuff heartily, it was sufficient. He would understand, by analogy, the pungency of other things beside Irish blackguard or Scotch rapee.

William Hazlitt
"On the Conversation of Authors"

I have heard what the talkers were talking, the talk of the
beginning and the end,
But I do not talk of the beginning or the end.

There was never any more inception than there is now,
Nor any more youth or age than there is now,
And will never be any more perfection than there is now,
Nor any more heaven or hell than there is now.

Walt Whitman, "Song of Myself"
Leaves of Grass

Perhaps none of the poems is more purely and typically Shelleyan than "The Cloud," and it is interesting to note how essentially it springs from the faculty of make-believe. The same thing is conspicuous, throughout his singing; it is the child's faculty of make-believe raised to the nth power. He is still at play, save only that his play is such as manhood stops to watch, and his playthings are those which the gods give their children. The universe is his box of toys. He dabbles his fingers in the day-fall. He is gold-dusty with tumbling amidst the stars. He makes bright mischief with the moon. The meteors nuzzle their noses in his hand. He teases into growling the kennelled thunder, and laughs at the shaking of its fiery chain. He dances in and out of the gates of heaven: its floor is littered with his broken fancies. He runs wild over the fields of ether. He chases the rolling world. He gets between the feet of the horses of the sun. He stands in the lap of patient Nature and twines her loosened tresses after a hundred wilful patterns to see how she will look nicest in his song.

Francis Thompson
Shelley

While always holding fast to his own personality, a personality so strong that he could not have concealed it even if he had wanted to, yet to each one of his friends Keats turns a different side. To Bailey, he philosophizes and opens up the heart of his spiritual puzzles; to Haydon, he chats about art, gossips of mutual friends, and falls in, as far as may be, with what he knows Haydon to be preoccupied with at the time; to Reynolds, he talks pure poetry, and often merely wanders on after the thread of his wandering fancies, certain that Reynolds will understand; to his brother he is everything by turns, but always in a taken-for-granted sort of way, quite unlike his attitude toward anyone else.

Amy Lowell
John Keats

God keep me from ever completing anything. This whole book is but a draft—nay, but the draft of a draft. Oh, Time, Strength, Cash and Patience!

Herman Melville
Moby Dick

Give me Chaucer in preference. He slaps us on the shoulder and makes us spring up while the dew is on the grass, and while the long shadows play about it in all quarters. We feel strong with the freshness round us, and we return with a keened appetite, having such a companion in our walk.

Walter Savage Landor
Imaginary Conversations

All beauty comes from beautiful blood and a beautiful brain.

Walt Whitman
Preface to *Leaves of Grass,* 1855

I can see no reason why man will not presently give up all major beliefs, and simply surrender himself to what is perhaps the first principle of his own present state as a conscious creature—an insatiable curiosity.

Conrad Aiken
"What I Believe"

It is not that poets are lonely. They are alone in the countries of the mind when they go there to get their poems and bring them back. They would allow no company there, and what they do there may be guessed by the more ingeniously inventive critics. But their speculations will be in error if they prove the poet unhappy in his solitary journey. And the poet would not ordinarily be lonely in this world's company, except that he sees too clearly the webs and veils, the nakedness and its poor disguise, that complicates ordinary acquaintance. Who ever knows another human being? The poet, naturally a warm and friendly sort, agonizes over the silences, the delays, the awkward aims of his personal relationships. A friend said of Henry James, "In spite of admiration and curiosity, I left our meetings entirely to chance, for I soon discovered two daunting facts about him. Firstly, that he was easily bored (not merely in an ordinary but in an excruciating sense of the word); and secondly, that he minded intensely the dislocations and disappointments which are inevitable in all human relations. They made him groan and writhe and worry. The measure of how much he minded them could be read in the frequency, extravagance, and emphasis of signals that all was really well, across even those small rifts (to him they had the horror of gulfs) which absence and accident open up between people."

John Holmes
"Nothing Is Lost"

We live in a web of associated memories; our general map—the chart thanks to which we know more or less clearly where we put what, recognize analogies, form classes, make order out of chaos and accumulate experience—is a network of memories. And one of ourselves, the loudest voiced one, the one we usually think of when we say I, corresponds to the spot on that map where the most frequent and familiar memories cross each other, as the railroads of a country cross at its capital.

H. B. Brewster
The Prison

A great poet, who appears in illiterate times, absorbs into his sphere all the light which is anywhere radiating. Every intellectual jewel, every flower of sentiment, it is his fine office to bring to his people; and he comes to value his memory equally with his invention.

Ralph Waldo Emerson, "Shakespeare"
Representative Men

. . . man was to be treated as a musical instrument, and if any viol was to be made of sound timber and kept well tuned always, it was he, so that when the bow of events is drawn across him he may vibrate and resound in perfect harmony. A sensitive soul will be continually trying its strings to see if they are in tune. A man's body must be rasped down exactly to a shaving. It is of far more importance than the wood of a Cremona violin.

Henry David Thoreau
Journals

I hope I have some range in the appreciation of Beauty. I can see it all the way from exquisite through homely and mean, even to vile.

Robert Frost
From notes on a lecture

Upon wild plains omnipotent
A conquering quality Danger was.
You saw it always imminent,
A sly shadow on the grass.
It was an agent in the air,
Active as sunshine, yielding health
And Death, but not Death everywhere.

Welborn Hope
"Danger"

There are moments when Dickens is possessed by the power of writing: he is carried away. That is bliss. It certainly is not shared by writers today. The death of Cheedle: dawn falling upon the edge of night. One realizes exactly the mood of the writer and how he wrote, as it were, for himself, but it was not his will. He *was* the falling dawn, and he *was* the physician going to Bar.

Katherine Mansfield
Journals

If a sparrow comes before my window, I take part in its existence and pick about the gravel.

John Keats
Letters

I do not ask the wounded person how he feels—I myself become the wounded person.

Walt Whitman, "Song of Myself"
Leaves of Grass

Not I, not I, but the wind that blows through me!
A fine wind is blowing the new direction of Time.
If only I let it bear me, carry me, if only it carry me!
If only I am sensitive, subtle, oh, delicate, a winged gift!
If only, most lovely of all, I yield myself and am borrowed
By the fine fine wind that takes its course through the
    chaos of the world
Like a fine, an exquisite chisel, a wedge-blade inserted;
If only I am keen and hard like the sheer tip of a wedge
Driven by invisible blows,
The rock shall split, we shall come to wonder, we shall
    find the Hesperides.
Oh, for the wonder that bubbles into my soul,
I would be a good fountain, a good well-head,
Would blur no whisper, spoil no expression.

D. H. Lawrence
"Song of a Man Who Has Come Through"
Look! We Have Come Through

He gloried in the strong sensory-stimulus of glowing color, of dazzling light; in the more complex motory-stimulus of intricate, abrupt and plastic form. . . . He delighted in the angular, indented, interwining, labyrinthine varieties of line and surface which call for the most delicate, and at the same time the most agile, adjustments of the eye. He caught at the edges of things. . . . Spikes and wedges and swords run riot in his work. . . . He loved the grinding, clashing and rending sibilants and explosives as Tennyson the tender-hefted liquids.

C. H. Herford
"Browning"

Of Hopkins' imagery, there is not much in general to be said, but that "not much" is all. He had that acute and sharp sensuous awareness essential to all great poets. He was physically aware of textures, surfaces, colors, patterns of every kind; aware acutely of the earth's diurnal course, of growth and decay, of animality in man and of vitality in all things. Everywhere there is passionate apprehension, passionate expression and equally that passion for form without which these other passions are spendthrift. But the form is inherent in the passion. For, as Emerson remarked with his occasional deep insight, "It is not metres, but a metre-making argument, that makes a poem—a thought so passionate and alive, that, like the spirit of a plant or an animal, it has an architecture of its own, and adorns nature with a new thing."

Herbert Read
Form in Modern Poetry

It matters not where or how far you travel—the farther commonly the worse—but how much alive you are. All that a man has to say or do that can possibly concern mankind—is in some shape or other to tell the story of his love—to sing, and if he is fortunate and keeps alive, he will be forever in love.

Henry David Thoreau
Journals

As our blood labours to beget
Spirits, as like souls as it can,
Because such fingers need to knit
That subtile knot, which makes us man:
So must pure lovers' souls descend
To affections and to faculties,
Which sense may reach and apprehend,
Else a great Prince in prison lies.

John Donne
"The Ecstasy"

It isn't the money that makes people start writing, and stick to it; it is the hope of publication. In its highest phase the writing mania proceeds from the wish to break down, somehow, the awful barrier which exists between soul and soul, and share even bitterness, if there is neither knowledge nor joy to be shared; in its lower manifestations it may be merely exhibitionism, and yet, there too, is the wistful hope of being better understood.

Don Marquis

And cared it into song—strict care, strict joy!
Caring for grief he cared his grief away:
And those sad songs, tho' woe be all the theme,
Do not make us grieve who read them now
Because the poet makes grief beautiful.

James Stephens
Strict Joy

But what are you going to do about people when you're not with them? Into what faraway loneliness do their minds travel? What uncanny thoughts do they think? You can visualize them, see them walking, laughing, sulking; see their amusing clothes (so remarkably a part of themselves), the delicate way their hair grows, their bright serious eyes; hear their unmistakable voices repeating favorite opinions. Does all that go on, just the same, and you not there? Yes, they are pursuing their own relentless privacies, but are they real? Even if they were dead, would they be any farther away? You grope clumsily toward them, but is it really they you seek, or some new reassurance of yourself? . . . The phantoms of so many friends rise before you. What's happening to them? Tell me, tell me everything (you'd like to say): I'll never hold it against you. I'll match each grief that plagues you with grievances of my own. Ring, telephone; come, letter; I need you.

Christopher Morley
Human Being

A great and available reserve of sheer intensity—intensity of perception and emotion—it is in his possession of this that a great artist differs most deeply from his fellows. In no vague or rhetorical sense of the words, he sees and hears more intensely.

C. E. Montague, "The Last Question of All"
A Writer's Notes on His Trade

I have a hunger food is gall to—
It starves more sweetly on the thought
Of that light thing I could but call to,
That glimmering image scarcely caught.

George Dillon, "The Mad Hunter"
The Flowering Stone

Poor human nature, so richly endowed with nerves of anguish, so splendidly organized for pain and sorrow, is but slenderly equipped for joy. . . . A sense of ineffable joy, attainable at will, and equal in intensity and duration to (let us say) an attack of sciatica, would go far to equalize the one-sided conditions under which we live.

George du Maurier
Peter Ibbetson

In good health, the air is a cordial of incredible virtue. Crossing a bare common, in snow puddles, at twilight, under a clouded sky, without having in my thoughts any occurrence of special good fortune, I have enjoyed a perfect exhilaration. I am glad to the brink of fear.

Ralph Waldo Emerson, "Nature"
The Conduct of Life

Snow falling and night falling fast oh fast
In a field I looked into going past,
And the ground almost covered smooth in snow,
But a few weeds and stubble showing last.

The woods around it have it—it is theirs.
All animals are smothered in their lairs.
I am too absent-spirited to count;
Their loneliness includes me unawares.

And lonely as it is that loneliness
Will be more lonely ere it will be less—
A blanker whiteness of benighted snow
With no expression, nothing to express.

They cannot scare me with their empty spaces
Between stars—on stars where no human race is.
I have it in me so much nearer home
To scare myself with my own desert places.

Robert Frost, "Desert Places"
A Further Range

To be normal is to be a standard, but not, as things are and are likely to remain, an average; and to inquire into the characters of the norm or to ask who are normal is to raise a question as to value. The artist departs from the average, but so do other people. His departure, however, is one of the reasons why we attend to his work; other people's departures may be reasons why we should not. If the artist's organism is such as to allow him a fuller life than the average, with less unnecessary interference between its component impulses, then plainly we should do well to be more like him, if we can and as far as we can.

I. A. Richards, "The Normality of the Artist"
Principles of Literary Criticism

Emily Dickinson had a genius for trifles, peculiar to herself—in her poetry she was always proving the importance of the homely, the neglected detail, as if it were her chief business on earth. She was high-strung—life, every morsel of it, was momentous. And so, when she wrote to friends, she conveyed a breathless attitude. Her wit loved the material at hand.

Anonymous

Man with his burning soul
Has but an hour of breath
To build a ship of truth
In which his soul may sail—
Sail on the sea of death
For death takes toll
Of beauty, courage, youth,
All but truth.

John Masefield, "Truth"
The Widow in the Bye Street

There are people who appear to think only with the brain, or with whatever may be the specific thinking organ; while others think with all the body and all the soul, with the blood, with the marrow of the bones, with the heart, with the belly, with the lungs, with the life.

Miguel de Unamuno
The Tragic Sense of Life

I hate people who meet Time half-way. I am for no compromise with that inevitable spoiler.

Charles Lamb, "My Relations"
Last Essays of Elia

At first I shouted: "God," I cried,
"My valuable dream has died!"
He did not even look aside,
So I went nearer. "God," I said,
"I suppose you know my dream is dead."

Roberta Teale Swartz, "Preoccupation"
Liliput

Today I am hardening my heart. I am walking all around my heart and building up the defences. I do not mean to leave a loophole even for a tuft of violets to grow in. Give me a hard heart, O Lord! Lord, harden thou my heart!

Katherine Mansfield
Journals

I have relapsed into those abstractions which are my only life. I feel escaped from a new strange and threatening sorrow, and am thankful for it. There is an awful warmth about my heart like a load of immortality.

John Keats
Letters

Index

ABBOTT, CHARLES D., 131
Abbott, E. A., 161
Abercrombie, Lascelles, 209
"Adagia," 91
AE (George Russell), 232
Age, of poets, 85
Aiken, Conrad, 6, 63, 156, 249, 257, 299
"All's Well That Ends," 42
Allusion, 125
Analysis, by writers, 120; popularity of, 126
Anderson, Sherwood, 183
Andrewes, Bishop, 119
Anonymous, 151, 179, 218, 307
Anthologies, value of, 80
Antithesis, for precision, 113, 114
Arnold, Matthew, 80, 85, 128
Art, of the fugue, 119
Artistic future of poetry, the, 150
Arts, interrelation of, 60
Atlantic Monthly, 41
Auden, W. H., Oxford lecture of, 79; 104, 114, 125, 230
Audience, importance of, 15, 16, 17; Wilbur on, 123, 124
Aurelius, Marcus, 271
Austin, Mary, 186

BABBITT, IRVING, on style, 53
Bach, J. S., 119
Bacon, Francis, 71, 118
Bagehot, Walter, 291
Beaumont, Francis, 151
Becker, May Lamberton, 223
Belden, H. M., 157
Bemelmans, Ludwig, 116
Benét, Stephen Vincent, on not writing, 27
Benét, William Rose, 115, 202
Benson, Stella, 276, 290
Berryman, John, 63
Blackmur, R. P., 131-140
Blake, William, 105, 185, 188, 296
Blodgett, Ruth, 199, 255
"Body of the Roots," 6
Book of Words, A, 148
Booth, Philip, 42
Borrowing, from other languages, 125
Braithwaite, W. S., 18
Breton, Nicholas, 248
Brewster, H. B., 300
Bridges, Robert, study of Milton, 61
Brontë, Charlotte, 204
Brooke, Rupert, 4
Browne, Thomas, 295
Browning, Robert, 31
Burke, Kenneth, 116
Burr Oaks, 87
Burroughs, John, 223
Butler, Samuel, 201
Bynner, Witter, 256
Byrd, William, 114

CAESURA, 69
"Caged Skylark, The," 67
Canby, Henry Seidel, 186, 219, 284
Carlyle, Thomas, 146, 152, 158, 252, 283, 286, 288

Carroll, Lewis, 164
"Chair in the Field," 40
Chance, flowers into choice, 135, 140
Chapman, John Jay, 289
"Charterhouse of Parma, The," 106
Chaucer, Geoffrey, 63, 115, 152
Chekhov, Anton, 236, 268, 275, 281
Ciardi, John, 120
Clarity, 123
Climax, Marianne Moore on, 116
Clubs, on value of, 18, 28
Cocteau, Jean, 202
Coleridge, Samuel Taylor, 162, 168, 183, 258
Color, in imagery, 72
"Come Hither," 80
"Command of the Dead," 112
"Common Reader, The," 150
Communication, 150
Composition, in graphic arts, 57
Connick, Charles, 31
Conrad, Joseph, 193, 231
Contests, 18
Cournos, John, 202
Cowley, Abraham, 272
Cowley, Malcolm, 222, 225, 226
Cox, Sidney, 291
Cremieux, Benjamin, 232
Crosland, T. W. H., 216
Cummings, E. E., 116
Curie, Eve, 113

DANIEL, BOOK OF, 113
Daudet, Alphonse, 275
de la Mare, Walter, 80, 253, 276
Devices, misuse of, 126
Difficulty, of poetry, 123
Dillon, George, 305
"Discovering Poetry," 149
Discrimination, poet's job of, 147
Dixon, Richard Watson, 156
Donne, John, 62, 65, 66, 145, 161, 163, 224
"Double Man, The," 114
Dowd, Harrison, 232
Dream, use in poem of, 43-45
Drew, Elizabeth, 149, 155, 166
Dryden, John, 117
Duggan, Eileen, 282

EASTMAN, MAX, 279
Eberhart, Richard, on reasons for poetry, 87-90
"Education by Poetry," 150
"Elegie XVI, On His Mistris," 65
Eliot, Thomas Stearns, 28, 104, 117, 119, 126, 281
Ellis, Havelock, 163, 269, 277
Emerson, Ralph Waldo, 63, 164, 165, 193, 194, 198, 229, 240, 261, 287, 300, 305
Ennis, George, 182
Experiment, limitations on, 59; by Whitman, 102

FACT, poets and, 105-106
Feltham, Owen, 283
Ferry, David, 42
Ficke, Arthur Davidson, 217
Figgis, Darrell, 249
"Fighting Faith Saves the World," 113
"Finnegan's Wake," 125
Ford, Ford Madox, 115, 119, 202
Foreign, words, 125
Forms, 129
Forster, E. M., 181
Free verse, difficulty of, 83
Frost, Robert, 31, 63, 84-86, 150, 157, 158, 187, 190, 194, 195, 208, 221, 275, 280, 285, 288, 296, 301, 306

GALSWORTHY, JOHN, 233
Genealogy, of poets, 30-31
Gide, André, 192, 199, 200
Gilchrist, Marie, 151
Gilkes, Martin, 167
Ginsberg, Louis, 112
"Golden Nightingale, The," 74
Grahame, Kenneth, 192
Graphic arts, lesson from, 57
"Gratification Unto Master John Case, A," 114
Gray, Thomas, 62
"Great Praises," 87

HALL, DONALD, 42, 84
Handbooks, value of, 52
Hardy, Thomas, Auden on, 82
Hazlitt, William, 176, 196, 228, 238, 239, 292, 297
Hebbel, Friedrich, 194, 196
Henri, Robert, 187, 207
Henryson, 115
Herbert, George, 227
Herford, C. H., 302
Herrick, Robert, 127, 231
Herzburg, M. J., 161
Hewlett, Maurice, 260
Hofmannsthal, Hugo von, 189
Holmes, Edmond, 230
Holmes, John, 165, 300
Holmes, Oliver Wendell, on rules, 69
"Holy Sonnet XIV," 66
Honig, Edwin, 42
Hope, Welborn, 301
Hopkins, Gerard Manley, 5, 63, 67, 68, 69, 112, 147, 152, 181, 184, 234, 254, 256, 258, 259, 261
"Hot Afternoons Have Been in Montana," 8
Housman, A. E., 227
Howes, Raymond, 220
Hughes, Richard, 290
Hyperbole, 118

IAMBIC PENTAMETER, 60-67
Imagery, personal nature of, 71-72; stimuli for, 74; Wilbur on, 128
Imitation, danger of, 55; value of, 82
Incorrectness, fear of, 119
Individualism, Spender on, 108-110
Inner ear, 122
Irony, use of, 126

JAMES, HENRY, 118, 182, 184, 206, 207, 233, 262
Jespersen, Otto, 164
Johnson, Samuel, 116, 117, 189, 239
Jones, Robert Edmond, 183
Jonson, Ben, 199, 224
"Journey Among Warriors," 113
Joyce, James, 150, 249

KANT, EMMANUEL, 229
Keats, John, 4, 62, 192, 269, 270, 274, 282, 288, 290, 301, 308
Kipling, Rudyard, 148, 166, 241
Kunitz, Stanley, 287

LAMB, CHARLES, 198, 307
Landor, Walter Savage, 298; Frost on, 86
Language, for its own sake, 146; in poetry, 124-125
Lawrence, D. H., 223, 271, 302
Lee, Vernon, 189
Lewis, Wyndham, 118
Limerick, lesson of, 56, 59
Lion's leap, 112
Longfellow, H. W., 4
Longinus, 116, 118
Lowell, Amy, 180, 298
Lowell, Robert, 62, 67

MACHEN, ARTHUR, 154
MacLeish, Archibald, 4, 7, 31, 156, 188, 210, 225, 233
"Madeline," 116
Magazines, 17, 18, 28
Mansfield, Katherine, 195, 200, 258, 295, 301, 308
Maritain, Jacques, 119
Marquis, Don, 223, 304
Masefield, John, 63, 307
Masters, as models, 55; Auden's view of, 81-82
Masters, Edgar Lee, 230
Mather, Frank Jewett, 236
Matisse, Henri, 208
du Maurier, George, 305
Maurois, André, 232
"Maybe For Love," 46
Measure, W. C. Williams on, 101-102
Melville, Herman, 298
Menander, 252
Mencken, H. L., 225
Meredith, George, 62
Meyer, Richard Moritz, 284
Meynell, Alice, 259, 274
"Mid-Century American Poets," 120
Millay, Edna St. Vincent, 32, 63

Milton, John, 16, 63, 105, 127; studies of, 61; use of iambics in, 61
"Missa Vocis," 131-140
Mitchell, Ik, 238
Models, value of, 55
Monro, Harold, 230, 270
Montague, C. E., 154, 159, 179, 228, 252, 305
Montaigne, 195
Moore, Marianne, 111-119, 128
Morley, Christopher, 15, 163, 179, 201, 227, 288, 305
Morse, Samuel French, 91
Mozart, 193
Mullins, Helene, 255
Murray, Gilbert, 191, 203
Music, lessons from, 57

NASH, OGDEN, Marianne Moore on, 114
Nashe, Thomas, 117
Nerval, Gerard de, 275
Nettleship, R. L., 296
"New Poets of England and America," 84
"New View, The," 36
"New Year Letter," 114
New York *Times* Book Review, 87, 104
Norm, 129; variations on, 57, 63-64
North, Jessica Nelson, 287

OBSCURITY, in poetry, 123
Old age, 38
"On Heaven," 118
"Opus Posthumous," 91
"Orpheus and Eurydice," 115
O'Sheel, Shaemas, 250
Owen, Wilfred, 278

PACK, ROBERT, 84
Painting, lessons from, 57
Paradox, 126
Pepys, Samuel, 253
Plato, 104, 114, 118
Poet, the, prejudices against, 3, 4; special senses of, 5-10; his audience. 15; first book, 19; ancestors, 30; his gifts, 32-35; contemporary ideal of, 126-127
Poetics, study of, 52
Poetry, not writing it, 24-30
Poetry, 28
"Poets At Work," television program, 42; book, 131
Pope, Alexander, 62, 80
"Portrait of the Artist As a Young Man," 150
Pound, Ezra, 118, 234
Powys, John Cowper, 253
Powys, Llewelyn, 251
"Prayer In Time of War," 117
Preciosity, 118
Precision, Marianne Moore on, 112
Price, Lucien, 197
Principles, Wilbur on, 120-121
Prosody, Milton's, 61
Punctuation, at caesura, 70

"QUAKER GRAVEYARD AT NANTUCKET," 67
Quennell, Peter, 292
Quiller-Couch, Arthur, 186, 235

RANSOM, JOHN CROWE, 62, 117, 182
Read, Herbert, 108, 303
Reading, good as well as great, 80-81
Reading aloud, Wilbur on, 121-122
"Reading the Spirit," 87
"Red Wheelbarrow, The," 112
Reference, to other literature, 125
Reynolds, Joshua, 205
Rhodes, Eugene Manlove, 152
Rhyme, 126
Rhythm, description of, 9; sprung, 68
Rich, Adrienne, 42
Richards, I. A., 156, 205, 306
Rilke, Rainer Maria, 194, 268, 273
Rimbaud, Arthur, 261
Robinson, Edwin Arlington, 62
Roethke, Theodore, 260
"Rugby Chapel," 128
Rules, O. W. Holmes on, 69; source of, 51; need for, 52

Ruskin, John, 286
Russell, Bertrand, 256, 270

"SAILING TO BYZANTIUM," 135
St. John, 149
Sandburg, Carl, on style, 53
Santayana, George, 221, 289
Sarton, May, 42
Scanning, in Hopkins, 68
Schnitzler, Arthur, 177, 219, 220
Scholars, compared with poets, 85
Schools, poetry in, 84
Schopenhauer, 224
Schroeder, Eric, 258
Scott, Geoffrey, 210
Sculpture, experiments in, 58
"Second World, The," 132
Senancour, Étienne de, 294
Seriousness, in poetry, 104, 107
Shakespeare, William, 62, 84, 105, 115, 118, 226
"Shakespeare's Imagery," 71-72
Shaw, Bernard, on rules, 52
Shelley, Percy Bysshe, 104, 105, 278, 281
Sidney, Philip, 62
Siegel, Eli, 8, 248
Simpson, Louis, 84
Sitwell, Edith, 108, 236
Skill, in imagery, 73; relation to style, 58
Smith, Logan Pearsall, 153, 160, 162, 189, 196, 228
Socrates, 114
Sonnet, for practice, 27
Sound, of poetry, 122
Spender, Stephen, 62, 104-110, 150, 167, 209, 293
Spingarn, J. E., 240
Spinoza, 271
Sprott, Ernest, study of Milton, 61
Sprung rhythm, 68
Spurgeon, Caroline, on imagery, 71
Stauffer, Donald A., 73, 131-140
Stendhal, 106
Stephens, James, 15, 177, 304
Sterne, Lawrence, 150
Stevens, Wallace, 62, 64, 91-98, 112
Stevenson, R. L., 30, 276
Strictness, of forms, 129
Strong, L. A. G., 226-227
Structure, 128
Style, development of, 52-54
Subject matter, 127
Sun, New York, 119
"Sunday Morning," 64
Swartz, Roberta Teale, 308
Symbols, as belief, 73
Synthesis, contemporary distrust of, 126-127

THIRLWALL, JOHN C., 99
Thomas, Dylan, 4, 21, 61
Thompson, Francis, 298
Thomson, James, 269
Thoreau, Henry David, 178, 192, 226, 228, 253, 255, 257, 262, 281, 293, 300, 303
Time, poet's sense of, 8
"Tom o' Bedlam," 295
Tomlinson, H. M., 234
Tone, as voice, 54
Traherne, Thomas, 251, 257
Training, validity of, 34
Tree stump, poem about, 36-39
Treece, Henry, 117
Twain, Mark, 5
"Tyro, The," 118

DE UNAMUNO, MIGUEL, 307
"U. S. Camera Annual," 29
Universality, 124
Untermeyer, Louis, 15, 157, 229

VAN DOREN, MARK, 4
Van Vechten, Carl, 185
Vaughan, Henry, 62, 251
Voice, uniqueness of, 54, 56
Voltaire, on enigmas, 114

WALEY, ARTHUR, 113
Watson, Thomas, 114
Watson, William, 248
Welles, Winifred, 5, 6, 250
Wescott, Glenway, 222

West, Rebecca, 220
Whitman, Walt, 16, 189, 219, 229, 239, 260, 272, 297, 299, 301; W. C. Williams on, 102
Wilbur, Richard, 4, 63, 120-130
Wilde, Oscar, 224
Wilder, Thornton, 223
Williams, Charles, 180
Williams, William Carlos, 99, 112, 207
Wilson, Edmund, 237
Winters, Yvor, 203
Wither, George, 115
Woolf, Virginia, 150, 156, 163, 176, 178, 197, 219, 274, 289
Words, poets' need for, 143; poets' sense for, 33
Wordsworth, William, 105, 277, 285

YALE SERIES OF YOUNGER POETS, 19
Yeats, William Butler, 30, 62, 73, 74, 135, 153, 185, 192, 196, 200, 201, 202, 222, 233, 234, 238, 277, 294, 295
"You, Andrew Marvell," 7
Young, Edward, 187, 290